WHAT'S THE HURRY?

WHAT'S THE HURRY?

Urgency in the New Zealand Legislative Process
1987–2010

Claudia Geiringer, Polly Higbee and Elizabeth McLeay

VICTORIA UNIVERSITY PRESS

Published with the assistance of the New Zealand Law Foundation

VICTORIA UNIVERSITY PRESS
Victoria University of Wellington
PO Box 600 Wellington
vuw.ac.nz/vup

Copyright © Claudia Geiringer, Polly Higbee & Elizabeth McLeay 2011
First published 2011

This book is copyright. Apart from any fair
dealing for the purpose of private study, research, criticism
or review, as permitted under the Copyright Act, no part
may be reproduced by any process without the
permission of the publishers

National Library of New Zealand Cataloguing-in-Publication Data

Geiringer, Claudia, 1968-
What's the hurry? : urgency in the New Zealand legislative
process 1987-2010 / Claudia Geiringer, Polly Higbee
and Elizabeth McLeay.
Includes bibliographical references.
ISBN 978-0-86473-772-4
1. Legislation—New Zealand. 2. Constitutional law—New Zealand.
3. New Zealand—Politics and government—1972-
I. Higbee, Polly. II. McLeay, E. M. (Elizabeth M.) III. Title.
328.93—dc 22

Printed by PrintStop, Wellington

Table of Contents

List of Figures and Tables	ix
Acknowledgements	xi

Chapter One: Introduction — 1

I	Methods and Data		6
	A	The Statistical Data	8
	B	The Interviews	10
II	Overview and Summary		11
III	The Principles of Good Law-Making		15
	A	The Ten Principles	16
		1 Legislatures should allow time and opportunity for informed and open policy deliberation	16
		2 The legislative process should allow sufficient time and opportunity for the adequate scrutiny of bills	16
		3 Citizens should be able to participate in the legislative process	17
		4 Parliaments should operate in a transparent manner	17
		5 The House should strive to produce high quality legislation	18
		6 Legislation should not jeopardise fundamental constitutional rights and principles	18
		7 Parliaments should follow stable procedural rules	19
		8 Parliament should foster, not erode, respect for itself as an institution	19
		9 The government has a right to govern, so long as it commands a majority in the House	19
		10 Parliament should be able to enact legislation quickly in (actual) emergency situations	19
	B	Conclusion	19

Chapter Two: Urgency and the Legislative Process — 21

I	The Origins and Historical Development of Urgency	22
II	The Procedures for Invoking Urgency	23

III	The Effect of Urgency Motions	25
	A The House's Sitting Hours and their Extension under Urgency	25
	1 The effect of (ordinary) urgency on the House's sitting hours	27
	2 The effect of extraordinary urgency on the House's sitting hours	28
	B Suspension of Other Business of the House	28
	C Removal of Legislative "Stand-Down" Periods	29
	D Omission of Select Committee Consideration	31
IV	What Urgency Does Not Do	32
V	Roles and Responsibilities	32
	A The Leader of the House	32
	B The Speaker	33
	C The Party Whips	34
	D The Business Committee	35
	E The Standing Orders Committee	36
VI	Urgency and the Allocation of Parliamentary Time	36
VII	Urgency in Comparative Perspective	40
VIII	Conclusion	44

Chapter Three: The Reasons Why Governments Use Urgency   45

I	The Formal Requirement to Give Reasons	46
II	Why New Zealand Governments Use Urgency: Searching for the Reasons	48
	A Specific Reasons to Expedite the Passage of Particular Legislation	48
	1 Minimising opportunities for speculative behaviour by market participants and providing certainty for financial markets	48
	2 Responding to an unexpected event	50
	3 Correcting errors	52
	4 Urgency driven by an external (or pre-set) deadline	53
	B Freeing up the Order Paper	54
	C Tactical Reasons for Using Urgency	57

	1	Strategic urgency to manage public sentiment	57
	2	Tactical reasons unrelated to the legislative agenda	59
	D	Budget Day Urgency	61
III	Conclusion	65

Chapter Four: How Governments Use Urgency   67

I	Parliaments, Governments and the Use of Urgency	68
	A Urgency Motions	68
	B Bills Accorded Urgency	70
	C Percentage of Sitting Time Taken under Urgency	70
	D Trends in the Data	74
II	Different Types of Urgency	75
	A Taking Only One Stage under Urgency	77
	B Removing the Stand-Down Period between Introduction and Initial Debate	77
	C Urgency for Remaining Stages	77
	D Taking Committee of the Whole House and Third Reading Together	78
	E Bills Taken Through All Stages and/or Bills Not Sent to Select Committee	78
III	Extraordinary Urgency	84
IV	Seasonal Patterns in the Use of Urgency	84
V	Policy Areas of Bills Accorded Urgency	88
VI	Conclusion	90

Chapter Five: The Constraints on the Use of Urgency   91

I	Extraordinary Urgency	92
II	(Ordinary) Urgency	93
	A Internal Factors that Can Constrain Urgency	94
	B External Factors that Can Constrain Urgency	97
III	Getting the Numbers – The Impact of Multi-Party Parliaments on the Use of Urgency	99
	A The Lead-Up to MMP (1993–1996)	103
	B The First MMP Government (1996–1999)	103
	C The Labour-led Governments (1999–2008)	105

	D The National-led Government (2008–2010)	109
	E Conclusions on the Impact of Multi-Party Parliaments	112
IV	Urgency and Evolving Parliamentary Culture	115
V	Ideology, Personality and Internalised Constraints	119
VI	Conclusion	121

Chapter Six: Urgency, Time and Democratic Legitimacy   123

I	Time and the Legislative Process	124
	A Does the House Have Insufficient Capacity to Process Government Business?	124
	B Possible Solutions	130
	1 Extending the House's sitting hours	130
	2 Streamlining the House's business	132
	C Urgency as a Tool for Making Progress	139
II	Urgency and Democratic Legitimacy	139
III	Conclusion	146

Chapter Seven: Conclusion and Options for Reform   149

I	A Review of Parliamentary Time?	150
II	Separate Provision for Extended Hours	151
III	Reserving Urgency for Urgent Situations	153
IV	Additional Controls for Elimination of Select Committee Stage	157
V	Possibilities for Future Reform of the Standing Orders	160
VI	The Term of Parliament	161
VII	Conclusion	162

The Research Team	165

Appendix A: List of Interviewees and Interview Topics		167
I	List of Interviewees	167
	A MPs and Former MPs	167
	B Clerks of the House of Representatives	167
II	Topics Covered in the Interviews	168

Appendix B: Bills Not Sent to Select Committee 1996–2010	171
Appendix C: Portfolio Groupings	175

Figures and Tables

Figures

4.1	Urgency Motions Moved by Year 1987–2010	69
4.2	Urgency Motions Moved by Parliament 1987–2010	69
4.3	Bills Accorded Urgency (Attributed to Year of Introduction) 1987–2010	71
4.4	Bills Accorded Urgency by Parliament 1987–2010	71
4.5	Percentage of Bills Introduced that Were Accorded Urgency by Parliament 1987–2010	72
4.6	Percentage of Total Sitting Hours Taken under Urgency by Parliament 1987–2010	73
4.7	Bills not Sent to Select Committee by Year 1987–2010	80
4.8	Bills Accorded Urgency with No Select Committee Stage by Parliament 1987–2010	80
4.9	Bills Accorded Urgency by Year of Electoral Cycle 1987–2010	85
4.10	Bills Accorded Urgency First Six Months of New Parliament 1987–2010	86
4.11	Average Number of Urgency Motions by Month 1987–2010	87
4.12	Bills Accorded Urgency by Portfolio Areas 1987–2010	88
5.1	Question Time Provided for at the Time of Urgency Motion 1987–2010	118
5.2	Leave not Sought for Question Time when Urgency Motion Moved (Urgency for Three Days or More)	119

Tables

1.1	Parliaments and Governments 1987–2010	20
4.1	Percentage of Bills Introduced that Were Accorded Urgency by Parliament 1987–2010	72
4.2	Percentage of Total Sitting Hours Taken under Urgency by Parliament 1987–2010	73
4.3	Stages Taken under Urgency by Year	76
4.4	Bills Not Sent to Select Committee by Parliament and Category 1996–2010	83

5.1	Support Parties' Voting Patterns on Urgency Motions after 1996	101
5.2	Bills Passed Through All Stages and Bills Not Sent to Select Committee (Highest Post-1993 Years)	110
6.1	Parliamentary Sitting Hours 2008	128

Acknowledgements

This research project was conducted under the institutional auspices of the New Zealand Centre for Public Law and the Rule of Law Committee of the New Zealand Law Society. We thank both institutions for their support.

A huge debt of gratitude is owed to the principal funder for the project, the New Zealand Law Foundation. Its generous support enabled us to employ a research fellow (Polly Higbee) for the equivalent of six months fulltime work on the project. Without that funding, the in-depth empirical work that is at the heart of the study would not have been possible. A special thank you to Director Lynda Hagen and Executive Assistant Dianne Gallagher, for their support and practical assistance.

Thanks also to the Victoria University of Wellington Law Faculty, which provided additional financial assistance, as well as office space.

The research project team was guided by a reference group of eminent researchers and practitioners: Professor Andrew Geddis (School of Law, University of Otago); Professor Robert Hazell (Director of the Constitution Unit, University College London, United Kingdom); David McGee QC (Ombudsman; Former Clerk of the House of Representatives); and Professor Tony Smith (Dean of the Faculty of Law, VUW; Director of New Zealand Centre for Public Law; member of the Rule of Law Committee of the New Zealand Law Society). We are grateful for their expert guidance and, most especially, for their comments on drafts.

We are also grateful to the 22 senior civil servants, lawyers, academics and journalists who gave up an afternoon to attend an expert roundtable in November 2010 to discuss the provisional results of our empirical research: Rod Alley, Jonathan Boston, Ross Carter, Mai Chen, Tom Frewen, Briar Gordon, Cheryl Gwyn, Andrew Geddis, Jeremy Hammington, Colin James, Dean Knight, Ivan Kwok, Andrew Ladley, David McGee QC, John Martin, Kristina Muller, David Noble, Sir Geoffrey Palmer SC, Matthew Palmer, Tony Smith, George Tanner QC and David Wilson. Thanks also to Olivia James, the Law Faculty's Events and Centres Coordinator until August 2011, who organised this event, as well as a number of other events for the project.

Thank you to Lani Inverarity, who got us started with an initial literature survey, to Janet Coburn for her help with Elizabeth's research on parliamentary committees, and to Amy Dixon for assistance with referencing and style-guide compliance.

The helpful staff at the Parliamentary Library and the Office of the Clerk (including Debra Angus, David Bagnall and David Wilson) have provided invaluable assistance in various forms. A special thanks to Clerk of the House,

Mary Harris, for her support and assistance, including invaluable comments on a draft.

The wonderful cover design is courtesy of Kitty Higbee and the cover photograph is courtesy of Ben Moore. Thanks also to Kathy Scott Dowell for additional assistance with the photography.

Thanks to cartoonist Tom Scott, who waived his copyright to allow us to reproduce two of his cartoons.

Others who have provided invaluable feedback and assistance in various forms include Ross Carter, Rachel Lawson, Sir Kenneth Keith, Peter Lorimer, Ryan Malone, John Martin, Steven Price, Gareth Richards, John Uhr and Margaret Wilson.

As always, it was a pleasure to deal with Fergus Barrowman and his wonderful team at Victoria University Press. Especial thanks go to Kyleigh Hodgson for her cheerfulness in the face of adversity, typesetting our hellish figures and tables. And to Pamela Strike (from Proofreading and Copy Editing Services Ltd) for her sensitive copy editing suggestions.

Finally, a special debt is owed to 19 current and former politicians and senior parliamentary officials (listed in Appendix A), who not only agreed to be interviewed for this project but, without exception, agreed to have their answers attributed. The insights into parliamentary culture and practice that we gleaned from those interviews were invaluable, and we are deeply appreciative of the spirit of candour in which those insights were offered.

1

Introduction

Between 1987 and 2010, the New Zealand House of Representatives went into urgency or extraordinary urgency 230 times. It accorded urgency to more than 1600 bills – many of them on more than one occasion. Close to half the legislation introduced to the House between 1987 and 2010 had urgency accorded to it at some stage.

"Urgency motions" have been a prevalent feature of New Zealand parliamentary practice for more than a hundred years, employed by governments on both sides of the House to exert control over the legislative timetable. Urgency motions (put forward by members of the government and passed by a simple majority vote) force the House of Representatives to sit for longer hours and enable the executive government to dictate the business that the House will consider during those hours.

Governments put the House into urgency because urgency enables them to pass more legislation, more quickly. Sometimes, they use it because they believe (or they think that the public will believe) that a particular law needs to be passed in a hurry. For example, perhaps a bill responds to a civil emergency, or reverses an unexpected court decision, or fixes a mistake that has been found in earlier legislation. Sometimes, though, governments use urgency simply because they are frustrated with the pace at which their legislation is progressing through the House. Understandably perhaps, governments want to have something to show for their time in office. They see urgency as a legitimate and time-honoured mechanism to enable them to achieve more, during their term in government, than they might otherwise be able to achieve.

Undoubtedly, there are times when we would wish our governments to be able to act fast. But urgency comes at a cost. When urgency is taken, the public can be left with a sense that Parliament is not following its own rules and that legislation is not receiving proper scrutiny. In some instances, that concern is not borne out by closer analysis – putting the House into urgency does not necessarily reduce the amount (or quality) of scrutiny and deliberation that particular bills receive as they proceed through the legislative process. In other instances, though, there is real reason for disquiet. Urgency can be used (and sometimes is used) to dispense with certain mandated pauses (or "stand-down periods") that have been inserted between the different stages of legislative deliberation. These are there to ensure that bills proceed through the system at a leisurely pace, with adequate opportunities for reflection and informed debate. Of even more concern, urgency can be used (and sometimes is used) to dispense with the select committee stage of legislative consideration in its entirety. When that happens, opportunities for policy deliberation, legislative scrutiny and public input are all significantly reduced.

For these reasons, the use of urgency is an issue of major public importance with significant implications for the quality and integrity of New Zealand's lawmaking processes, as well as for public confidence in our democratic institutions. Urgency motions can be a means to foreshorten democratic deliberation – both amongst parliamentarians and within the wider community. Even when urgency does not have that effect, the damage to the reputation of Parliament, flowing from the public perception that legislative processes have been undermined, is real.

Perhaps because of a perception (borne out by this study) that the 2008–2011 Parliament was freer in its use of urgency than were other parliaments in recent times, public expressions of unease about the use of urgency appear to be on the rise. In 2011, over one third of submitters to the Standing Orders Committee's tri-annual review of the Standing Orders of the House of Representatives (the House's self-imposed procedural rules) sought amendments to the regulatory framework governing the use of urgency.[1] Also in 2011, right-wing political blogger David Farrar teamed up with Labour MP Grant Robertson to present statistics on the use of urgency during the previous decade. They both expressed particular concern about an apparent increase (again, confirmed by this study) in the use of urgency to bypass select committee scrutiny during the 2008–2011 term of Parliament.[2] Even the mainstream media – sometimes slow to report on parliamentary procedure – have been moved to occasional expressions of concern about the use of urgency during the last few years.[3]

Surprisingly, though, there has been little in the way of in-depth study of the use of urgency.[4] Indeed, although commentators have expressed dismay over the years about its use, there have been limited data published on the topic.[5]

---

1 See <www.parliament.nz>.
2 David Farrar, "Use of Urgency" (13 April 2011) <www.kiwiblog.co.nz>; Grant Robertson, "Urgency – Some Real Information" (12 April 2011) <blog.labour.org.nz>.
3 See, for example, "Bulldozed Rush of Legislation Makes Mockery of Democracy" in *The New Zealand Herald* (14 December 2008); Claire Trevett, "National's List of Laws Passed under Urgency" in *The New Zealand Herald* (14 April 2011); Tracy Watkins, "Urgency Erodes Right of Scrutiny" in *The Dominion Post* (16 April 2011).
4 For a similar observation in the United Kingdom context, see House of Lords Select Committee on the Constitution, "Fast-Track Legislation: Constitutional Implications and Safeguards" (HL Paper 116-I, 2009) at 6.
5 Two exceptions to this are data published by Ryan Malone, contrasting the use of urgency during three periods of 109 sitting days under first-past-the-post government, MMP coalition majority government and MMP minority government (Ryan Malone, *Rebalancing the Constitution: The Challenge of Government Law-Making under MMP*

The research reported here aims to fill that gap in our knowledge by providing a contextualised account of the use of urgency by the New Zealand Parliament, with a particular focus on the years 1987–2010. Our research findings identify trends in the use of urgency and the constraints on its use. We comment on the constitutional implications of the use of these powers and suggest reforms to the regulatory matrix in which they occur. Questions that this study is concerned with include:

- What exactly is urgency and what are its effects on the legislative process?
- Why do governments use urgency? What motivates or drives them?
- How much is it used and what constrains its use?
- In particular, what effect did the introduction of mixed-member proportional representation (MMP) have on the use of urgency? Do the multi-party governments that typify the MMP Parliament use urgency less than the single-party majority governments that were the norm under the first-past-the-post electoral system? If so, how might we account for this?
- If governments feel that they need more time to progress their legislative programmes in the House, is urgency the best method of achieving this? If not, what other means might be available?
- Should we be worried about the use of urgency and, if so, why?
- How robust is the regulatory framework that governs the use of urgency? Should it be amended and, if so, how?

At its simplest, this book is an in-depth empirical examination of an important but under-explored aspect of New Zealand's parliamentary procedure that aims to advance understanding of, and promote debate on, a matter of significant public concern. Additionally, this book offers a window onto wider themes in New Zealand politics and legislative practice. One of these relates to a broader debate about how parliamentary time is best apportioned. The urgency motion is only one of an array of tools – albeit one of the most dramatic and controversial – that is available to New Zealand governments seeking to engineer more time in the House to progress their legislative business. This study into the use of urgency thus provides a lens through which to examine broader underlying questions about the way the House manages and distributes the scarce resource of parliamentary time. How easy (or difficult) should it be for the executive to exert control over the legislative timetable? Are the House's regular sitting hours

---

(Institute of Policy Studies, Wellington, 2008) at 205–212); and the data jointly published by Farrar and Robertson on use of urgency between 1999 and 2010 (David Farrar, "Use of Urgency" (13 April 2011) <www.kiwiblog.co.nz>; Grant Robertson, "Urgency – Some Real Information" (12 April 2011) <blog.labour.org.nz>).

insufficient? Could the House make better use of the hours that are available to it? Does the House spend too much time scrutinising particular legislative proposals? Or not enough? What other activities do we expect our MPs to perform, and how much time should they be devoting to them? Do we want to encourage more legislating on the part of our governments? Or discourage it? If more time is needed to devote to Parliament's legislative business, is the periodic use of urgency motions really the best way of finding that time?

Although we seek to locate our discussion of the use of urgency within the parameters of this broader set of questions, we do not presume to offer definitive answers to all of them. Ultimately, ours is a focused examination of one aspect of New Zealand parliamentary procedure. Nevertheless, we hope and expect that the study will offer the reader insights into the terms of the wider-ranging and multi-faceted debate over parliamentary time.

On yet another level, this book can be viewed as a window onto power relationships between the executive and the legislature within New Zealand's system of parliamentary government. The urgency motion is a mechanism by which the political executive exerts dominance over the legislature by prioritising its own business over the other activities that MPs perform (whether inside or outside the House) and, in some cases, by reducing the level of scrutiny and deliberation that particular bills receive. For that reason, the use of urgency can be seen as part of a wider narrative about executive dominance and parliamentary control in New Zealand politics – a narrative that is as old as Parliament itself.[6]

Our study begins during the period of "executive paradise" that characterised the pre-MMP era of New Zealand government.[7] Between 1935 and 1994, New Zealand's unicameral Parliament was commanded by a series of single-party majority governments, able to exert near total control of the House through absolute parliamentary majorities, dominated by powerful Cabinets and a robust system of party discipline. In 1992, writing as this era drew to an end, Sir Geoffrey Palmer identified the "central feature of the New Zealand system of government" as being "a concentration of power in the central government".[8]

---

6   For discussion of how this narrative about House time, executive dominance and parliamentary control played out in battles over parliamentary procedure during the nineteenth and early twentieth centuries, see: John E Martin, "From Talking Shop to Party Government: Procedural Change in the New Zealand Parliament, 1854-1894" (2011) 26 Australasian Parliamentary Review 64; John E Martin, "A Shifting Balance: Parliament, the Executive and the Evolution of Politics in New Zealand" (2006) 21 Australasian Parliamentary Review 113.

7   Lesley Zines, *Constitutional Change in the Commonwealth* (Cambridge University Press, Cambridge, 1991) at 47.

8   Geoffrey Palmer, *New Zealand's Constitution in Crisis: Reforming our Political System* (John McIndoe, Dunedin, 1992) at 1.

MMP changed the terms of engagement. Between 1994 (two years before MMP was introduced) and 2010 (the final year of our study), no one party achieved an absolute majority in the House of Representatives. Instead, the larger parties (National and Labour) had to collaborate with minor parties in order to maintain the confidence of the House and to achieve the requisite support for particular legislative proposals. In the language sometimes adopted in the political science literature, under MMP, minor parties have the potential to act as "veto players", able to block the adoption of particular policies or, in the case of urgency, particular procedural strategies.[9]

This book can be viewed as a case study of the extent to which, in practice, minor parties exert this veto power. Our research shows that, following the introduction of MMP, minor parties exerted a significant effect on the ability of the major parties to rely on urgency to push their legislative programmes through the House. On the other hand, the effect of MMP on the use of urgency was not consistent. In some cases, minor parties did not want, or did not feel able, to exercise their "veto" power in deciding whether or not to support urgency motions in the House. The reasons why that might be so are explored in the account that follows.[10]

In short, the use of urgency is part of a wider story of a small parliament, historically dominated by strong executives, and lacking the checks and balances (such as bicameralism, federalism or a judicially enforced higher-law constitution) that are common in many other jurisdictions. Against that background, the ultimate question for this study was whether the institutional constraints on the use of urgency (and, most especially, the multi-party make-up of the House that typifies MMP politics) are sufficient to control its abuse. The conclusion that we reach is that those constraints are not sufficient.

In early 2011, the authors of this book made a number of recommendations to the Standing Orders Committee's tri-annual review of the Standing Orders. We proposed amendments to the Standing Orders that might better regulate the urgency power.[11] Shortly before this book went to press, the Committee reported to the House.[12] It accepted that there was a need for better regulation of the urgency power and it agreed with some (but not all) of our recommendations for how to do so. The House has adopted the Committee's proposed amendments to the Standing Orders, and they will be in force when the House sits following

---

9   See, for example, George Tsebelis, "Decision Making in Political Systems: Veto Players in Presidentialism, Parliamentarism, Multicameralism and Multipartyism" (1995) 25 BJ Pol S 289.
10 See, especially, Chapter Five.
11 Claudia Geiringer, Polly Higbee and Elizabeth McLeay, "The Urgency Project: Revised Submission to Standing Orders Committee" (2011).
12 Standing Orders Committee, "Review of Standing Orders" [2011] AJHR I.18B ["Standing Orders Review 2011"].

the November 2011 election.[13]

This is a welcome development but does not, in our view, go far enough. In particular, the new package of reforms does not alleviate significant concerns about the extent to which urgency can be used to eliminate the select committee stage of legislative consideration. Perhaps the most troubling data produced by our study relate to the failure of MMP – at least during the forty-fifth and forty-ninth parliaments (1996–1999 and 2008–2011) – to act as an effective constraint on this type of urgency. In our view, a major cultural shift is needed in order to diminish reliance on this particular practice. The Standing Orders Committee's somewhat cautious package of recommendations is unlikely to achieve that shift.

These points are developed in the account that follows. In the rest of this introductory chapter, we begin by discussing our methodology and the data that we have relied on, before offering an overview and summary of our main findings. Finally, we leave the reader with 10 principles of good law-making that, if respected by parliaments when making laws, will maximise the chances of achieving high quality legislative outcomes. These principles serve as markers, which we will use in later chapters to test our empirical findings on the use of urgency and its implications for New Zealand democracy.

I *Methods and Data*

At the outset we realised that we needed a mixed method approach to understanding the use of urgency, using both quantitative and qualitative methods.[14] In the absence of full statistical data on the topic, we needed to design databases that mapped how urgency was used through time. Without this information we could not know how frequently urgency was used, for what stages of the legislative process, by which governments and under which circumstances. Statistical data, however, would provide only part of the story, albeit a crucial part. Interviews with participants in the legislative process were essential to fill in the full context and provide an understanding of the culture around the use of urgency.

At the heart of this project, therefore, were two empirical research exercises: the creation of statistical databases mapping the use of urgency across time; and in-depth interviews of participants in the political system. Vital primary sources for the study included the New Zealand Parliamentary Debates, the Journals of the New Zealand House of Representatives, the Schedule of

---

13 (5 October 2011) 676 NZPD 21758–21765.
14 See Melvyn Read and David Marsh, "Combining Quantitative and Qualitative Methods" in David Marsh and Gerry Stoker (eds), *Theory and Methods in Political Science* (2nd ed, Palgrave McMillan, Basingstoke, 2002) 231.

Legislation, the Standing Orders of the House of Representatives, the Standing Orders Committee's reports on its periodic reviews of the Standing Orders, and the Speakers' Rulings. In addition to providing the source material for the databases, these official records provided information and context – on, for example, the stated reasons for moving urgency, the substance of the bills to which urgency was accorded and the reasons for changes over time to the regulatory framework.

A snapshot approach (perhaps examining the use of urgency during just one parliamentary term) clearly would have been inadequate. Given that one of the goals of the research was to compare the use of urgency before and after the introduction of MMP, we needed to adopt a longitudinal strategy. The data, and the narrative, needed to include examples of both pre-1996 and post-1996 parliamentary terms. On the other hand, there is a limit to how far back statistical comparisons can usefully be made. The 1985 review of the Standing Orders brought in significant changes to the rules governing urgency, rendering statistical comparisons with the use of urgency prior to that date of little benefit.[15] For that reason, our story begins at the start of 1987 and ends at the conclusion of 2010.[16]

The 1987–2010 time period included three terms of parliaments elected under the simple plurality, single-member constituency electoral system. During that time there were two single-party majority governments and one parliamentary term (1993–1996) that saw a range of types of government. Labour held the treasury benches between 1987 and 1990 – its second parliamentary term after being elected in 1984. National defeated Labour in the 1990 general election and, like its predecessor, governed for the ensuing parliamentary term with an easy majority. In 1993, the year of the binding referendum that brought in MMP, National was very narrowly returned to power but lost its majority the following year.

Since that time, there have been no single-party majority governments in the New Zealand Parliament. National, supported by independents and minor parties, led the government until the 1996 general election.[17] Between 1996 and 2010, New Zealand was governed by both National- and Labour-led governments with a range of minority and coalition arrangements. Thus, the study includes four full parliaments elected under the MMP rules and one further parliament that had one year to run before the 2011 general election.

15 See Chapter Two, Part I.
16 1987 was the first year in which almost all of the legislation being processed by the House under urgency had been introduced to the House under the new rules.
17 See Jonathan Boston and others, "Experimenting with Coalition Government: Preparing to Manage Under Proportional Representation in New Zealand" (1997) 35 Journal of Commonwealth and Comparative Politics 108 at 110.

A fuller account of the government arrangements during the 24 years of the study is set out at the end of this chapter as Table 1.1.

A *The Statistical Data*

We created two databases, documenting every use of urgency by the New Zealand House of Representatives between the years 1987–2010. The first and smaller database (the motions database) contains all but one of the 222 urgency motions moved in the House between 1987 and 2010. The urgency motion that we did not include was a motion from 1996 in which none of the items of business to which urgency was accorded were bills.[18] Although, as will be explained in Chapter Two, urgency can be sought in relation to any item of business before the House, this study focuses exclusively on the most common usage – to advance the progress of legislation.

In the period studied, there were eight extraordinary urgency motions. The phenomenon of extraordinary urgency – which enables the House to sit through the night – is explained in Chapter Two. In order to maintain the technical distinction between extraordinary urgency motions and (regular) urgency motions, we did not include the extraordinary motions in the urgency motions database. In succeeding chapters, the phenomenon of extraordinary urgency is analysed separately, as and where appropriate.[19]

The second and larger database (the legislation database) includes the details of all bills to which either urgency or extraordinary urgency was accorded between 1987 and 2010.[20] This produces a different (and much higher) figure because one urgency motion may contain a number of different items of legislative business (that is, it may comprehend a number of separate bills). The 222 urgency motions and eight extraordinary urgency motions collectively dealt with 1953 items of legislative business, relating to 1608 bills. The reason for the variation between the number of bills and the items of legislative business is that some bills were accorded urgency on more than one occasion (for different stages of the legislative process). This means that some bills appear as an item of business in more than one urgency motion.[21]

Although the total number of bills that were accorded urgency between 1987 and 2010 was 1608, only 830 bills were *introduced* to the House between 1987 and 2010, and accorded urgency at some stage. This is because sometimes bills

---

18   This was the only urgency motion passed in 1996.
19   See, for example, Chapter Two, Parts II and III.A.2; Chapter Three, Parts I and II.A.1; Chapter Four, Part III; Chapter V, Part I.
20   Any reference to bills includes government bills, members' bills, local bills and private bills.
21   For example, of the 830 bills that were introduced during the period of the study and accorded urgency at some stage, 272 were accorded urgency on more than one occasion.

are divided or split after introduction into more than one enactment (indeed, in some circumstances, multiple enactments).[22] The figure of 1608 total bills accorded urgency during the period of the study includes both the 830 "bills introduced" and an additional 767 bills that were created at a later point, when a parent bill was divided or split.[23]

Bills often take more than one year to proceed through the House and, as noted above, can be accorded urgency more than once during that time. However, in order to produce figures and tables that reflect the changing use of urgency across time, each bill that has been accorded urgency must be assigned to a particular year. The obvious choices are either the year of introduction or the year of enactment. While there are difficulties with either approach,[24] we have preferred to assign bills to the former.[25] There are two reasons for this. The first is that, if the enactment date is used, one large bill that is divided into many can radically distort the data. Alternatively, if the enactment date is used but divided bills are eliminated, then an initial bill that has subsequently been divided would not be represented in the sample at all.

The second reason is that the government that has introduced the bill is likely to be the one most closely identified with the legislation. Accordingly, it seems most appropriate to attribute the use of urgency to that government.

Despite the advantages of the above method of assignment, it does also have drawbacks. One is that it results in an abridged collection period for bills introduced to the House during the final few years of the study. This is because urgency shows up on the graphs, not in the year that it is taken, but in the year that the bill to which it relates was introduced. If the study had continued to collect data for the final year of the 2008–2011 parliamentary term, the figures for "bills introduced" in 2008–2010 would have increased to reflect occasions on which bills that were introduced during those years were accorded urgency during the course of 2011.

The collation and analysis of raw data on the use of urgency was complex for a number of reasons, including the relative frequency with which some form of urgency was taken and the length of the time period for which the data

---

22 See Chapter Six, Part I.B.2 for discussion of "omnibus bills", which are the most common situation in which this occurs.
23 Eleven bills that were introduced prior to 1987 (but accorded urgency within the period studied) were captured in the data collection but are not included in the graphs and tables in this document because they fell outside of the date range for our data analysis.
24 See, for example, David McGee QC, "Concerning Legislative Process" (2007) 11 Otago LR 417 at 418–419 ["Concerning Legislative Process"]; George Tanner QC, "Confronting the Process of Statute-Making" in Rick Bigwood (ed), *The Statute: Making and Meaning* (LexisNexis, Wellington, 2004) 49 at 105–106.
25 Compare the following two sources, which adopted the yardstick of bills enacted: Malone, above n 5, at 202–205; McGee, "Concerning Legislative Process", above n 24, at 418–419 and 431.

was collected. In particular, changes to the Standing Orders throughout the period meant that a number of bills included in the database straddled different versions of the Standing Orders for different parts of their consideration by the House. Another major challenge in recording data on the use of urgency is the peculiarity of date recording when the House sits under urgency. The House is considered to have one continual sitting day once it enters urgency, even if it actually sits under urgency for a number of calendar days.[26]

A full account of the methodology adopted and the effect of these complexities on the gathering, recording and analysis of the data is available on request and will eventually be published on the New Zealand Centre for Public Law website.

B *The Interviews*

The second prong of the empirical research consisted of interviews with 18 current and previous members of Parliament and senior parliamentary officials on their experiences and perceptions of the use of urgency both before and after the introduction of MMP. One further person, Richard Prebble, was not able to be interviewed in person but provided us with written answers to the questions posed through an exchange of emails. Appendix A lists the names of interviewees and the topics covered in the interviews.

The interviews were taped and then transcribed.[27] Although some of the interviews were conducted by two or three of the researchers, research fellow Polly Higbee interviewed all of our participants, thereby helping to ensure that the interviews were conducted in as uniform a manner as possible. Having said that, as is usual with elite and in-depth interviewing, the interviews were conducted with a degree of flexibility in order to account for the fact that different experiences lead to different observations.[28]

The interviewees were selected on the basis of their representativeness across the pre- and post-MMP periods, in terms of the roles that they had played in the legislative process and in terms of their political affiliations. The interviewees collectively had careers spanning the full 24-year period under study and beyond, and had fulfilled a number of parliamentary roles: Speaker; junior or senior whip; Leader of the House; minister; and Clerk of the House. We spoke with past and/or current parliamentary members of the following parties: Labour, National, ACT, the Māori Party, the Green Party, and United Future.[29]

---

26 See Chapter Two, Part III.A.1.
27 The transcripts will be lodged in due course in the Alexander Turnbull Library.
28 The classic text is Lewis Anthony Dexter, *Elite and Specialized Interviewing* (Northwestern University Press, Evanston, Illinois, 1970). See, also, Janet Buttolph Johnson and Richard A Josling, *Political Research Methods* (3rd ed, Congressional Quarterly Inc, Washington DC, 1995) at 262–265.
29 We were unable to arrange an interview with a member of New Zealand First.

We asked interviewees whether they would agree to attribution of their disclosures or whether they would prefer to speak in confidence. All interviewees indicated that they were happy for some or all of the content of the interviews to be attributed. All transcripts were sent to the interviewees for their approval. Minor corrections only were requested and made.

Interviewees were asked a range of questions concerning the roles that they themselves played (or were playing) in relation to the use of urgency motions. In addition, they were asked about their perceptions of the way that urgency had been used by governments, past and present, the reasons for its use, the constraints that exist (or existed) upon its use and the legitimacy of its use.

II *Overview and Summary*

If this book is to achieve nothing else, we hope that it will contribute to better public understanding of urgency and its impacts on the legislative process. In Chapter Two, we explain how urgency works. In brief, urgency is a mechanism by which governments can engineer an ad hoc extension to the House's sitting hours and can prioritise certain items of business within those hours. Urgency motions require the House to sit for longer hours, and can require it to sit on days that it would not normally sit. Urgency also enables the government to dictate the business that the House will progress during those hours.

Some additional (and significant) impacts of urgency have already been adverted to above. Although this does not happen in every case, urgency enables governments to dispense with the prescribed stand-down periods between the different stages of the legislative process and/or to dispense with the select committee stage in its entirety. In this way, urgency motions can be a means to reduce the level (and quality) of scrutiny that particular bills receive and, thus, to fast-track particular laws through the legislative process.

We explain these impacts in more detail in Chapter Two. Additionally, we trace aspects of the historical, thematic, comparative and cultural context in which the modern urgency motion operates. Importantly, we introduce the central motif of scarce parliamentary time. We set out the broad contours of the debate over parliamentary time and we familiarise the reader with the range of techniques that legislatures, both in New Zealand and elsewhere, deploy in order to manage and apportion their limited sitting hours.

In Chapter Three, we turn to the question *why* governments use urgency. In short, there are multiple interlocking reasons. Some of these relate to a genuine need to expedite the passage of particular legislation and some relate to perceived tactical advantages to be gained, in certain situations, from putting the House into urgency. Additionally, though, urgency is driven by a more general perception that the House has insufficient regular sitting hours to get through government business. Governments often take urgency to make progress with their legislative programmes generally, rather than because any particular piece of legislation genuinely needs to be fast-tracked.

No doubt because of the range of interlocking advantages that governments can gain by putting the House into urgency, the urgency motion has proved to be a resilient feature of the New Zealand legislative process, employed by governments of all stripes over the course of many decades. In Chapter Four, we present and discuss the bulk of our statistical data on the use of urgency. We have already seen that, during the 24 years of our study, urgency was used a great deal – in relation to nearly 2000 items of legislative business, pertaining to more than 1600 bills. The use of urgency was not, however, distributed evenly across various parliaments and governments, and there was a marked difference between the periods of highest and lowest use. We explore these variations in Chapter Four by mapping the use of urgency across time (by year and by parliament). In order to dig more deeply into the data, we also analyse the different ways in which urgency was used (for example, we provide separate analysis of the occasions on which urgency was used to avoid select committee scrutiny). Finally, Chapter Four also documents seasonal variations in the use of urgency (at different times of the year or different times of the electoral cycle) and provides a breakdown of the policy areas accorded urgency.

The data presented in Chapter Four provide the foundations for a more extended analysis, located in the following chapter, of the impact of proportional representation on the use of urgency. These data show that MMP had a profound impact on the use of urgency, as well as on the cultural norms that operate when urgency is taken. That said, the pattern of use of urgency following the introduction of MMP was not even. In particular, two post-MMP parliaments stand out for the comparatively high use of urgency motions: the forty-fifth Parliament (1996–1999) and forty-ninth Parliament (2008–2011). These parliaments also stand out for the highest use, during the entire period of the study, of urgency to avoid select committee scrutiny.

It seems, then, that not all minor parties have availed themselves of the opportunities produced by their potential bargaining positions in the MMP Parliament and that the constraint imposed on the use of urgency by the multi-party environment is sometimes weak or even absent. In Chapter Five, we consider why that is so. In order to account for the impact of multi-party parliaments on the use of urgency, we look beyond the formal designation of governance arrangements (for example, majority coalition versus minority) to a complex list of factors, including the particular makeup of the governing majorities, the personalities of key figures (such as the Prime Minister), the ideological perspectives of support parties and the people who comprised them, and the overarching support arrangements that were entered into.

Also in Chapter Five, we consider a range of other factors that can and, on occasion, do constrain excessive uses of urgency – most especially, the role of the opposition, and the role of the media and public opinion. But here, too, the effect of these constraints is somewhat erratic and unpredictable. Importantly, the ultimate constraint on political behaviour – the ballot box – does not always operate effectively in the case of urgency. The media may sometimes take an interest in the fact, or perceived fact, that Parliament is "ramming through" legislation but the occasions on which it does so are irregular and not always well-informed. The public has a limited interest in, and an even more limited understanding of, parliamentary procedure – a matter that, we suggest, is not assisted by the confusing regulatory framework in which urgency operates. A particular problem in this regard is the hybrid role played by urgency as both a general "overtime" mechanism and as a device for expediting particular legislative proposals (by removing standdown periods and/or eliminating select committee scrutiny). This can result in "urgency" sometimes attracting negative public attention in relatively benign circumstances – when all that has happened is that the House has decided to sit for slightly longer hours. On the other hand, the frequency with which urgency is taken, and the sheer number of bills to which urgency is accorded, may serve to camouflage its more democratically troubling uses (for example, to bypass select committee scrutiny).

All of this raises the question whether further regulation is required. That depends, to a large extent, on whether one considers that the use of urgency is something to be avoided. Our interviews indicate that many politicians do not take that view. They see urgency as a valid procedural device for extending the House's sitting hours and pushing forward with the government's legislative programme. Their concern is that there are insufficient scheduled sitting hours for the House to get through government business and they view urgency as a legitimate device for ameliorating this problem.

In Chapter Six, we consider whether or not we agree. We begin by tackling the perceived problem of insufficient legislative capacity, which is a significant driver for the use of urgency. The wide-ranging and multi-faceted debate over parliamentary time that underlies this perceived problem demands far more comprehensive examination than this focused study on the use of urgency can provide. Nevertheless, in Chapter Six, we sketch in more detail the dimensions of that debate and we also consider a package of relevant recommendations, made by the Standing Orders Committee in its 2011 review of the Standing Orders, to streamline the House's business and free up additional legislative capacity.[30] Those recommendations (released shortly before this book went to

---

30 "Standing Orders Review 2011", above n 12.

press) were adopted by the House and will be in force when Parliament meets following the November 2011 election.[31]

The reason for our dalliance into the broader debate over parliamentary time is to underscore one point: if there is a problem with insufficient capacity in the House to progress the government's legislative business, there are a range of reforms that could be investigated to address that problem. For the purposes of this study, however, the key point is this: reliance on urgency to address the perceived problem of insufficient legislative capacity is undesirable. We explore that proposition in Chapter Six by evaluating the use of urgency against the yardstick of 10 principles of good law-making (which are first set out later in this chapter). We conclude, on the basis of those 10 principles, that any use of urgency comes at a cost to the integrity of the legislative process. That cost may be higher or lower depending on the circumstances. For example, it is likely to be higher when urgency is used to bypass select committee scrutiny and lower when urgency is taken for only one stage of a bill (and, therefore, does not interfere with the stand-down periods between the legislative stages). Even relatively benign uses of urgency, however, contribute to a public perception – whether fair or not – that Parliament is not following its own rules and that legislation is being "rammed through" the House at the will of the executive.

This does not, of itself, mean that the use of urgency is always inappropriate. There will always be situations in which the benefits outweigh the disadvantages. However, in our view, reliance on urgency as a mechanism to address the perceived problem of insufficient legislative capacity is undesirable. Further, there is a need for effective disincentives against it being used too much or in the absence of appropriate justification.

In our view, the current constraints (explored in Chapter Five) are insufficient. In the final chapter, we consider what might be done about this. In early 2011, the authors of this study made a submission to the Standing Orders Committee.[32] We put forward a package of reforms, designed to prise apart "overtime" (when the House simply decides to sit for longer) from "urgency" (when the House wants to fast-track particular bills) and to improve the incentives for governments to limit reliance on the latter to genuinely urgent situations. For the most part, our proposed reforms sought to enhance the political sanctions for the use of urgency, and accepted as their underlying premise that the justifiability of urgency in any particular case is a political question. In the case of urgency to eliminate the select committee stage, however, we went further. We suggested that the time had come to accord a role to the Speaker in approving this form

---

31 (5 October 2011) 676 NZPD 21758–21765.
32 Geiringer, Higbee and McLeay, above n 11.

of urgency (a role that the Speaker already plays in relation to extraordinary urgency).

In Chapter Seven, we document our recommendations to the Standing Orders Committee and the Committee's response to them, as reflected in its report on the 2011 review of the Standing Orders (now adopted by the House).[33] The Committee accepted the general thrust (but not the detail) of two of our recommendations: to introduce a separate "extended sitting" power into the Standing Orders; and to require greater specificity in the reasons given in urgency motions. Both of these reforms are to be welcomed, as is the broader acknowledgement in the Committee's report that the use of urgency can detract from the reputation of Parliament.

Nevertheless, for reasons analysed in Chapter Seven, the Committee's recommendations were, in other respects, disappointing. Most regrettably, the Committee resisted calls to place special controls around the most troubling use of urgency – to eliminate select committee scrutiny. The importance of the select committee stage in New Zealand's unicameral legislative process, together with worrying data from our study on the overuse of this type of urgency during some recent parliamentary terms, make more effective regulation of this type of urgency a matter of pressing concern. In our view, a major cultural shift is required in relation to this type of urgency, and we doubt that the reforms instigated as a result of the 2011 review will be sufficient to engineer that shift.

For this, and other reasons, a further round of reforms to the Standing Orders may need to be contemplated in the near future. In Chapter Seven, we suggest what these may be.

III The Principles of Good Law-Making

In a 2009 report on expedited legislation, the House of Lords Select Committee on the Constitution identified five constitutional principles that should "underpin the consideration of fast-track legislation". These concerned: "effective parliamentary scrutiny"; maintaining "good law"; "providing interested bodies and affected organisations with the opportunity to influence the legislative process"; ensuring that legislation is a "proportionate, justified and appropriate response to the matter in hand and that fundamental constitutional rights and principles are not jeopardized"; and the "need to maintain transparency".[34]

These principles are as relevant to New Zealand as they are to the United Kingdom but, in our view, could helpfully be expanded. Drawing on the House of Lords' suggestions, we end this introductory chapter by setting out

---

33   "Standing Orders Review 2011", above n 12.
34   House of Lords Select Committee on the Constitution, above n 4, at 8.

10 principles, against which to evaluate the use of urgency. We note that there is some overlap among the various principles and that they relate just to the House's legislative role, not to its other functions.

We do not examine here the extent to which urgency implicates or offends these 10 principles – that is reserved for discussion in Chapter Six. Nevertheless, it is helpful to set these principles out at this early stage so that the reader can bear them in mind throughout the succeeding analysis.

A The Ten Principles

1 *Legislatures should allow time and opportunity for informed and open policy deliberation*

Public, full and open policy deliberation is an important democratic principle. In systems of representative democracy, with laws made by elected representatives rather than by citizens, it is vital that political representatives articulate the arguments for and against bills. One of the key justifications for democratic deliberation is that, through debate, people provide reasons for their actions.

The media are part of this process of democratic deliberation, relaying, interpreting and criticising policies.[35] Additionally, the growth of non-mediated communication (for example, social networking sites) means that citizens can also have direct access to the deliberations of their MPs.

2 *The legislative process should allow sufficient time and opportunity for the adequate scrutiny of bills*

Providing effective scrutiny of the government, including the government's legislative agenda, is one of the House of Representatives' constitutional functions.[36] In order to fulfil this role, opposition MPs need to question ministers, examine bills closely and listen to expert and citizen advice. In New Zealand's unicameral system, there is no second house to assist with this scrutiny function and so there must be adequate opportunities for it to take place as legislation proceeds through the single chamber. Select committee examination of bills and the orderly progression of bills through the House enable MPs to perform their scrutiny role.[37]

It is vital to a healthy democracy that minority and opposing voices have the opportunity to express their views on bills. Her Majesty's Loyal Opposition is a significant part of New Zealand's constitutional arrangements, as in other

---

35   Richard Mulgan, *Politics in New Zealand,* updated Peter Aimer (3rd ed, Auckland University Press, Auckland, 2004) at 288–289.
36   David McGee QC, *Parliamentary Practice in New Zealand* (3rd ed, Dunmore, Wellington, 2005) at 4.
37   See Mulgan, above n 35, at 124–128.

Westminster systems, and plays a particularly important role in the scrutiny of legislation. As noted by Wheare:[38]

> [I]n the legislature itself, though government supporters may grumble behind the scenes and occasionally in public, it is the members of the Opposition who are charged with the duty of examining and criticising what the government has done and proposes to do.

3 Citizens should be able to participate in the legislative process

All citizens should be able to participate in and attempt to influence the legislative process – whether directly or indirectly.[39] Indirect participation is facilitated when minority rights are respected in the House. Minority parties – those that are not part of the government – need to have opportunities to express their views, opinions and criticisms.

Direct participation may involve citizens (individuals and groups) lobbying MPs directly, or taking the opportunity to influence bills during the select committee process.[40] Opportunities for direct involvement are particularly vital for members of minority groups whose views may not be represented by the parliamentary parties.[41]

All participants need time to consider the implications and details of bills and to work within their organisations to produce informal and formal submissions to ministers, MPs and select committees.

4 Parliaments should operate in a transparent manner

Transparency is a democratic value in its own right.[42] MPs and citizens alike depend on the legislative process being conducted in an open and accessible way, with government intentions made public so that all the relevant issues and implications of bills can be considered carefully. Bills should proceed

---

38 K C Wheare, *Legislatures* (Oxford University Press, London, 1963) at 118.
39 See, for example, Philip Parvin and Declan McHugh, "Defending Representative Democracy: Parties and the Future of Political Engagement in Britain" (2005) 58 Parliamentary Affairs 632 at 632. Broadly speaking political participation can be justified either in terms of its individual personal benefits (education about politics, identification with the polity and so forth) or through an instrumental justification, in terms of the different views and ideas that citizens can bring to the decision-making process: see David Held, *Models of Democracy* (3rd ed, Polity Press, Cambridge, 2006) at 231.
40 See Tim Barnett and Polly Higbee, "Engaging in the Future: Overcoming the Limitations of Parliamentary Representation" (2009) 24 Australasian Parliamentary Review 61 at 67–70; Mulgan, above n 35, at 124–125.
41 Barnett and Higbee, above n 40, at 62.
42 See, for example, International Institute for Democracy and Electoral Assistance, "Basic Principles and Mediating Values" <www.idea.int>; Consultative Steering Group on the Scottish Parliament, "Shaping Scotland's Parliament" (December 1998), Section 2.2; House of Lords Select Committee on the Constitution, above n 4, at 8.

at a measured pace through the legislature and there should be opportunity for submissions through committee consideration of bills. These submissions should be heard publicly wherever possible. The public nature of the legislative process also allows the media to report on parliamentary proceedings.

5 *The House should strive to produce high quality legislation*

A key role of the New Zealand Parliament is to make good law. In New Zealand, that responsibility falls on the House of Representatives because no other body, such as an upper house or judges (except indirectly), can improve it. The quality of legislation can be detrimentally affected by: (a) inadequate and abbreviated pre-introduction scrutiny; (b) insufficient time for MPs to give bills adequate consideration; or (c) insufficient time for the public, including expert submitters, to provide advice, feedback and new ideas.[43]

6 *Legislation should not jeopardise fundamental constitutional rights and principles*

One of the principles enunciated by the House of Lords in its report on fast-tracking legislation was that legislation should be a "proportionate, justifiable and appropriate response to the matter in hand and that fundamental constitutional rights and principles [should not be] jeopardised".[44] Some commentators have suggested that the New Zealand Bill of Rights Act 1990 in fact places a substantive obligation on Parliament not to trench on the rights protected in that instrument.[45] Others would say that legislative breaches of fundamental rights offend the rule of law.[46] Still others would say that there is a constitutional convention that Parliament does not legislate for "tyrannical or oppressive purposes".[47] Although each of these characterisations may, in itself, be controversial, few would disagree with the bare proposition that legislation should not trench on constitutional rights or principles without justification. The more that legislation affects individual and group rights, the more important it is that it is accorded due process and is carefully considered.

---

43 See, for example, Mulgan, above n 35, at 121–122.
44 House of Lords Select Committee on the Constitution, above n 4, at 8.
45 Contrast Andrew Butler and Petra Butler, *The New Zealand Bill of Rights Act: A Commentary* (LexisNexis, Wellington, 2005) at 87–89; with Claudia Geiringer, "The Dead Hand of the Bill of Rights? Is the New Zealand Bill of Rights Act 1990 a Substantive Legal Constraint on Parliament's Power to Legislate?" (2007) 11 Otago Law Review 389.
46 See, for example, Paul Craig, "Formal and Substantive Conceptions of the Rule of Law: An Analytical Framework" [1997] PL 467, which compares "substantive" conceptions of the rule of law of this kind with more procedural or formal conceptions. The latter would not regard intrusions on human rights as offending the rule of law per se.
47 See the discussion in Philip A Joseph, *Constitutional and Administrative Law in New Zealand* (3rd ed, Thomson Brookers, Wellington, 2007) at [8.5.2].

7 *Parliaments should follow stable procedural rules*

Leaving aside the situations that truly need an immediate legislative response, most law-making should be conducted according to Parliament's regular (not exceptional) procedural rules. This is conducive to a stable policy-making environment. In New Zealand, the House of Representatives may change its rules "but the House has recognised that when playing its part in making law it ought to act according to a more deliberate set of procedures than when enacting other business."[48]

8 *Parliament should foster, not erode, respect for itself as an institution*

Following due process and regular legislative stages helps maintain respect for parliaments, parliamentarians, and the bills that become law. The fact that correct procedures have been followed helps the courts and the community to accept statutes as binding and as the highest form of law.[49]

9 *The government has a right to govern, so long as it commands a majority in the House*

Under New Zealand's parliamentary system of government, with its partial fusion of the executive and the legislature, governments ultimately have the right to implement their policy programmes through legislation. Respect for this principle, however, has to be balanced against the others outlined here.

10 *Parliament should be able to enact legislation quickly in (actual) emergency situations*

We need our governments to be responsive. For that reason, legislatures need rules that allow normal processes to be bypassed in exceptional situations.

B Conclusion

The democratic and constitutional principles explained above provide high normative standards against which the use of urgency in the New Zealand House of Representatives can be judged. We return to such an assessment in Chapter Six after, first, reporting on and analysing our empirical findings.

Next, though, we turn to consider in more detail what urgency is and how it works.

---

48 David McGee, "The Legislative Process and the Courts" in Philip A Joseph (ed), *Essays on the Constitution* (Brookers, Wellington, 1995) at 86 ["The Legislative Process and the Courts"].
49 McGee, "The Legislative Process and the Courts", above n 48, at 86.

Table 1.1: Parliaments and Governments 1987–2010

Parliament and Dates	Parties in Government and Prime Ministers	Description of Governing Arrangements
42nd 1987–1990	*Labour (4th)* Lange –08/08/89 Palmer 08/08/89–04/09/90 Moore 04/09/90–02/11/90	*Single-party majority government.* Labour won the 1987 election with a substantial majority. (It had also been in government during the forty-first Parliament).
43rd 1990–1993	*National (4th)* Bolger	*Single-party majority government.* National won the 1990 election with a substantial majority.
44th 1993–1996	*National (4th)* Bolger	*Single-party majority government initially, and then a range of governing arrangements.* National won the 1993 election with a narrow majority. From September 1994, it became a minority government, remaining in that position for most of the rest of that parliamentary term. It had two formal coalition agreements, first with the Right of Centre Party and then with the United Party (two of the parties formed during the unsettled period between 1993 and 1996, the first MMP election).
45th 1996–1999	*National (4th)– New Zealand First* Bolger –08/12/97 Shipley 08/12/97–05/12/99	*Majority coalition government formed after the first MMP general election, then a minority coalition government.* The government lost its majority in July 1998 when an MP left NZ First. In August 1998, NZ First split up, leaving a rump of MPs, plus ACT and a couple of others, to support the government.
46th 1999–2002	*Labour (5th)– Alliance* Clark	*Minority coalition government supported by the Green Party.* In April 2002 the Alliance split up, although Alliance ministers remained in office. Clark called an early general election.
47th 2002–2005	*Labour (5th)– Progressive* Clark	*Minority coalition government supported by the United Future Party.*
48th 2005–2008	*Labour (5th)– Progressive* Clark	*Minority coalition government supported by New Zealand First and the United Future Party and with agreement not to oppose on confidence and supply from the Green Party.* NZ First and United Future each had a minister outside Cabinet who was bound by collective Cabinet responsibility only on the policy issues for which they had ministerial responsibility. This was effectively, although not officially, a majority coalition government since Labour, with the two support parties, could command a majority of the House.
49th 2008–2011	*National (5th)* Key	*Minority single-party government supported by the ACT Party, the Māori Party and United Future.* ACT and the Māori Party each had two ministers outside Cabinet and United Future had one. The minor party ministers were bound by collective Cabinet responsibility only on the policy issues for which they had ministerial responsibility. Again, this was effectively, although not officially, a majority coalition government.

2

Urgency and the Legislative Process

For a lay person, the term "urgency" (when used in a parliamentary context) is generally synonymous with rushed law-making. When members of the public hear that the House has gone into "urgency", they assume (if they assume anything at all) that this means that legislation is being pushed through Parliament without the usual opportunities for scrutiny and debate. And, indeed, urgency *can* have that effect. Importantly, though, it does not always do so. At its heart, urgency is a technique for extending the House's sitting hours and for prioritising certain items of government business within those hours. In some cases, the way that urgency is taken will result in reduced opportunities for reflection and deliberation; in others, it is simply a case of more House time being freed up for that legislative deliberation to occur.

This chapter serves two purposes. The first is to explain the regulatory framework within which urgency operates. During the course of the chapter, we cover such matters as when and how urgency can be taken, and precisely how it impacts on the legislative process. Our account is based primarily on the 2008 edition of the Standing Orders (the House's self-imposed rules of procedure). Following significant reforms to the Standing Orders in the mid-1980s (discussed below), the procedures for invoking urgency and extraordinary urgency were fairly stable throughout the period of the study (1987–2010). Where there were changes during the period, we detail them to the extent appropriate in the account given below.

As noted in Chapter One, shortly before this book went to press, the Standing Orders Committee released its report on the 2011 review of the Standing Orders.[1] Its recommendations have been adopted by the House of Representatives and will be in force when Parliament meets following the November 2011 election. Analysis of those recommendations, and of the changes to the Standing Orders that will result from them, is reserved for Chapter Six and does not generally form part of the account given in this chapter.[2]

The second aim of this chapter is to assist the reader to locate urgency in a broader historical, thematic, comparative and cultural context. We begin the chapter by explaining the origins and development of the urgency motion in

---

1   Standing Orders Committee, "Review of Standing Orders" [2011] AJHR I.18B ["Standing Orders Review 2011"].
2   However, where those changes directly affect the account given in this chapter, the reader is alerted to that in a footnote.

the New Zealand Parliament. Later in the chapter (once we have explained how urgency works), we place urgency in a cultural context by considering the roles and responsibilities of respective parliamentary actors in relation to urgency motions. We then suggest that, for the significance of the urgency motion to be properly appreciated, it needs to be understood as one of a number of techniques available to the House to ration the scarce resource of parliamentary time, and we introduce the reader to some of the other available techniques. Finally, we offer a brief explanation of some similar processes in selected other jurisdictions (as well as touching on the difficulties of comparative analysis).

I *The Origins and Historical Development of Urgency*

The use of urgency motions to extend the House's sitting hours and to fast-track particular items of legislative business is a resilient feature of New Zealand parliamentary practice, employed by governments on both sides of the House over the course of more than a century. Even before urgency motions appeared in the Standing Orders, the House had adopted a de facto practice of fast-tracking legislation. John E Martin notes that by the turn of the twentieth century:[3]

> ... a tradition had been established that the government, in the last two weeks of a session, could have bills read a second time, committed, and passed on the same day. This was the precursor to moving urgency in the House, and it led to numerous late-night sittings towards the end of sessions.

In 1903, procedural revisions recommended by the Standing Orders Committee and accepted by the House included new Standing Order 95A:

> When urgency in the public interest is claimed by the Government for any matter or proceeding, a Motion that urgency be accorded shall be moved by a Minister, and the Question shall be decided without Debate other than the speech of the Mover.

Although there was a continuing battle at that time about the desirability of measures to curtail the length of debates in the House (such as "closure motions" – unsuccessfully pushed around that time by Richard Seddon – and time limits on speeches and debates),[4] new Standing Order 95A passed with little comment. Despite being formally contested, the parliamentary debates in

---

[3] John E Martin, *The House: New Zealand's House of Representatives 1854–2004* (Dunmore, Palmerston North, 2004) at 120 [*The House*].

[4] See Martin, *The House*, above n 3, at 121–123. For an explanation of the range of techniques available to curtail debate and otherwise apportion scarce parliamentary time (including "closure motions"), see Chapter Two, Part VI.

1903 reveal no particular criticisms of the new urgency rule, no discussion of what might constitute "urgency" and no discussion of its likely consequences.[5]

Evidently, governments did not use urgency often until the ministry led by George Forbes (Prime Minister 1930–1935). From that time, it became "a key tool for effecting government business."[6] Martin reports that this was not without criticism from Labour MPs – most notably, when the Public Safety Conservation Act 1932 was passed in one sitting.[7] Nevertheless, when the Labour Party took office in 1935, it also "used urgency regularly".[8]

The 1903 urgency rule appeared in successive versions of the Standing Orders in essentially the same form, albeit with added detail, until 1985.[9] From then onwards, the House's ability to sit all night – formerly a consequence of the use of urgency motions – was relegated to the narrow category of "extraordinary urgency".[10] The instigator of the reform, then Minister of Justice and Attorney-General, Geoffrey Palmer, argued that the new provisions provided "a reasonable compromise between the desire and the need of the Government to get its business through and the rights of the minority to express its opposition when it feels it must do."[11]

II *The Procedures for Invoking Urgency*

The procedures for invoking urgency and extraordinary urgency are set out in the House's Standing Orders. Those procedures were fairly stable throughout the period of this study: 1987–2010. At the outset, though, it is important to understand that the Standing Orders (and the procedures that are set out in them) can be overridden in a number of ways. The Standing Orders themselves authorise departures from the procedures stipulated in them in a number of circumstances, either by motion of the House (that is, by majority vote)[12] or by decision of the Business Committee.[13] Even outside these circumstances, the procedures specified in the Standing Orders can always be varied by leave of the House (that is, if

5   The new Standing Orders were considered in the Committee of the whole House. The debate was not recorded but SO 95A was approved by 36 votes to 17: (17 August 1903) 125 NZPD 598. Later that year, there was a lively (reported) debate on the Standing Orders that revisited some of the clauses but the urgency provision was not addressed directly in that debate: (1 October 1903) 126 NZPD 137–164.
6   Martin, *The House*, above n 3, at 193.
7   Martin, *The House*, above n 3, at 193–197.
8   Martin, *The House*, above n 3, at 210.
9   See, most recently, Standing Orders (1979), SO 46(2).
10 See Standing Orders (1986), SO 50.
11 (23 July 1985) 464 NZPD 5853.
12 For example, Standing Orders (2008), SO 45.
13 For example, Standing Orders (2008), SOs 76 and 77. The role of the Business Committee is discussed further below: see Chapter Two, Part V.D. It makes decisions by unanimity or near unanimity.

no member present dissents).[14] Finally, the Standing Orders themselves can be suspended by motion of the House but this is a rare occurrence.[15]

Only a minister can move urgency or extraordinary urgency and urgency motions can be moved without notice.[16] Urgency can be sought in relation to any item of business before the House. Most commonly, though, urgency is sought in relation to the passage of legislation, and that is the exclusive focus of this study.

An urgency motion may relate to one item of business or to several, meaning that ministers may (and often do) move urgency for a number of bills in one motion. Urgency may be moved for any or all stages of a bill or bills.[17] A motion for urgency may only be moved after "general business" has concluded for the day,[18] and it may not interrupt a debate on a bill or other item of business which the House has already entered upon.[19]

Until 1996, the minister moving urgency was required to claim urgency "in the public interest by the Government".[20] That requirement was removed in 1996, leaving only the stipulation that the minister who moves the motion must inform the House "with some particularity of the reasons why such urgency is being claimed."[21] On the other hand, for extraordinary urgency, the minister must inform the House of the nature of the business and the circumstances that warrant the claim for extraordinary urgency.[22]

In the case of (ordinary) urgency, the Speaker has no role in assessing the soundness of the reasons given. Since 1996, though, the Speaker has been required to approve extraordinary urgency,[23] which may only be claimed: "if the Speaker agrees that the business to be taken justifies it."[24] There appears to be general agreement that extraordinary urgency is only justified for a bill that is to come into force immediately after enactment.[25]

14 David McGee QC, *Parliamentary Practice in New Zealand* (3rd ed, Dunmore, Wellington, 2005) at 117 [*Parliamentary Practice*]; Standing Orders (2008), SO 3(1).
15 Standing Orders (2008), SO 4(1). McGee notes that this "is looked upon as a procedure to be adopted only in exceptional circumstances or as a precursor to an amendment of the Standing Orders": McGee, *Parliamentary Practice*, above n 14, at 116–117.
16 Standing Orders (2008), SOs 54(1) and 56(1).
17 McGee, *Parliamentary Practice*, above n 14, at 154.
18 Standing Orders (2008), SO 54(2). For an explanation of "general business", see Chapter Two, Part III.A.
19 See Standing Orders (2008), SO 128.
20 For example, Standing Orders (1986), SO 50(1).
21 Standing Orders (1996), SO 56(2); Standing Orders (2008), 54(3). As a result of the 2011 review of the Standing Orders, this provision will be further amended: see Chapter Seven, Part III.
22 Standing Orders (2008), SO 56(2).
23 Contrast Standing Orders (1992), SO 52(5); with Standing Orders (1996), SO 58(3).
24 Standing Orders (2008), SO 56(3).
25 McGee, *Parliamentary Practice*, above n 14, at 155; Standing Orders Committee, "Review of Standing Orders" [1995] AJHR I.18A at 20 ["Standing Orders Review 1995"]. But see

The motion to move into urgency or extraordinary urgency requires a simple majority of the members to vote for it.[26] No amendment or debate on the question is allowed.[27]

Urgency (and extraordinary urgency) is terminated when either the business for which it is accorded has been completed or the House takes a positive decision to end it (for example, by adjourning).[28] It is also deemed to have ended if the government indicates to the Speaker that its ministers do not intend to move any more motions relating to the business for which urgency has been accorded.[29]

If the House is sitting outside normal hours when urgency ends, it adjourns.[30] Otherwise, it carries on with the business on the order paper. An urgent sitting is interrupted if the House is still sitting at midnight on a Saturday.[31] The House never sits on a Sunday.[32]

III *The Effect of Urgency Motions*

In every case where urgency is taken, urgency overrides the House's standard legislative procedures in two significant respects: first, by extending the House's normal sitting hours (and days); and secondly, by giving priority to the matters accorded urgency over other business. Additionally, in some (but not all) cases, urgency motions can have two further significant impacts: they can remove the routine scheduled "stand-down" periods (or enforced pauses) that would otherwise apply between the different stages of consideration of a bill; and they can result in the select committee process being bypassed.

Each of these potential impacts is now discussed in turn.

A *The House's Sitting Hours and their Extension under Urgency*

One of the key effects of moving an urgency motion is that it extends the House's normal sitting hours. In order to understand how this works, "normal" sitting hours must first be explained. At the beginning of each year (or the end of the previous year), the House adopts a "sitting programme", which specifies the weeks and days on which it intends to sit during the forthcoming year.[33]

Chapter Five, Part I, discussing two occasions on which discrete aspects of legislation accorded extraordinary urgency did not, in fact, come into immediate effect.

26 See Standing Orders (2008), SO 135(2).
27 Standing Orders (2008), SOs 54(3) and 56(2).
28 (9 December 1997) 565 NZPD 6106; McGee, *Parliamentary Practice*, above n 14, at 156.
29 McGee, *Parliamentary Practice*, above n 14, at 156.
30 (23 June 1998) 569 NZPD 10121.
31 Standing Orders (2008), SOs 46, 49 and 50.
32 See Standing Orders (2008), SO 46.
33 Standing Orders (2008), SO 78; McGee, *Parliamentary Practice*, above n 14, at 157–158. McGee notes that this obviates the need for the House to pass separate adjournment motions each time it wishes to adjourn for an extended period.

Generally, the House sits for around 30 weeks each year. Its regular "sitting days" on those weeks are Tuesdays, Wednesdays and Thursdays.[34] Even on those days, it does not sit in the mornings. On Tuesdays and Wednesdays, it sits from 2pm–10pm and, on Thursdays, from 2pm–6pm.[35] At the end of each sitting, the House "adjourns" until its next sitting day.[36] Additionally, on Tuesdays and Wednesdays, the sitting is "suspended" (rather than adjourned) from 6pm–7.30pm for dinner.[37]

It may be helpful to state at the outset that, when the House is not sitting, this does not mean that MPs are idle. Attending plenary sessions of the House of Representatives is only part of the role of an MP. For example, during a sitting week, there are a number of other regular activities that must be fitted into the parliamentary calendar. Government ministers must attend Cabinet, which usually meets on a Monday. Political parties hold regular meetings of their parliamentary members (the "caucus") and these are generally fitted in on the Tuesday morning. Select committees hold their regular meetings on Wednesday and Thursday mornings and, on Fridays, MPs often return to their constituencies, where they are expected to be available for consultation and to attend community functions. These are only some of the routine functions of an MP.[38]

Returning, though, to the House's routine sitting schedule, sitting days normally commence (following the Speaker's prayer) with "general business".[39] This includes: the announcement of petitions, papers and select committee reports that have been presented, and bills that have been introduced, since the House last sat;[40] questions for oral answer; debates on matters of urgent public importance; debates of reports of the Privileges Committee; and, on Wednesdays, the weekly general debate. The House then considers the "orders of the day", including bills set down for consideration by the House.[41] Generally speaking, government orders of the day have precedence.[42] However, every

---

34   Standing Orders (2008), SO 43. The House may order any other day (other than Sunday) to be a sitting day: SO 45.
35   Standing Orders (2008), SO 43.
36   Standing Orders (2008), SO 47.
37   Standing Orders (2008), SO 43.
38   See, for example, Geoffrey Palmer and Matthew Palmer, *Bridled Power: New Zealand's Constitution and Government* (4th ed, Oxford University Press, Melbourne, 2004) at 143–145.
39   Standing Orders (2008), SO 63.
40   The introduction of bills is an administrative step that can be done when the House is not sitting: see Chapter Two, Part III.C.
41   See, generally, McGee, *Parliamentary Practice*, above n 14, at 161–165.
42   Standing Orders (2008), SOs 72 and 73. Government orders of the day consist of government bills; the Address in Reply debate; the debate on the Prime Minister's statement; consideration of the performance and current operations of Crown entities, public organisations and State enterprises; and government notices of motion: SO 64.

second Wednesday is "members' day". On this day, private and local orders of the day, followed by members' orders of the day, have precedence.[43]

It will be clear from this account that the scheduled hours that the House has available to it each year to progress the government's legislative agenda are not, in fact, substantial. The House only has around 90 scheduled sitting days each year and, even on those days, sits for only part of each day. The urgency motion is a tool by which the government can engineer an ad hoc extension of these sitting hours on a case by case basis. In order to explore the precise effect of urgency in this respect, it is helpful to address (ordinary) urgency and extraordinary urgency separately.

1 *The effect of (ordinary) urgency on the House's sitting hours*

On the days following the passing of an urgency motion (and until urgency is terminated), the House sits each day (regardless of whether it would otherwise have been a sitting day) and for extended hours: from 9am until midnight, with one-hour breaks for lunch and dinner.[44]

Before 1996, urgency operated to extend the sitting hours of the House on the day on which the House was put into urgency as well as on subsequent days. Since 1996, that has not been the case.[45] On the actual day on which urgency is moved, the sitting hours remain the same.[46] Thus, members have adequate notice for changing their travel arrangements.[47] The only exception is that, if a minister moves the House into urgency on a Thursday and advises the Business Committee in advance of his or her intention to do so, the sitting hours may be extended on that Thursday until 10pm.[48] As the Business Committee usually sits on a Tuesday, this means that members have two days' notice of the extended sitting.[49]

A sitting under urgency may extend for several calendar days. For the purposes of the House, however, all of the business transacted at that sitting is regarded as having occurred on the same "sitting day" on which urgency

---

43 Standing Orders (2008), SO 73. Members' orders of the day consist, in addition to members' bills and notices of motion, of the reports of select committees on a briefing, inquiry, international treaty examination or other matter, and reports of the Regulations Review Committee.
44 Standing Orders (2008), SO 55(2)(c).
45 Contrast Standing Orders (1992), SOs 52(2) and (4); with Standing Orders (1996), SO 57(2)(a).
46 Standing Orders (2008), SO 55(2)(a); McGee, *Parliamentary Practice*, above n 14, at 154.
47 Standing Orders Committee, "Review of Standing Orders" [2003] AJHR I.18B at 10 ["Standing Orders Review 2003"].
48 Standing Orders (2008), SO 55(2)(b). This provision was added to the Standing Orders on the recommendation of the Standing Orders Committee in 2003: see "Standing Orders Review 2003", above n 47, at 10–11.
49 See below for discussion of the role of the Business Committee: Chapter Two, Part V.D.

was taken.[50] Therefore the records of the House will report business that has, in reality, taken a number of days to complete as having all occurred on one calendar date.

This also means that urgency can have the effect of overriding previously scheduled "sitting days". For example, if the House goes into urgency on a Tuesday and continues to sit under urgency all week, then the "sitting days" scheduled for the Wednesday and the Thursday of that week will simply be lost.[51]

As noted above, if the House is still sitting under urgency at midnight on a Saturday, the period of urgency is interrupted and the House adjourns.[52] If the government wishes to continue to consider an item or items under urgency, it is required to move a new urgency motion on the next sitting day (generally a Tuesday). The House never sits on a Sunday.[53] It has sat on a Monday on only two occasions since 1958, and on only one of those occasions under urgency.[54]

2 *The effect of extraordinary urgency on the House's sitting hours*

The key difference between urgency motions and extraordinary urgency motions lies in the magnitude of their impact on the House's sitting hours. Under extraordinary urgency, the House sits through the night.[55] Additionally, when a motion for extraordinary urgency is carried, the extended sitting hours come into effect that day rather than on the following day.[56] Even under extraordinary urgency, though, the House may not sit past midnight on a Saturday.[57]

B *Suspension of Other Business of the House*

As will be apparent from the account just given of the House's regular business, even when the House is sitting, not all of its time is dedicated to progressing the government's legislative agenda. Rather, the House ordinarily devotes time each sitting day to other activities, such as scrutinising the government's activities

---

50 McGee, *Parliamentary Practice*, above n 14, at 148.
51 McGee, *Parliamentary Practice*, above n 14, at 148.
52 Standing Orders (2008), SOs 46, 49 and 50.
53 See Standing Orders (2008), SO 46.
54 This was the occasion of the "Mother of All Budgets" in 1991, discussed at Chapter Three, Part II.D and Chapter Five, Part II.A. The House also sat on a Monday in 2000 to debate the Employment Relations Bill, which had been considered under urgency the previous week. In that case, though, the Monday sitting was not itself under urgency.
55 Standing Orders (2008), SO 57.
56 On the day extraordinary urgency is taken, the House takes its ordinary dinner break of 6pm–7.30pm. On subsequent days, it breaks between 8am–9am, 1pm–2pm and 6pm–7pm: see Standing Orders (2008), SO 57(2)(a); "Standing Orders Review 2011", above n 1, at 19.
57 Standing Orders (2008), SOs 46 and 57(2)(b).

through question time and the weekly general debate. When the House is sitting under urgency, however, these other activities take a back seat. While an urgency motion is in place, no business other than that for which urgency has been accorded may be transacted by the House without leave.[58] For example, unless leave has been given:

- general business will not be transacted;
- members' day will be bypassed; and
- question time will not be held.

It will be remembered that the House gives "leave" when no member present dissents. Opposition members are, though, unlikely to object to any of these activities taking place while the House is sitting under urgency. In practice, therefore, whether or not they do take place is generally at the will of the executive.

Similarly, during the hours that the House is sitting under urgency, select committees do not generally meet.[59] There are, though, two ways to overcome this rule. First, a select committee may meet if the committee itself gives leave.[60] Secondly, a select committee may consider a bill or other item of business when the House is sitting under urgency if the House authorised the committee to do so at the time the item of business was referred to the committee.

It is worth noting that, whereas it is generally in the opposition's interest for other business (such as question time) to be transacted when urgency is taken, it is more likely to be in the government's interest for select committees to continue to meet. That is because if select committees meet, the government can get the benefit of extra time in the House without disruption to the progress of its legislative business through the select committee stage.[61]

C *Removal of Legislative "Stand-Down" Periods*

Urgency motions list the particular bill or bills that are to be accorded urgency and also specify, in relation to each bill, the stages of legislative consideration to which urgency is to be accorded. Sometimes urgency is only accorded to one stage of a bill. When that happens, the fact that urgency has been accorded to

---

58   Standing Orders (2008), SO 58.
59   Standing Orders (2008), SO 190(1)(b). So long as notice requirements are met, select committees can still sit prior to 9am in the morning, when the House commences for the day: see SOs 190(1)(c) and 201.
60   Standing Orders (2008), SO 190(1)(b). As a result of the 2011 review of the Standing Orders, non-voting members of a committee will now not be entitled to participate in leave decisions: "Standing Orders Review 2011", above n 1, at 31–32. Subject to that qualification, "leave" of a select committee means if no member present dissents.
61   See Chapter Six, Part I.B.2 for further discussion.

that bill does not alter the legislative process to which that bill will be subject. On the other hand, if an urgency motion includes more than one stage of legislative consideration of a bill, urgency removes the routine "stand-down" periods that would ordinarily apply between the legislative stages.

In order to understand this point better, it is necessary to recall the usual process through which legislation passes in order to become law. The stages through which legislation ordinarily passes are: introduction, first reading, select committee, second reading, Committee of the whole House and third reading.[62] The order in which these stages are proceeded through and the time spent on each stage has not remained static during the period under study.[63] These changes necessitate care being taken in the analysis of urgency statistics across time and so are noted, to the extent necessary to make sense of the data, in later chapters. However, since 1999, government legislation has proceeded through the House in the following manner.[64]

- The introduction of a government bill is an administrative step, done by advice to the Clerk of the House. A government bill can therefore be introduced on any working day, regardless of whether it is a sitting day.[65] If a government bill is introduced on a sitting day, it cannot ordinarily be read a first time until the next Tuesday on which the House sits.[66] In other cases, it cannot ordinarily be read a first time until the third sitting day following its introduction.[67]
- Unless it is an appropriation bill or an imprest supply bill, a bill is referred to a select committee for consideration after its first reading.[68] Unless the House fixes a different time or the Business Committee

---

62 Following the third reading stage, legislation is presented to the Governor-General for royal assent.
63 Between 1993 and 1999 (but not before or since), the second reading stage occurred prior to a bill being referred to select committee. Before 1996, there was an introduction debate, at which point, a bill was read a first time as a matter of course with no first reading debate: see, for example, Standing Orders (1992), SO 215. From 1996 to 1999, a bill was introduced by being read a first time. During that time (which coincided with the period when bills were sent to select committee after the second reading stage), there was no debate on introduction or first reading: Standing Orders (1996), SO 271.
64 See Standing Orders Committee, "Review of the Operation of the Standing Orders" [1999] AJHR I.18B at 22–24 ["Standing Orders Review 1999"].
65 Standing Orders (2008), SO 270. Business of the House (such as the introduction of government bills, select committee reports, and so on) can be transacted on any working day, even though the House is not sitting: McGee, *Parliamentary Practice*, above n 14, at 147. See, also, Standing Orders (2008), SO 3(1) for the definition of "working day".
66 Standing Orders (2008), SO 277(1). This rule was introduced following the 2008 review of the Standing Orders: see Standing Orders Committee, "Review of Standing Orders" [2008] AJHR I.18B at 26–27 ["Standing Orders Review 2008"]. It is the only alteration in the procedures set out here during the period 1999–2011.
67 Standing Orders (2008), SO 277(1).
68 Standing Orders (2008), SO 280.

permits an extension of time, select committees must report back to the House on bills within six months.[69]
- After the presentation of a select committee report on a bill, the House must wait to read the bill a second time until the third sitting day after the report.[70]
- The House may not move into the Committee of the whole House stage until the next sitting day after the second reading of a bill.[71]
- The House must then wait until the next sitting day before the bill may be read a third time.[72]

It will be clear from the above that the Standing Orders mandate breathing periods (or "stand-down" periods) between each legislative stage in order to give legislators, officials and interested members of the public the opportunity to keep abreast of, and respond to, developments in the House. A motion for urgency that encompasses more than one stage of legislative consideration of a bill removes these compulsory stand-down periods. A bill that is already in a stand-down period cannot be brought back prematurely before the House.[73] However, once the bill is before the House, the usual stand-down periods between the stages to which urgency has been accorded do not need to be adhered to. The House may proceed with the bill's stages continuously in the one "sitting day".[74]

D *Omission of Select Committee Consideration*

Finally, urgency enables the government to move a bill immediately on from its first reading to its second reading without it being considered by a select committee.[75] Prior to 2003, the Standing Orders provided for this to occur if the motion accorded urgency to the bill's "passing" (meaning that it accorded urgency to all of the bill's remaining stages).[76] Since that time, bills have skipped the select committee stage whenever urgency has been accorded to both their first and second reading.[77]

---

69 Standing Orders (2008), SO 286. Following the changes to the Standing Orders to be implemented as a result of the 2011 review, the Business Committee will now also have the power to truncate the length of time for which bills are referred to select committee: see Chapter Six, Part I.B.2.
70 Standing Orders (2008), SO 287.
71 Standing Orders (2008), SO 290.
72 Standing Orders (2008), SO 301.
73 As a result of the 2011 review of the Standing Orders, this position will change in relation to the stand-down period between the introduction and the first reading stage: see Chapter Six, Part II.
74 McGee, *Parliamentary Practice*, above n 14, at 154.
75 Standing Orders (2008), SO 280(1).
76 See, for example, Standing Orders (1996), SO 279(1).
77 This is the effect of Standing Orders (2008), SO 280. See J F Burrows and R I Carter, *Statute Law in New Zealand* (4th ed, LexisNexis, Wellington, 2009) at 75.

As will be seen below, this is a relatively uncommon use of urgency. On the other hand, it is also the use of urgency that is of most concern in terms of its impact on the legislative process. Where legislation is not sent to select committee, the opportunities for policy deliberation, legislative scrutiny and public participation are significantly reduced.

IV What Urgency Does Not Do

Given the misperceptions that exist about urgency, it is helpful to state briefly what urgency does not do, or does not do in all cases.

First, urgency is not a technique for foreshortening the length of time for debate at each stage of the legislative process. As we explain below, the Standing Orders place limits on the length of debate allowed at various stages of legislative deliberation.[78] These limits remain unchanged when urgency is taken.

Secondly, except where extraordinary urgency has been moved, urgency no longer allows the House to sit through the night. Thirdly, although urgency *can* result in the select committee stage of legislative consideration being omitted, it does not do so in all cases. It is only when an urgency motion includes both the first and second readings of a bill that referral to select committee is bypassed. Fourthly, although urgency *can* result in legislation being introduced and enacted through all stages in one sitting, it does not do so in all cases. Urgency may only be accorded to some stages of a bill, in which case, the ordinary stand-down periods will apply for the remaining (or previous) stages.

Accordingly, in evaluating the use of urgency in later chapters, it will be important to distinguish between the different ways in which urgency can be, and has been, used over time.

V Roles and Responsibilities

In order to put urgency in context, it is helpful to have a sense at the outset of the main players involved in the timetabling of bills, including in making the decision whether or not to invoke urgency. We also briefly discuss here the roles of the Business Committee and the Standing Orders Committee.

A The Leader of the House

The Leader of the House plays the key role in deciding when a government should take urgency. Prime Ministers assumed this strategically important position until 1979.[79] Since then, the role has been assumed by a senior Cabinet minister who, as well as holding ministerial portfolios, chairs the Cabinet Legislation Committee.

---

78 Chapter Two, Part VI.
79 Martin, *The House*, above n 3, at 286.

Cabinet as a whole plays only a minor role in deciding when urgency is to be taken, although it is usually (but not always) informed in advance. Individual ministers often want their legislation to take priority but it is the Leader of the House, in consultation with the Prime Minister, who has the responsibility of managing the legislative programme.

The negotiation role played by the Leader of the House was key even in the two-party dominated House prior to the introduction of MMP but it became even more important after the advent of coalition and minority governments. It is the Leader of the House who must ensure that the government has enough support from its legislative partners to pass an urgency motion.

The Leader of the House is advised by the Clerk of the House. The Leader generally meets with the Clerk on the Monday of a sitting week to "discuss the Government's business and give advice."[80] The Clerk drafts the urgency motion and checks that it is procedurally correct (for example, that the stages of the bill are correctly identified). The Clerk does not, of course, propose that urgency be taken. Rather, he or she advises on wording and procedures (for example, how other House business such as question time can be achieved – should the government wish it to be – when urgency is taken).[81]

B *The Speaker*

The Speaker is also an important figure in the urgency process. As a non-partisan actor, the Speaker plays no role in the decision to take urgency: that decision is a political one. But the Speaker needs to be informed of the government's intentions. That is especially so if a government is intending to take extraordinary urgency, when the Speaker plays an important role in determining whether the prescribed conditions for taking urgency are met.[82] In fulfilling that role, the Speaker will be assisted by advice from the Clerk of the House. Ultimately, though, the decision whether or not extraordinary urgency is justified is for the Speaker himself or herself.

The Speaker also has a role in ensuring that the House runs smoothly when under urgency. As one former Speaker observed to us: "The House, like most contentious institutions, runs according to routine, and once the routine is broken, the children play up so to speak. So there was always a potential for trouble [when the government sought to put the House into urgency]".[83]

Speakers also have an administrative role because they must ensure that parliamentary staff and assistant speakers are available for the extended

---

80 Harris interview.
81 Harris interview.
82 See Chapter Two, Part II and Chapter Five, Part I.
83 Wilson interview.

hours.[84] In 1996, the Speaker acquired the additional role of chairing the Business Committee, which was created after the 1995 review of the Standing Orders.[85]

C *The Party Whips*

Another important role in the urgency process is played by the "whips", especially the government whips. The whips (or "musterers", as they are known in the Green Party) are parliamentary members of the party that have the responsibility of managing the party's tactics in the House. The role of the whips changed somewhat after the 1995 review of the Standing Orders before the first MMP election. Before 1995, the House operated on the basis of personal votes or "divisions". So that this system could function effectively, the House operated a "pairing" system, where "the effect of a member who is absent from the House is cancelled out by a member from another party agreeing not to vote while the other member is absent."[86] This arrangement enabled members to be away from the House on ministerial or constituency business, or when they were ill, without disadvantage to the party in the House.[87] When urgency was taken, though, the opposition would generally stop pairs.[88] The whips, therefore, had the vital role of keeping members present.

The 1995 changes to the Standing Orders replaced "divisions" with party voting and also provided for a proxy voting system, authorising the party to vote in the name of its members.[89] This meant that pairing was no longer necessary and, as such, "whipping" became somewhat less demanding. Even under this system, though, there are restrictions on the number of proxy votes that a party is entitled to cast on behalf of members who are not present in the precincts of Parliament (or deemed to be present because they are away on authorised business).[90] Accordingly, the whips still have an important role in ensuring that the party voting system operates smoothly, as well as in developing House tactics such as who will speak for the party in each debate.

---

84   Wilson interview.
85   See "Standing Orders Review 1995", above n 25, at 20–21.
86   "Standing Orders Review 1995", above n 25, at 29. For a history and description of pairing, see David McGee, *Parliamentary Practice in New Zealand* (2nd ed, Government Printer, Wellington, 1994) at 183–184. See, also, J L J May, "The Whip" in A Mitchell (ed), *Government by Party: Parliament and Politics in New Zealand* (Whitcombe and Tombs, Wellington, 1966) 135.
87   "Standing Orders Review 1995", above n 25, at 29.
88   Sowry interview.
89   See Standing Orders (2008), SOs 135–151.
90   Standing Orders (2008), SOs 150–151. See McGee, *Parliamentary Practice*, above n 14, at 206.

The whips, like the Leader of the House, are members of the Business Committee. Both in the Committee and behind the scenes, they take an active part in inter-party negotiations over House business and strategy.

D *The Business Committee*

The Business Committee was created in its contemporary form by the amendments resulting from the 1995 review of the Standing Orders. It includes representatives from all (or almost all) the parliamentary parties.[91] The Committee is a forum in which discussions can be held among the parties as to the organisation of the business to be transacted in the House.[92] It is empowered by the Standing Orders to make decisions in relation to a number of specific matters, such as the order and timing of business to be transacted in the House.[93]

The Business Committee makes its decisions on the basis of "unanimity or, if this is not possible, near-unanimity having regard to the numbers in the House represented by each of the members of the committee."[94] This means that, while its powers are extensive, it can only exercise them when there is something close to full agreement among the parties as to how to proceed.

The Committee does not, itself, decide whether or not urgency is to be sought. That is a decision for the government. However, because the Committee has a role in determining the order and timing of House business, it inevitably has a part to play in the urgency process. The changes resulting from the 2011 review of the Standing Orders will augment significantly the role of the Business Committee in relation to decisions to extend the House's sitting hours. These changes are discussed in Chapter Six.

The Business Committee is also important as a site for the exchange of information between the government and opposition parties. Increasingly, over the years, its members have been informed in advance of the government's intention to take urgency (if not the actual bills that will be included in the urgency motion). This cultural evolution will be explored further in Chapter Five.[95]

---

91 This has been the formal position since the Standing Orders (2008) came into effect: SO 74(2). Prior to that, it was the informal practice.
92 For general discussion, see McGee, *Parliamentary Practice*, above n 14, at 166–169.
93 See, for example, Standing Orders (2008), SO 76. The power to determine when the business will be transacted in the House (SO 76(b)) was added in 2008: see "Standing Orders Review 2008", above n 66, at 11. Some of the other functions of the Business Committee are discussed in the next section: Chapter Two, Part VI.
94 Standing Orders (2008), SO 75(1). "Near-unanimity" means "agreement has been given on behalf of the overwhelming majority of members of Parliament" and is judged by the Speaker: SO 75(1) and (2).
95 Chapter V, Part IV.

E The Standing Orders Committee

As already explained, the procedures for invoking urgency and extraordinary urgency are contained in the Standing Orders of the House of Representatives. The Standing Orders Committee is a parliamentary committee that is charged with the oversight of the House's Standing Orders, procedures and practices.[96] Usually towards the end of each parliamentary term, the Committee conducts a review of those Standing Orders, procedures and practices. The House then generally adopts a new version of the Standing Orders, reflecting any changes recommended by the Committee, in time for the commencement of the new Parliament.

The Standing Orders Committee usually contains representatives from each party and is almost always chaired by the Speaker. For example, during the 2008–2011 parliamentary term, all parties represented in the House had one or more members on the Committee. Of the voting members, the ratio between government (and government supporters) and opposition members was 5:4, excluding the Speaker, who was in the chair. The Committee was dominated by senior MPs, including those with experience of being Leader or deputy Leader of the House, and/or party whip.

The House regards the Standing Orders as akin to "constitutional rules" and so the Committee operates, where possible, by consensus. Its aim is "to arrive at an overall package of proposals that enjoys the overwhelming support of members around the House, even if full unanimity cannot always be reached."[97]

VI Urgency and the Allocation of Parliamentary Time

It will, by now, be apparent that urgency is a tool by which governments (through their majorities in the House) seek to influence and apportion the scarce resource of parliamentary time. By using urgency motions, governments can engineer the ad hoc extension of the House's regular sitting hours, can prioritise their own business over other parliamentary activities within the hours that are available and can truncate the legislative process in relation to particular bills (by removing stand-down periods and/or eliminating the select committee stage).

It will also be apparent that the resource of parliamentary time is, indeed, a limited one. To recapitulate, the House sits for around 90 scheduled sitting days a year and for only part of each day. When it is sitting, it must divide its attention between the government's legislative agenda and other business (for example, question time, members' days and general debates). When the House is *not*

---

96 See Standing Orders (2008), SO 7.
97 "Standing Orders Review 2011", above n 1, at 7. See, also, McGee, *Parliamentary Practice*, above n 14, at 118.

sitting, its members have a number of other tasks that they must perform. These include select committee membership, constituency work, policy development and, in the case of government ministers, running the country.

For these reasons, any discussion of the role of urgency needs to be located in a broader debate about how the House manages the limited resource of parliamentary time. That debate has at least two distinct dimensions to it. The first concerns whether the House should sit for longer hours. As we will see in the next chapter, many politicians see urgency as a technique to address a perceived shortfall in the House's regular sitting hours. This raises a series of questions. Are the House's (plenary) sitting hours, indeed, insufficient? If so, is urgency the best method of addressing that shortfall? If not, what other methods are available?

These questions, in turn, expose a series of underlying tensions. First there is the normative tension between the idea of legislation as the primary means to advance solutions to social problems and the concern expressed by some commentators that New Zealand parliaments, in fact, legislate too much.[98] As the Standing Orders Committee acknowledged in its 2011 review of the Standing Orders, the limited time available to the House to conduct its business may, in fact, provide "a safeguard against unfettered legislative activity."[99]

Secondly, there is the political tension between the desire of governments to be seen to achieve as much as possible during their three-year terms and the desire of opposition parties to inhibit them from doing so. Thirdly, there is the more prosaic tension between MPs' activities in the House and competing demands on their time (be that other parliamentary activities, constituency duties, ministerial responsibilities or, indeed, family).

To complicate matters further, there is a second dimension to the debate over parliamentary time. It concerns the question of how the House manages and apportions the limited hours that are available to it. During the course of the twentieth century, the House has made a number of changes to its legislative procedures in order to streamline the way that it performs its business (and, thereby, to free up additional legislative capacity). Some key examples are as follows:

- Legislation used to be debated clause by clause in the Committee of the whole House. By the 1990s, however, it had become standard practice instead to debate legislation part by part. This was regularised in the Standing Orders in 2005.[100]

---

98 For example, Palmer and Palmer, above n 38, at 183–188; David McGee QC, "Concerning Legislative Process" (2007) 11 Otago Law Review 417 at 429–430 ["Concerning Legislative Process"].
99 "Standing Orders Review 2011", above n 1, at 14.
100 Standing Orders (2005), SO 298. See McGee, "Concerning Legislative Process", above n 98, at 424.

- As already mentioned, prior to 1995, the House voted by personal vote or "divisions".[101] The move to party voting following the 1995 review of the Standing Orders significantly streamlined the voting process.
- Over the course of a century, the House progressively introduced limits to the length of time for which any one member may speak in a debate and (except in the case of the Committee of the whole House) to the maximum number of speeches in the debate.[102] For example, since 1999, the Standing Orders have allocated a maximum of 12 speeches of 10 minutes for each of the first, second and third readings of government bills.[103]
- Over the last few decades, the House has reduced the time devoted to its non-legislative business and, thus, freed up more of its time for legislating. For example, until 1984, each calendar year began with a new parliamentary session, which included a full State opening and an extended general debate (called the Address in Reply debate). Since 1984, the practice is, instead, to hold only one parliamentary session in each three-year term (and, thus, to eliminate two out of three of the Address in Reply debates). Significant reductions have also been made to the length of the yearly Budget and estimates debates.[104]

The House also has available to it a number of ad hoc techniques for expediting the legislative process still further in particular cases.[105] For example:

- The Business Committee (which, it will be remembered, operates by unanimity or "near unanimity") has significant powers to streamline the passage of particular legislation. It can, for example, determine "the time to be spent on an item of business" and "the speaking times of individual members on an item of business."[106] It can also decide that a particular bill does not require consideration in the Committee of the whole House at all.[107]

---

101 Chapter Two, Part V.C.
102 For discussion of this trend, see, for example, McGee, *Parliamentary Practice*, above n 14, at 177–182; John E Martin, "A Shifting Balance: Parliament, the Executive and the Evolution of Politics in New Zealand" (2006) 21 Australasian Parliamentary Review 113.
103 See "Standing Orders Review 1999", above n 64, at 56–57; Standing Orders (2008), SO 117 and Appendix A.
104 See McGee, "Concerning Legislative Process", above n 98, at 420.
105 We do not discuss here the extreme device of suspending the Standing Orders altogether. See footnote 15 above.
106 Standing Orders (2008), SO 76.
107 Standing Orders (2008), SO 290. See Chapter Six, Part I.B.2 for discussion of relevant additional powers to be given to the Business Committee as a result of the 2011 review of the Standing Orders.

- Under the Standing Orders, a member can attempt to curtail a debate by moving: "that the question be now put".[108] This is what is known as a "closure motion". Closure motions are not available "if the time for the debate is prescribed by the Standing Orders or by a determination of the Business Committee."[109] This means that they are principally now relevant at the Committee of the whole House stage.[110]

  The Speaker may accept a closure motion "if, in the Speaker's opinion, it is reasonable to do so."[111] McGee explains that the Speaker or chairperson will decide whether to accept a closure motion having considered the time already spent on the debate, who has been involved, whether each party has had its opportunity to contribute, and the extent to which members have been "relevant or repetitious".[112] If the Speaker accepts the closure motion, it must then be put to the House.[113]
- Although the starting point is that bills are referred to select committee for six months, the House is able to fix whatever timeframe for report back that it chooses.[114] By curtailing the time that particular legislation sits with select committee, the House can, if it wishes, significantly reduce the overall time that it takes to enact the legislation.
- The House can vary its procedures by leave (that is, if no member present dissents).[115] So, for example, the Canterbury Earthquake Response and Recovery Act 2010 passed through all of its stages in one sitting by leave, without an urgency motion.[116]

There is an ongoing debate as to whether these various efficiency measures go too far, or not far enough.[117] Underlying that debate are yet further tensions. First, there is the tension between the House's role in supporting

---

108 Standing Orders (2008), SO 132(1).
109 Standing Orders (2008), SO 132(2).
110 McGee, *Parliamentary Practice*, above n 14, at 199.
111 Standing Orders (2008), SO 132(3).
112 McGee, *Parliamentary Practice*, above n 14, at 200.
113 Standing Orders (2008), SO 133.
114 Standing Orders (2008), SO 286(1). See, also, SO 286(2), empowering the Business Committee to extend the timeframe for reporting. Following the changes to the Standing Orders to be implemented as a result of the 2011 review, the Business Committee will now also have the power to truncate the length of time for which bills are referred to select committee: see Chapter Six, Part I.B.2.
115 The House may, for example, give leave to dispense with the Committee of the whole House stage and to proceed forthwith (on that day) with the bill's third reading: see McGee, *Parliamentary Practice*, above n 14, at 367.
116 See (14 September 2010) 666 NZPD 13899.
117 For a strongly worded contribution to that debate, see Jeremy Waldron, "Parliamentary Recklessness: Why We Need to Legislate More Carefully" (Maxim Institute Annual John Graham Lecture, Auckland, 2008).

the government's legislative agenda, and other important House functions (such as its constitutional role in scrutinising and controlling the government through, for example, question time and general debates). Secondly, there is the tension between flexibility and efficiency, on the one hand, and the quality of legislative scrutiny on the other. In general, the more time that is spent debating a particular item of legislative business, the more opportunities there are for high quality scrutiny and deliberation. On the other hand, the less time that is spent debating a particular item of legislative business, the more additional capacity is freed up to push through the government's legislative agenda.

We return to these themes later in the book.[118] At the outset, though, it is important to appreciate that urgency is one of a range of techniques for managing the scarce resource of parliamentary time. Urgency straddles both dimensions of the debate over parliamentary time: it is a technique for extending the House's sitting hours; but it is also a technique for rationing the House's time within the hours that are available. As such, the debate over urgency embodies the full range of tensions identified above: between government and opposition agendas; between legislative progress and legislative restraint; between deliberation and efficiency; and between House business and other activities.

This book can, therefore, be viewed as an in-depth examination of one aspect of a broad and multi-faceted debate over how the House manages its time. We do not purport to provide comprehensive solutions to all of the wider issues raised by this debate. On the other hand, in making sense of the phenomenon of urgency, the wider contours of the debate must constantly be borne in mind.

VII *Urgency in Comparative Perspective*

The final aspect of the broader context that it is helpful to bear in mind is the comparative dimension. Many parliaments have some means of expediting the passage of legislation.[119] Further, as in New Zealand, such mechanisms are often highly contested and debated, simply because they are part of the battle between the political executive and the legislature. As one writer put it: "Since time is a scarce resource of parliaments, the question of what will be debated and put up for decision both on each sitting day and during the sessional calendar is a highly pertinent one."[120]

---

118 See, especially, Chapter Six, Part I.
119 For a survey of comparative approaches to fast-tracking legislation across a range of Westminster-influenced legislatures, see House of Lords Select Committee on the Constitution, "Fast-Track Legislation: Constitutional Implications and Safeguards" (HL Paper 116-I, 2009) Appendix 6 at 66.
120 Herbert Döring, "Parliamentary Agenda Control and Legislative Outcomes in Western Europe" (2001) 26 Legislative Studies Quarterly 145 at 148.

There are a range of weapons available to political executives in New Zealand and elsewhere by which they can advance their legislative programmes. A number of these were touched on above by reference to the New Zealand context. Even more broadly, they may include the power to determine the plenary agenda, to veto money bills, to restrict initiatives, to control the composition of parliamentary committees and to curtail debate.[121] Specifically in relation to the latter technique, one study of 17 European countries found that only the German, Greek, Irish and United Kingdom legislatures had the power to curtail legislative debate. New Zealand would take its place in this small grouping. However, as the author of that study acknowledged: "The rich nuances of different countries' peculiarities cannot be captured by a simple 'yes' or 'no'".[122]

One reason for this is that formal rules do not always accord with actual practices, making uninformed comparison a dangerous endeavour. More generally, legislative processes need to be understood in their broader institutional contexts. Institutional design choices – including whether legislatures are unicameral or bicameral, whether they are large or small, and whether their executive/legislative relationships follow a parliamentary, semi-presidential or presidential pattern – all affect how legislatures operate. How they are elected also influences their processes: proportionally elected institutions tend to develop different rules than do those elected through majoritarian electoral systems.

For these reasons and others, comparing processes and outcomes across legislatures in different polities is a notoriously difficult enterprise. For all that, a brief survey of three jurisdictions (all with Westminster heritages, thus somewhat easing the difficulties of comparison) may be of some interest. We do not purport here to provide a comprehensive account of the full range of methods available to political executives in each of these jurisdictions to exercise dominance over the legislative timetable. Rather, by giving a selective account of some of the methods deployed in each of these jurisdictions, we hope to provide a further window into the breadth of the mechanisms that are available and the highly contextual nature of the phenomenon of urgency.

Australia is an interesting comparison because of its shared United Kingdom heritage and its close links with New Zealand (including frequent contact among parliamentarians). In both houses of the Australian federal Parliament, ministers can declare bills to be "urgent".[123] This process is known as the "guillotine" because it enables the government, if the accompanying motion is

---

121 Döring, above n 120, Table 1 at 148.
122 Döring, above n 120, at 148.
123 Australian House of Representatives, "Standing and Sessional Orders" (10 October 2010), SOs 82–85; Australian Senate, "Standing Orders and Other Orders of the Senate" (June 2009), SO 142.

agreed to, to set time limits for each stage of the debate. Interestingly, if more than one bill is to be included in a declaration of urgency, the Standing Orders must be suspended. We understand, though, that there have been many cases over the years when that has occurred.[124]

One interesting contemporary development in Australia that is worth noting is the creation, in 1994, of the "Main Committee" system. This system enables the Committee of the whole House to sit concurrently with the House itself in order to debate uncontroversial legislation, thereby relieving time pressure in the House and freeing up additional legislative capacity. Interestingly, one commentator has noted that, following the creation of the Main Committee in Australia, fewer bills were declared "urgent" by the Australian Parliament (although she also acknowledges that this may have been due to other factors).[125]

The United Kingdom House of Commons is another obvious choice of comparison because its procedural rules influenced New Zealand's (although New Zealand also borrowed many ideas from European states when it reformed its Standing Orders in preparation for the first MMP election). The House of Commons has a number of means of fast-tracking legislation. Taking one of the more extreme measures – bills that go through their two main stages (second and third reading) on the same day – a House of Commons briefing paper documented 70 bills between 1979 and July 2011 that fell into that category.[126]

In the Commons, expedition of legislation can also be achieved through a number of other mechanisms. One fairly recent innovation is programme orders, by which bills are timetabled through the House. A programming committee, appointed by the Speaker for each bill, agrees on the timetable. Guillotine motions (setting limits for particular stages of bills) are also employed, though only rarely since programme orders became routine at the start of the 2000–2001 session.[127] Closure motions are also part of the available armoury. Finally, there is the "wash-up" – a convention by which outstanding legislation is rapidly passed through the House just before the House dissolves for a general election, through agreement between the government and the opposition.[128]

---

124 House of Lords Select Committee on the Constitution, above n 119, Appendix 6 at 67. In contrast, in New Zealand, suspension of the Standing Orders is an infrequent occurrence: see McGee, *Parliamentary Practice*, above n 14, at 116–117.

125 Sonia Palmieri, "Cooperation or Consideration: An Analysis of the Main Committee in the Australian House of Representatives" (1998) 13 Legislative Studies 64 at 66–68.

126 Charley Coleman, "Expedited Legislation: Government Bills Receiving their Second and Third Reading on the Same Day in the House of Commons" (2011) <www.parliament.uk>. As we will explain in later chapters, in New Zealand 88 bills between 1987 and 2010 received no select committee scrutiny as a result of being taken under urgency – a roughly equivalent procedure.

127 House of Commons Information Office, "Programming of Government Bills" (August 2010) <www.parliament.uk>.

128 See Ruth Fox and Matt Korris, "Hansard Society: Reform of the Wash-up: Managing the Legislative Tidal Wave at the End of a Parliament" (2010) 63 Parliamentary Affairs 558.

The Scottish Parliament provides our third and final comparator. It is of interest because of its similar size and method of election to New Zealand and because, as a new parliament (established in 1998), it attempted to create a newly democratic legislature that did not simply follow in the pathway of its mother parliament. Its governing committee, the Parliamentary Bureau, plays a similar role in legislative programming to New Zealand's Business Committee.[129]

An interesting feature of the Scottish approach to fast-tracking legislation is that, unlike the other jurisdictions discussed, its parliamentary procedures explicitly recognise the concept of an "emergency bill".[130] That term is not defined. Rather:[131]

> An emergency bill can be any Executive bill which, subject to the Parliament's agreement, undergoes a faster legislative process. For example, all stages of the bill are considered by the whole Parliament rather than by a specific committee, and the usual requirements of intervals between stages do not apply.

As in New Zealand, the Scottish Parliament has the power to extend its sittings beyond the usual hours. For example, the Parliamentary Bureau can decide that the Parliament will sit for extra hours to deal with members' business or a member of the executive can move to sit for extended hours or on other days. Further, the Presiding Officer (the Speaker) can recall Parliament in emergencies.[132] However, unlike the New Zealand urgency motion, the procedure for extending hours is separate from the question whether the legislative process can be varied in relation to a particular bill (for example, by skipping particular stages or removing stand-down periods between the stages). For that to happen, the bill must be declared to be an "emergency bill".

In Scotland, executive dominance over the legislative timetable can also be exercised through the setting of the business timetable established for each bill. This is set by the Parliamentary Bureau, though its motions must be put to Parliament.[133] Closure motions and adjournment motions during debates are also available (subject to the approval of the Presiding Officer).[134]

This brief comparative survey serves to highlight four points. First, the techniques that are potentially available to legislatures in order to manage and apportion parliamentary time, and to fast-track particular legislative proposals, are wide-ranging and varied. Secondly, the New Zealand Parliament is not alone

---

129 "Standing Orders of the Scottish Parliament" (4th ed, 2011), Rules 5.1–5.9.
130 "Standing Orders of the Scottish Parliament" (4th ed, 2011), Rule 9.21. See, also, House of Lords Select Committee on the Constitution, above n 119, Appendix 6 at 66.
131 House of Lords Select Committee on the Constitution, above n 119, Appendix 6 at 66.
132 See "Standing Orders of the Scottish Parliament" (4th ed, 2011), Rule 2.2.
133 See "Standing Orders of the Scottish Parliament" (4th ed, 2011), Rule 9.5(3); Meg Russell and Akash Paun (eds), *Managing Parliament Better? A Business Committee for the House of Commons* (The Constitution Unit, London, 2006) at 23.
134 "Standing Orders of the Scottish Parliament" (4th ed, 2011), Rules 8.14 and 8.15.

in having adopted a number of such techniques. Thirdly, such mechanisms are often highly contested and debated because they form part of the armoury by which political executives, within parliamentary systems of government, seek to exert their dominance over legislative institutions. Fourthly, urgency itself is a highly contextual phenomenon that is imbedded into a complex and nuanced political system.

For all these reasons, caution must be taken in drawing specific lessons from the experience of other jurisdictions. In this study, we draw on the comparative experience only sparingly and with great care.

VIII Conclusion

For over one hundred years New Zealand governments have been able to fast-track their legislative programmes through the use of urgency. Urgency motions achieve the goal of speeding the passage of legislation in three ways: by compelling the House of Representatives to sit for longer hours; by prioritising government business over other parliamentary activities; and by facilitating the omission of stand-down periods and select committee referral. Along with other useful rules for expediting the parliamentary process (such as closure rules and time limits on speeches and debates), urgency has become a vital tool by which political executives exert dominance over Parliament.

Urgency, then, is an extremely useful tool. But what precisely are the factors that motivate governments to take urgency on any particular occasion? That is the subject of the next chapter.

3

The Reasons Why Governments Use Urgency

Sometimes, legislation needs to be passed in a hurry. Perhaps there has been an unexpected event (such as a civil emergency). Perhaps an error or omission has been exposed in existing legislation. Perhaps there is an upcoming event (such as a major sports tournament) for which the existing regulatory framework is, for some reason, inadequate. In these and other similar circumstances, we hope and expect that our governments have sufficient flexibility to be able to respond to contingencies in a timely manner. As might be supposed, urgency is one of the key tools available to governments to enable them to do so.

It may, though, come as something of a surprise to many members of the public to discover that the majority of parliamentarians (past and present) do not believe that a contingency of this kind is, or ought to be, a prerequisite for taking urgency. Certainly, politicians see urgency as a tool that is available for responding to genuine emergencies. But they also see urgency as a device to enable governments to push forward with their legislative agendas more generally. In short, they see urgency as a legitimate and time-honoured mechanism to supplement the House's regular sitting hours from time to time in order to ensure that governments achieve more during their term in office than they might otherwise be able to.

In this chapter, we explore in some depth the reasons why governments take urgency. The starting point in identifying those reasons is the formal justifications put forward by successive leaders of the House in urgency motions themselves. However, those formal reasons are often brief, general and imprecise – a point that is explored in the next section. In order to look behind those stated reasons into politicians' deep-seated motivations for using urgency, we draw heavily in this chapter on the interviews that we conducted with participants (past and present) in the political system.

These sources disclose multiple interlocking reasons why New Zealand governments use urgency, which we categorise below under four headings. We have already touched on the first two of those headings: specific reasons to expedite the passage of particular legislation; and the desire to make faster progress with the government's overall legislative agenda. The remaining two headings relate to the perceived tactical advantages to be gained from using urgency and to the distinctive practice of Budget day urgency.

The purpose of this chapter is to explore what motivates the politicians themselves. For the most part, we refrain from commenting on the validity or otherwise of those motivations in this chapter, leaving that for subsequent analysis.¹

I *The Formal Requirement to Give Reasons*

As explained in the foregoing chapter, the Standing Orders require the minister moving urgency (who will generally be the Leader of the House) to inform the House "with some particularity" why the motion is being moved.² In the case of extraordinary urgency, the Standing Orders require the minister to inform the House of the "nature of the business and the circumstances that warrant the claim for extraordinary urgency."³

In accordance with this formal requirement, respective leaders of the House provided at least some explanation of the reasons for moving urgency in all but five urgency motions during the period under study. There was no set pattern for the giving of reasons for an urgency motion, although particular leaders of the House displayed distinctive styles. It was during Don McKinnon's period as the Leader of the House that five urgency motions were moved with no reason being given at all.⁴ Wyatt Creech (1996–1998), Roger Sowry (1998–1999) and Gerry Brownlee (2008–) tended to give the most detailed explanations, sometimes running to several paragraphs.⁵ Jonathan Hunt (1987–1990), Paul East (1990–1992), Don McKinnon (1993–1996) and Dr Michael Cullen (1999–2008) tended to be very brief – often expressing their reasons in one sentence.⁶ Jonathan Hunt's reasons occasionally involved a dig at the opposition, for example: "That motion is to ensure that the Bill will be referred to a select committee so that the Opposition can do some work during the recess."⁷

Even when expressed at some length, the formal reasons given to justify the use of urgency were often general and imprecise. Where (as was often the case) a motion accorded urgency to a number of items of business, separate reasons were generally not given for all of those items.⁸ Despite a Speaker's ruling in the 1980s that a reason must be more than a "bald statement that progress needed

---

1   See, especially, Chapter Six.
2   Standing Orders (2008), SO 54.
3   Standing Orders (2008), SO 56.
4   (27 April 1993) 534 NZPD 14897; (1 June 1993) 535 NZPD 15339; (1 July 1993) 536 NZPD 16490; (27 July 1993) 537 NZPD 16902; (5 July 1994) 541 NZPD 2597.
5   For example, (9 December 1997) 656 NZPD 6105; (29 September 1998) 572 NZPD 12368; (24 November 2009) 659 NZPD 7900.
6   For example, (27 July 1989) 499 NZPD 11560; (18 August 1992) 528 NZPD 10618; (22 July 1993) 536 NZPD 16727; (16 March 2006) 629 NZPD 1904.
7   (5 May 1988) 488 NZPD 4017. See, also, (21 July 1988) 490 NZPD 5268; (6 December 1988) 495 NZPD 8454; (18 May 1989) 498 NZPD 10606; (19 October 1989) 502 NZPD 13308.
8   For example, (10 October 2001) 595 NZPD 12221.

to be made",⁹ many of the reasons given were, in truth, little more than that. Most commonly, the reasons given simply reflected the government's wish to make progress with its legislative agenda.¹⁰

Turning to extraordinary urgency, formal reasons were given in each of the eight cases in which extraordinary urgency was moved during the period under study but, again, the quality of the reasons given was often lacking. In three of the eight cases, it was considered sufficient simply to refer to the subject-matter of the proposed measure and to the fact that it was to come into effect at midnight;¹¹ and in a fourth, it was considered sufficient to assert that the measures were "major matters" and that it was "essential that they are passed into law as quickly as possible."¹² In three cases, an actual reason for urgency was clearly articulated – in each case, to minimise the consequences of pre-emptive behaviour by consumers following the announcement of a proposed change in excise duties.¹³ The most recent use of extraordinary urgency documented in the study (again involving the imposition of an excise – on tobacco) noted that the legislation itself was "in the interests of public health" and simply asserted that: "Procedurally, it is desirable that this bill is passed as quickly as possible in order that it can be given assent and that new tax provisions can be applied."¹⁴

In general, therefore, governments throughout the period under analysis failed to explain to Parliament exactly why it was necessary to expedite the passage of particular pieces of legislation through the use of urgency. Nevertheless, the explanations that were supplied were generally regarded as acceptable interpretations of the Standing Orders or, in any event, as unimpeachable.¹⁵ It seems that this is an area where established practices have led to operating norms that only partially satisfy the written rules.

---

9   (19 November 1985) 467 NZPD 8181.
10 For example, (16 May 1989) 498 NZPD 10458; (22 June 1993) 536 NZPD 15959; (24 November 1998) 573 NZPD 13404; (12 April 2005) 625 NZPD 19757; (16 December 2008) 651 NZPD 728.
11 (14 May 1988) 490 NZPD 5594; (20 May 1999) 577 NZPD 16618; (6 May 2003) 608 NZPD 5358.
12 (30 July 1991) 517 NZPD 3287–3288. In that case, after questioning by an opposition member, the Leader of the House went on to elaborate slightly.
13 (28 July 1988) 490 NZPD 5594; (9 May 2000) 583 NZPD 1983; (28 February 2002) 598 NZPD 14767. This explanation for resort to urgency is explored further: Chapter Three, Part II.A.1 and Chapter Five, Part I.
14 (28 April 2010) 662 NZPD 10559.
15 See, for example, (16 December 2008) 651 NZPD 728. Dr Michael Cullen raised a point of order, arguing that an urgency motion moved by the Leader of the House, Gerry Brownlee, did not comply with the Standing Orders as it contained no explanation whatsoever as to why urgency was being sought. The Speaker's response was that, if the opposition felt that inadequate reason had been given, its remedy was to refuse to support the motion.

II Why New Zealand Governments Use Urgency: Searching for the Reasons

The formal reasons provided in Hansard paint, at best, an incomplete picture of the factors that motivate New Zealand governments to use urgency. An additional and more fruitful source is the interviews that we conducted with participants in the political system – past and present politicians and senior parliamentary officials. Drawing on both those sources, in the remainder of this chapter we categorise politicians' motivations for using urgency under four heads: a specific need, or perceived need, to expedite the passage of a particular piece of legislation; making progress with the "order paper"; seeking tactical advantage; and Budget day urgency.

These categories are not watertight. In each case where urgency is used, one or more of a range of reasons may be at play. For example, whereas a generalised desire to expedite the legislative programme may provide the backdrop against which a decision to move urgency is made, other factors will necessarily dictate which items of legislative business are prioritised by inclusion in the urgency motion.

A Specific Reasons to Expedite the Passage of Particular Legislation

As might be expected, and as its name suggests, in some (but by no means all) cases during our period of study, the use of urgency was motivated by factors giving rise to a need (or perceived need) to expedite the passage of a particular piece of legislation.[16] There is a range of circumstances – some more compelling than others – in which such a need may arise or be thought to arise. It would be unwise to attempt an exhaustive list.[17] Some recurring examples, though, are as follows.

1 Minimising opportunities for speculative behaviour by market participants and providing certainty for financial markets

A repeated justification for using urgency during the period studied was to minimise the potential for speculative behaviour from consumers and other market participants that might follow the announcement of change to fiscal policy. The concern in these cases is that, if the change is not brought into immediate effect, there will be the opportunity for interference with the financial markets or a "run" on a particular product.[18] A concern about pre-

---

16   For example, Sowry, Dunne, Creech and East interviews; Prebble email exchange.
17   See House of Lords Select Committee on the Constitution, "Fast-Track Legislation: Constitutional Implications and Safeguards" (HL Paper 116-I, 2009) at [25].
18   For example, Kidd and Shirley interviews.

emptive behaviour of this kind appears to have been the sole motivation for six of the eight extraordinary urgency motions taken during the period under study.[19]

The most common situation in which a concern about pre-emptive behaviour of this kind was used to justify urgency (and generally extraordinary urgency) was an increase to the excise rates on alcohol, tobacco or petrol.[20] The pre-emptive behaviour concern appears to have become so accepted in such cases that it was sometimes not even considered necessary to spell out the concern in the urgency motion. For example, an extraordinary urgency motion in 2010 involved an excise tax on tobacco products and so was presumably motivated by the pre-emptive behaviour concern. In the urgency motion, however, the Leader of the House Gerry Brownlee did not find it necessary to articulate that concern, referring simply to the public health justification for the legislation (a matter that hardly explained the need to rush it through the House).[21]

Rodney Hide suggested to us in his interview that the use of urgency for all stages of the Local Government (Tamaki Makaurau Reorganisation) Act 2009 (amalgamating the various local councils in the Auckland region) was motivated by analogous reasoning.[22] In his view, once the intention to amalgamate the councils had been announced, there was a danger that individual councils would no longer feel constrained by the ordinary political processes from incurring debt.

There was a high level of acceptance from interviewees of the legitimacy of this "pre-emptive behaviour" justification for expediting legislation, including as a reason for extraordinary urgency.[23] Some of our interviewees, though, wondered whether this justification for the use of urgency is less compelling in modern times than it may have been previously.[24] Peter Dunne, for example, questioned whether "panic buying" of consumer goods really does occur in any significant amount and pointed out that many changes to fiscal policy (for example, increases to GST) are now pre-announced without deleterious consequences. In a similar vein, Roger Sowry suggested that extraordinary

---

19 (28 April 2010) 662 NZPD 10559; (6 May 2003) 608 NZPD 5358; (28 February 2002) 598 NZPD 14766; (9 May 2000) 583 NZPD 1983–1984; (14 May 1998) 568 NZPD 8581; (28 July 1988) 490 NZPD 5594–5595. In addition, the extraordinary urgency motion moved on 30 July 1991 seems to have been partially motivated, at least, by the same concern: (30 July 1991) 517 NZPD 3287.
20 See, for example, (2 July 1992) 526 NZPD 9728–9729; (14 May 1998) 568 NZPD 8581; (9 May 2000) 583 NZPD 1983.
21 (28 April 2010) 662 NZPD 10559.
22 Introduced as the Local Government (Auckland Reorganisation) Bill 2009.
23 For example, Shirley, McGee, East, Hughes, Katene, Palmer and Brownlee interviews.
24 For example, Kidd interview. Interestingly, this justification does not appear in the list of justifications for fast-tracking legislation given by House of Lords Select Committee on the Constitution, above n 17, at 10.

urgency is justified for "something substantial around the share market" but not for putting up the price of alcohol or tobacco.[25]

A related justification that appeared in urgency motions during the period of the study was to create certainty and clarity for the business community and market participants.[26] A relatively recent example of this formal justification being used was the passage of the Crown Retail Deposit Guarantee Scheme Bill in 2009, which extended the government guarantee on particular financial investments.[27] This justification also appeared in one of the eight extraordinary urgency motions during the period (abolishing a tax on the sale and lease of commercial land and buildings).[28]

2 Responding to an unexpected event

The second category falling under the broad rubric of specific reasons to expedite particular legislation is that of unexpected events that require, or are thought to require, an immediate legislative response. Civil emergencies might fall at the high end of this category[29] but, during the period studied, no legislation was, in fact, enacted under urgency to respond to a civil emergency. A number of interviewees put forward the legislation responding to the first Canterbury earthquake, the Canterbury Earthquake Response and Recovery Bill 2010, as an example where the use of urgency might have been justified.[30] However, that legislation was actually expedited by leave of the House rather than through urgency (illustrating the point made in Chapter Two that urgency is not the only device available to governments and parliaments to expedite the passage of legislation).[31] Although it falls outside the temporal scope of our study, it is worth noting that the following year, legislation to respond to the second Canterbury earthquake *was* expedited by way of urgency.[32]

Aside from civil emergencies, when the House of Lords Select Committee on the Constitution undertook a similar exercise in 2009 of documenting the situations that had been used to justify fast-tracking legislation in the United Kingdom, it identified two specific examples that might fall within the general

25 See, also, (30 July 1991) 517 NZPD 3287–3288 (where Richard Prebble suggested that the "speculative behaviour" justification is weaker now that shops and service stations are open after hours).
26 For example, (29 April 1997) 559 NZPD 1336; (24 March 1998) 567 NZPD 7695; (20 September 2001) 595 NZPD 11897.
27 (8 September 2009) 657 NZPD 6038–6039. A further historic example given to us by interviewees concerned legislative changes to interest rates during the period when they were regulated or fixed: Hughes and Kidd interviews.
28 (20 May 1999) 577 NZPD 16618.
29 Dunne and Shirley interviews.
30 Sowry, Dunne, Shirley and Palmer interviews.
31 See (14 September 2010) 666 NZPD 13899.
32 (12 April 2011) 671 NZPD 17898.

Tom Scott cartoon referencing the Canterbury Earthquake Recovery Act 2011, enacted under urgency in April 2011. The cartoon appeared in *The Dominion Post* and is reprinted with the permission of the artist.

category of unexpected events: "economic crises" and "to deal with a crisis in prisons as a result of industrial action".[33] In New Zealand, an example repeatedly given by our interviewees as to when urgency might be justified was legislation to prop up a failing financial institution, such as happened in relation to the Public Service Investment Society in 1979.[34] Another New Zealand example that might perhaps fit under the rubric of "economic crisis" was the use of urgency in 2009 to enact legislation to defer tax cuts because of "the difficult economic circumstances the country finds itself in".[35]

Another situation that might be thought to fall into the category of unexpected events is legislation enacted to respond to a court decision.[36] An example of this use of urgency was given to us by Wyatt Creech. He was the Minister of Education and the Leader of the House in 1998, when urgency was

---

33 House of Lords Select Committee on the Constitution, above n 17, at 10.
34 For example, East, Kidd and Dunne interviews; Prebble email exchange. For the urgency motions, see (28 June 1979) 423 NZPD 1175–1176; (28 June 1979) 423 NZPD 1176.
35 (28 May 2009) 654 NZPD 3958.
36 See House of Lords Select Committee on the Constitution, above n 17, at 10.

used to pass legislation to respond to a court case in relation to the merger of tertiary institutions.[37] A more recent and high profile example was the Foreshore and Seabed Act 2004, enacted in response to a Court of Appeal ruling that the Māori Land Court could determine whether the foreshore and seabed had the status of Māori customary land.[38] The Bill was accorded urgency for its remaining stages after returning from select committee.[39]

A final example during the period of the study of legislation to respond to an unexpected event can be found in the passage of the Immigration Amendment Bill (No 2) in 1999. The Government was made aware that a boat of 102 Chinese nationals was en route to New Zealand with the apparent intention of seeking refugee status on arrival. Legislation had been enacted to streamline New Zealand's refugee and immigration processes but its provisions were not due to come into force until later that year. A second bill was passed under urgency to provide for an earlier commencement date.[40]

3 Correcting errors

A third category in which there may be a real or perceived need to expedite the passage of a particular piece of legislation is where an anomaly, oversight or uncertainty has come to light in existing legislation.[41] There are numerous examples of urgency being used for this purpose throughout the period studied.[42] One example is the Summary Proceedings Amendment Bill (No 2) 2010. It was accorded urgency in order to correct an error in earlier legislation that had resulted in an unintended extension to the right to a jury trial.[43]

---

37 *Manawatu Polytechnic v Attorney-General*, Wellington High Court, CP324/97, 15 December 1997; (19 May 1998) 568 NZPD 8882.
38 *Ngati Apa v Attorney-General* [2003] 3 NZLR 643.
39 (16 November 2004) 621 NZPD 16929. An even more recent example falling outside the period of the study is the Video Camera Surveillance (Temporary Measures) Bill 2011, introduced at short notice to respond to a decision from the Supreme Court that cast into doubt the lawfulness of certain Police video surveillance practices: *Hamed v R* [2011] NZSC 101; (27 September 2011) 676 NZPD 21443; (6 October 2011) 676 NZPD 21804.
40 (15 June 1999) 578 NZPD 17350–17351.
41 See House of Lords Select Committee on the Constitution, above n 17, at 10; Wilson and Turei interviews.
42 For example, (18 August 1992) 528 NZPD 10619 (according urgency to the Summary Proceedings Amendment Bill (No 3) 1992); (23 June 1998) 569 NZPD 9890 (according urgency to the Oaths and Declarations (Validation) Amendment Bill 1998); (2 August 2001) 593 NZPD 10628 (according urgency to the Social Security (Residence of Spouses) Amendment Bill 2001).
43 (28 October 2010) 668 NZPD 14938; Brownlee interview.

4 Urgency driven by an external (or pre-set) deadline

Finally, urgency may be driven by an external deadline or earlier commitment which requires the legislation to be passed by a particular date. One example falling within this category is legislation that needs to be in force in time for a forthcoming event.[44] For example, in 1991, the Smoke-free Environments Amendment Bill was passed under urgency to allow for tobacco sponsorship of the World Cup Cricket Series.[45] In 1992, electoral legislation was accorded urgency to allow "the necessary machinery work to be undertaken prior to the next election."[46] Conversely, upcoming local government elections have sometimes been halted, altered or deferred by legislation accorded urgency – a recent example being the deferral of the Environment Canterbury elections in 2010.[47]

Another example falling within this category might be legislation to respond to a timeframe contained in an international agreement.[48] For example, in 2009, urgency was taken for the second reading of the Anti-Money Laundering and Countering Financing of Terrorism Bill because "we have some international obligations that mean we need to, at least by the middle of October, have reached a conclusion."[49]

Sometimes the source of the deadline is some other legislation that is about to enter into force. Perhaps the other legislation depends for its operative effect on the bill that is therefore being expedited,[50] or perhaps a change of government has prompted a desire to amend or repeal the enacted legislation before it enters into force.[51] Urgency can also be driven by the need to pass legislation before the expiry of regulations or state sector contracts,[52] or by the exigencies of the industry to which the bill relates,[53] or by broader commitments that the government has made.[54]

---

44 See House of Lords Select Committee on the Constitution, above n 17, at 10.
45 (4 June 1991) 515 NZPD 2034.
46 (28 April 1992) 524 NZPD 7999.
47 (30 March 2010) 661 NZPD 9929. See, also, (2 May 2000) 583 NZPD 1780–1781; (28 July 1998) 570 NZPD 10783; (13 May 2009) 654 NZPD 3175.
48 See House of Lords Select Committee on the Constitution, above n 17, at 10; Prebble email exchange.
49 (24 September 2009) 657 NZPD 6854. See, also, (6 December 1994) 545 NZPD 5370; (8 October 2002) 603 NZPD 923.
50 Hughes interview. For example, (24 July 1990) 509 NZPD 3010.
51 For example, the Climate Change Response (Moderated Emissions Trading) Amendment Bill 2009 was accorded urgency so that it would come into force rather than the previous Government's emissions trading scheme: (24 November 2009) 659 NZPD 7900.
52 For example, (26 February 1991) 512 NZPD 264–265; (15 December 1998) 574 NZPD 14564; (29 April 1997) 559 NZPD 1335.
53 Prebble email exchange; Cullen interview. See, also, (19 May 1998) 568 NZPD 8882 (citing the end of the dairy season).
54 Treaty of Waitangi settlements might be considered an example of this: see (31 March 1998)

It is not the purpose of this chapter to judge the validity of these or other justifications for the use of urgency.[55] Nevertheless, it is perhaps worth noting, with respect to uses of urgency that fell into this general category, that the circumstances creating urgency were not always outside the control of the government. Rather, many such examples appeared to involve the government being over-optimistic in the commitments that it had made and then relying on urgency to deliver on them.

That phenomenon was perhaps most especially evident in the numerous cases during the period of the study where the formal reason for seeking urgency invoked a deadline (such as a commencement date) contained in the legislation itself.[56] On its face, this is nothing more than bootstrapping and so it would be necessary to excavate further in each case, in order to determine the real cause, if any, of the perceived urgency.

B Freeing up the Order Paper

When the House of Lords Select Committee on the Constitution undertook a similar exercise in 2009, almost all of the situations that it identified involved specific reasons, of the kinds identified above, for expediting the particular legislation.[57] In the New Zealand context, however, it is important to understand that a genuine need to expedite the passage of particular legislation is not the only, indeed, not even the main reason why governments seek to utilise urgency motions. Urgency in the New Zealand Parliament is, at its heart, a technique for extending the House's sitting hours and prioritising government business over other House business. A key reason why governments use urgency motions is because they have a full order paper and want to push forward with their legislative programmes[58] – to get through the "legislative log jam", as one interviewee put it.[59] In other words, a significant factor that drives urgency is a

---

567 NZPD 7936 (relating to the Ngai Tahu Claims Settlement Bill); (3 December 1992) 532 NZPD 12813 (relating to the Treaty of Waitangi (Fisheries Claims) Settlement Bill).
55 For that, see Chapter Six.
56 See, for example, (2 April 1998) 567 NZPD 8115 ("In each case the Bills are required to be passed because of the operative dates within those particular measures"). For further examples, see (29 June 2004) 618 NZPD 13989; (26 March 2002) 599 NZPD 15290; (29 September 1998) 572 NZPD 12368; (22 June 1994) 541 NZPD 1966; (22 March 1988) 487 NZPD 2848. Seven of the eight examples of extraordinary urgency motions during the period refer to the fact that the legislation is to come into effect "at midnight tonight" or the following day and, in two of the eight, that is the only explanation given for the urgency of the matter: (14 May 1988) 490 NZPD 5594; (20 May 1999) 577 NZPD 16618; (6 May 2003) 608 NZPD 5358.
57 House of Lords Select Committee on the Constitution, above n 17, at 10.
58 Sowry, Wilson, Smith, Kidd, McGee, Harris, East, Creech, Dunne, Hughes and Brownlee interviews; Prebble email exchange.
59 Dunne interview.

perception that there are insufficient scheduled sitting hours to get through the government's legislative agenda.

Of all the parliamentarians that we interviewed, only three expressed discomfort with this reason for using urgency.[60] Most interviewees stressed to us that urgency was not only a tool but, in their view, a legitimate tool for the government to engineer extra sitting hours.[61] Underlying that view was a general perception that the House does not currently have enough hours to get through government business, that this is a significant problem and that the question of urgency needs to be addressed in that wider context. If urgency were to be constrained, we were told, the House would have to find other ways to extend its regular sitting time. In fact, the need for reforms to address more systemically the problem of insufficient time was a common theme in the interviews that we conducted.[62] Interviewees also made the point in this context that the three-year electoral term puts particular pressure on governments to expedite legislation.[63]

The "insufficient sitting hours" justification for urgency was also evident from the formal reasons given in Hansard for moving urgency which, most commonly, consisted of variations on the theme of the government's wish to "make progress".[64] Indeed, on one occasion in 2009, the Leader of the House, Gerry Brownlee, was moved to give a small treatise on the topic in the course of justifying an urgency motion:[65]

> I also say that it is not widely known that the House sits for only 17 hours a week. When we take out question time, the general debate, and quite often, the overrun of question time, or special debates such as were requested today, we get to the situation whereby between now and Christmas the scheduled sitting days available to the House are such that we have just 115-odd hours available for the passing of legislation. That means that from time to time the Government needs to seek extended hours, which is exactly what is being sought here through the provision of urgency.

The impetus to use urgency to push forward with a government's legislative programme may potentially arise at any period of the parliamentary year. However, our interviewees identified particular pressure points in the parliamentary calendar where a desire to extend the House's sitting hours is

---

60 Turei, Dunne and Katene interviews.
61 For example, Sowry, Wilson, McGee, Hunt and Cullen interviews.
62 For example, Sowry, Brownlee, Kidd, McGee and Dunne interviews.
63 For example, Wilson and Palmer interviews; Prebble email exchange.
64 For example, (12 May 1987) 480 NZPD 8918; (29 March 1994) 539 NZPD 798; (2 December 1997) 565 NZPD 5831; (13 December 2000) 589 NZPD 7378; (12 April 2005) 625 NZPD 19757; (20 October 2009) 658 NZPD 7195; (24 August 2010) 666 NZPD 13374.
65 (8 September 2009) 657 NZPD 6039.

particularly likely to arise. For example, one interviewee suggested to us that, because a large amount of legislation tends to be introduced at the front end of the parliamentary session, reports from select committees will sometimes pile up at around the same time (presumably around six months or so into the session), and there will be a perceived need for extra sitting days.[66] Another interviewee suggested to us that this may be a particular issue for new governments that have spent a long time in opposition and so tend to introduce a large amount of legislation when they are first elected.[67] Conversely, a government that is nearing the end of the parliamentary term may be motivated to use urgency to push through its legislative programme before the election – particularly if it is not doing well in the polls and is contemplating being voted out of office.[68]

Another interviewee suggested that there is often a wish to take urgency on the first readings of bills before a recess in order to get them off to select committee,[69] and this was borne out on occasion by the formal reasons given in Hansard.[70]

Finally, a number of interviewees referred to the phenomenon of pre-Christmas urgency, when there is a particular desire to clear the order paper before the long summer recess.[71] Again, this was borne out on occasion by the formal reasons given in Hansard.[72] Both the current and former Clerk of the House suggested to us that pre-Christmas urgency was even more of a feature prior to 1984, when Parliament only met for around seven months a year. That short sitting year heightened the perceived need to clear the order paper before the House "knocked off" for five months.[73]

---

66 Kidd interview.
67 Hughes interview.
68 Creech interview. Jonathan Hunt suggested to us (perhaps for this reason) that urgency taken early in a sitting year is an indication that a government may be considering holding an early election.
69 Dunne interview.
70 For example, (29 March 1994) 539 NZPD 798 ("to make progress, and in particular to introduce Government Bills for the select committees to consider"); (23 February 2010) 660 NZPD 9112 ("in order that the Bill gets to a select committee before we go into that long adjournment").
71 For example, Wilson, Hunt, Palmer, Creech and Hide interviews.
72 For example, (13 December 2000) 589 NZPD 7378 ("in order that the Government can complete its legislative business this week"); (2 December 1997) 565 NZPD 5831 ("because these are important pieces of legislation that we wish to advance or complete before the end of the parliamentary year"); (16 November 2010) 668 NZPD 15348 ("Although the content of the urgency motion has a number of bills that are controversial, it is largely driven out of the fact that we have just 11 House days left until the end of the year").
73 McGee and Harris interviews. Since 1984, Parliament has sat regularly throughout the year: Geoffrey Palmer and Matthew Palmer, *Bridled Power: New Zealand's Constitution and Government* (4th ed, Oxford University Press, Melbourne, 2004) at 145.

C Tactical Reasons for Using Urgency

Urgency, then, is both a way of expediting the passage of genuinely urgent legislation and a way of expediting the government's legislative agenda more generally. As well, there may also be a range of tactical reasons motivating the use of urgency in any particular case. These might include tactical decisions in relation to how best to manage a particular piece of legislation through the House and tactical decisions quite unrelated to the legislative agenda (for example, to avoid question time).

1 Strategic urgency to manage public sentiment

Urgency is sometimes motivated by a calculation from the government of the day that being seen to act decisively in relation to a particular piece of legislation, or at a particular time in the electoral calendar, will play well with the electorate. At one end of the spectrum, that may be because there is considerable public concern about the mischief that the legislation is designed to address, and the government perceives an electoral advantage in being seen to act quickly and decisively.[74] An example of this might be the Employment Relations (Film Production Work) Amendment Bill 2010, introduced to respond to public concerns over the industrial relations dispute that had threatened to prejudice the production of "The Hobbit" movies in New Zealand.[75] The legislation purported to "clarify" the law following the decision of the Supreme Court in *Bryson v Three Foot Six Ltd*.[76] However, as that decision had been released more than five years earlier, this instance of urgency being used can hardly be seen as an example of a genuine need to expedite legislation in response to a court decision.

More generally, a factor that appears on occasion to have motivated the decision to use urgency is the desire of new governments to be seen to be acting decisively in implementing their election promises.[77] This was clearly a significant feature driving the high reliance on urgency motions by the newly elected National Government in late 2008 and early 2009. The National Party had made election promises as to what it would achieve in its "first 100 days" in government and wanted to be seen to be decisive in implementing those

---

74 Harris and Creech interviews. See House of Lords Select Committee on the Constitution, above n 17, at 10, identifying "to respond to public concerns" as a category.
75 (28 October 2010) 668 NZPD 14938. Another example recounted to us by David McGee QC in his interview was the recurrent use of pre-Christmas urgency by governments in the 1970s and 1980s that wished to be seen to be responding decisively to the problem of the holiday road toll.
76 *Bryson v Three Foot Six Ltd* [2005] 3 NZLR 721.
77 See Smith and Harris interviews.

Tom Scott cartoon referencing legislation introduced (under urgency) in October 2010 to respond to public concerns over the industrial relations dispute that that had threatened to prejudice the production of "The Hobbit" movies in New Zealand. The cartoon appeared in *The Dominion Post* and is reprinted with the permission of the artist.

promises.[78] This was reflected in the formal reasons given for three urgency motions in 2009 (though not, interestingly, in either of the two urgency motions moved by the National Government in late 2008).[79] Similarly, in December 1999, the newly elected Labour-led Government moved an urgency motion referring to "a clear electoral pledge."[80]

Some interviewees were highly critical of this use of urgency by the National-led Government in 2008/2009.[81] However, in his interview with us, the Leader of the House Gerry Brownlee emphatically resisted these criticisms. In his view, this use of urgency was supported by the election promises that had been made and by the fact that the policy intention was well canvassed and supported.

78 See Brownlee and Katene interviews.
79 See (10 February 2009) 652 NZPD 1075–1076: "These bills are all part of the Government's 100-day programme. These matters were of prominence for members of the Government during the election campaign, so it is a matter of ensuring that we honour the commitments made to New Zealanders that these bills would be introduced and sent to select committees within the first 100-day period." See, similarly, (12 February 2009) 652 NZPD 1258; (15 October 2009) 658 NZPD 7113.
80 (22 December 1999) 581 NZPD 62.
81 For example, Turei interview.

At the other end of the strategic spectrum, another motivation for the use of urgency that was referred to repeatedly by our interviewees is political pragmatism or expediency from a government that is trying to guide controversial legislation through the parliamentary process. For example, in his interview, Sir Douglas Kidd referred to historic "ritual arena contests" between Labour and National over key points of ideological divide such as compulsory trade unionism – where the battle lines were clearly drawn, and: ". . . there has to be a mechanism, short of drawing guns and swords, of resolving things and so you basically put everybody inside and shut the door and tell them to go to it."[82] Other interviewees suggested that one motivating factor for urgency was to get controversial legislation off the political agenda well before the election.[83] Darren Hughes, Labour's junior whip at around that time, suggested to us that the Foreshore and Seabed Bill 2004 could perhaps be seen as an example of this phenomenon. In that case, the Bill had already been sent to select committee when urgency was accorded for its remaining stages.[84] However, one interviewee suggested that the controversial nature of legislation might also provide an impetus for governments to use urgency to seek to avoid the select committee process altogether.[85]

Interviewees rarely sought to positively justify the use of urgency for tactical reasons of this kind. On the other hand, nor did many of them volunteer concerns about the legitimacy of this practice. Of those interviewees who did express a view on this topic, it tended to be that, while perhaps not a "good practice", urgency might perhaps be justified "when an issue has gone on for a significant amount of time, where the political divides are drawn and clear and where the government is in for a major fight on the floor of the House."[86]

2 Tactical reasons unrelated to the legislative agenda

Urgency motions have also been used over time to gain a broader tactical advantage against the opposition, not directly related to the passage of legislation. In his interview, Ken Shirley, who was a Labour backbencher (and briefly a minister) during the Fourth Labour Government (as well as serving three terms more recently as an ACT MP), said of the use of urgency in the pre-MMP period:

> . . . it was essentially straight political expediency to get the business done. And sometimes expediency and sometimes opportunism. Sometimes just to irritate the opposition even. Back in the old Muldoon governments, he used to do it

---

82   For a modern analogue, see the urgency motion for the Injury Prevention, Rehabilitation, and Compensation Amendment Bill: (23 February 2010) 660 NZPD 9112.
83   Turei, Wilson and Harris interviews.
84   (16 November 2004) 621 NZPD 16929.
85   Dunne interview.
86   Hughes interview.

deliberately just to irritate them. Whenever there was a Labour Party conference, Muldoon would call urgency in the House . . .

Roger Sowry, who was part of the National Government throughout the 1990s, and served terms as junior and senior whip, as well as the Leader of the House, had this to say of the use of urgency during that period:[87]

> . . . it was a process of passing a lot of legislation, but it was also a process of breaking the morale of the opposition . . . it was tactical, so there was no notice given about it. It was used in those days because you could throw the House into urgency to stop question time, so you could get yourself out of a hole if there was a whole lot of questions. You'd say, "we'll bang the House into urgency; there'll be no more questions this week" . . . used properly in those days, you could boost the morale of your team, and damage the morale of the opposition. So it was purely tactical.

Sowry also described the tactical use of urgency to avoid members' day:[88]

> You could bang the House into urgency, bowl the private members' day – which becomes a government day – and then the following week you get another government week, so you're actually buying the government a *lot* of extra time . . . and then you could have a recess week or something, and you come back in and bowl out the next private members' day again.

As well as freeing up a number of extra hours for government business, this meant that the government could: "keep a [member's] bill out for a month or two, give yourself some space to deal with a tricky private member's bill."

Finally, Dr Michael Cullen described in his interview the "take the bastards by surprise" approach to urgency in the mid-1980s: to push through legislation before the opposition had time to organise its response.

These tactical uses did not feature as prominently in parliamentarians' perceptions of urgency in the post-MMP period. Sowry described the pre-MMP parliamentary environment (somewhat nostalgically) as "like a big chess game" and the MMP Parliament as "far more formulaic". He was the only one of our interviewees to speak approvingly of the use of urgency for tactical reasons of this kind, and it seems that such tactical uses of urgency are rarer in the post-MMP environment.[89] Some interviewees did suggest that governments continued to use urgency, on occasion, to avoid question time.[90] No interviewees, though,

---

87 Ken Shirley similarly suggested to us that urgency was used in this period to avoid question time.
88 Sowry interview.
89 For example, Richard Prebble suggested to us that MMP has "reduced the use of urgency as a bully boy tactic."
90 For example, Hughes and Shirley interviews. On the other hand, preservation of question time has become a feature of recent urgency motions – a phenomenon discussed further in Chapter Five, Part IV.

volunteered modern examples of governments deliberately using urgency to avoid members' day.

D *Budget Day Urgency*

The longstanding practice of taking urgency on Budget day does not fit easily within any of the above categories, though it overlaps with all of them.

Technically, Budget day is the day on which the Minister of Finance moves the second reading of the first and main Appropriation Bill for the upcoming government financial year.[91] More than that, though, Budget day is an important parliamentary occasion on which the government outlines a broad range of financial, economic and social policy measures that it sees as central to its legislative and policy programme for the upcoming year.[92]

Urgency was taken on 15 out of the 24 Budget days during the years studied and on all but one of the Budget days falling within a period of single-party majority government.[93] Of the eight extraordinary urgency motions during the period, four fell on Budget day.[94]

"Budget-related issues" was a common justification given by our interviewees for the use of urgency.[95] It was not, though, entirely clear to us what it was about Budget day that justified the use of urgency in the minds of our interviewees. To the extent that explanation was offered, interviewees tended to link Budget day urgency with the market distortion/commercial sensitivity justification explored above.[96]

Certainly, there are examples of Budget day urgency during the period under study that fall within the market distortion category. For example, of the four extraordinary urgency motions taken on Budget day, two concerned excise taxes, one a land tax and one was primarily concerned with a non-resident withholding tax.

Much Budget day urgency, though, was not as obviously linked to the market distortion justification. Indeed, over the years of the study, there were periods during which a wide range of legislation, not all of it financial, was enacted under the umbrella of Budget day urgency.

---

91 See Standing Orders (2008), SO 323. The Appropriation Bill is introduced and read a first time without amendment or debate. The Minister of Finance then moves the second reading of the Bill and delivers the Budget statement. This is followed by the Budget debate, which lasts for 14 hours and usually runs over several days.
92 See David McGee QC, *Parliamentary Practice in New Zealand* (3rd ed, Dunmore, Wellington, 2005) at 478.
93 1987–1993, 1998, 1999, 2002, 2004 and 2007–2010.
94 (28 July 1988) 490 NZPD 5594; (30 July 1991) 517 NZPD 3287–3288; (14 May 1998) 568 NZPD 8581; (20 May 1999) 577 NZPD 16618.
95 For example, Sowry, Kidd, Smith, Dunne, Shirley, Creech, East and Hide interviews. See, also, House of Lords, above n 17, at 10.
96 For example, Shirley and Kidd interviews.

The years 1988–1991 are particularly noteworthy (and troubling) because of the use of "finance bills" to enact a miscellany of legislation under urgency.[97] In each of those four years, the Budget day finance bill covered a haphazard collection of topics, many of which had little to do with the Budget itself. The subject matters covered included (but were not limited to): the amendment of the Earthquake and War Damage Act 1944, the powers of the Department of Conservation, the scope of accident compensation, the powers of the Housing Corporation, the importation of medicines, the name of the Government Life Insurance Corporation, the creation of new civil aviation rules and, infamously, the validation of the Tokelauan coin during the "Mother of All Budgets" in 1991.

Many of our interviewees referred to the "Mother of All Budgets" Finance Bill as a high water mark in the abuse of Budget day urgency.[98] It contained amendments to 25 separate acts, none of which, according to then Clerk of the House David McGee QC, were linked with the Budget.[99] In his interview, Paul East QC, who was the Leader of the House in 1991, told us:[100]

> The Treasury decided to bundle everything up that they wanted to get done, into the Budget legislation. Now if we'd been more up with the play, we would have told them to take a running jump, but we were rather naive about that . . .

After the 1991 Budget (and possibly as a result of the criticism that resulted from it) the use of Budget day urgency motions changed.[101] Certainly, finance bills were never again used in quite the same way to pass a hodgepodge of miscellaneous legislation. This change was initially a product of self-denial but was underpinned by amendments to the Standing Orders in 1995 that limited the permissible use of "omnibus" bills (that is, bills that relate to more than one subject area, of which, finance bills were a notorious example).[102]

More generally, the period between 1991 and 2010 was characterised by clear trends away from the use of Budget day urgency overall, and towards limiting its use to bills that were more closely connected to financial matters (such as taxation) or, at very least, to key Budget announcements.

The urgency motion passed on Budget day in 1992 accorded urgency to

---

97 Respectively, Finance Bill (No 3) 1988, Finance Bill (No 5) 1989, Finance Bill (No 2) 1990 and Finance Bill (No 2) 1991. In each case, the Finance Bill was taken through its first and second reading and Committee of the whole House stage and then divided into its constituent parts, which were passed as separate acts.
98 For example, East, Sowry, Dunne and McGee interviews.
99 David McGee QC, "Concerning Legislative Process" (2007) 11 Otago LR 417 at 428.
100 Dr Michael Cullen expressed similar sheepishness to us in his interview about the Finance Bill (No 3) 1988, introduced when he was Associate Minister of Finance.
101 For a discussion of the reaction to the "Mother of all Budgets" urgency motion, see Chapter Five, Part II.A. David McGee QC observed in his interview that his perception was that urgency was never again used quite so irresponsibly.
102 See, now, Standing Orders (2008), SOs 256–259. For further discussion of the regulation of omnibus bills, see Chapter Six, Part I.B.2.

only one piece of legislation – a tax measure.[103] One more piece of legislation was passed under urgency on Budget day in 1993. However, as the legislation was debated prior to the Budget statement being read, this was not, strictly speaking, an example of Budget urgency.[104] No urgency motion at all was passed on Budget days over the next four years.

In 1998 and 1999 (years characterised by a high use of urgency overall),[105] there was a brief spike in the use of Budget day urgency to facilitate the passage of a broad array of policy reforms.[106] The use of urgency motions in these years differed from its use during the 1988–1991 period in that the measures to which urgency was accorded were, at least, linked to policy announcements made in the Budget statement. Nevertheless, that can be a broad category. As the former Clerk of the House David McGee QC said to us:

> [T]here is no constraint on what the Minister of Finance might put in the Budget speech ... A Budget contains anything a government wants to put in it. It isn't just concerned with the appropriations from 1 July to 30 June. The Budget is a political announcement, not just a financial announcement.

From 2000, Budget day urgency was again used very sparingly. No urgency motion at all was taken on Budget day in 2000, 2001, 2003, 2005 or 2006. Budget day urgency was limited to just one bill in the years 2002,[107] 2004,[108]

---

103 (2 July 1992) 526 NZPD 9728, according urgency to the passing of the Transit New Zealand Amendment Bill (No 4) (which made changes to the operation of an excise duty on petrol).
104 (1 July 1993) 536 NZPD 16490, according urgency to the Committee of the whole House stage and third reading of the Resource Management Amendment Bill. The urgency motion came after Winston Peters refused to give leave to allow the two stages to be taken together, despite only a few minutes remaining from the Committee of the whole House stage from the night before.
105 See Chapter Four, Parts I and II; Chapter Five, Part III.
106 In 1998, Budget day urgency was accorded to the Social Security Amendment Bill (No 5), the passage of the Copyright (Removal of Prohibition on Parallel Importing) Amendment Bill, the Social Security (Work Test) Amendment Bill, and the Public Health Agencies (Re-designation and Taxation) Bill; and both urgency and extraordinary urgency were accorded to the Customs and Excise Amendment Bill: (14 May 1998) 568 NZPD 8580–8581. In 1999, Budget day urgency was accorded to the Taxation (Parental Tax Credit) Bill, the Broadcasting Amendment Bill (No 3), the Estate Duty Repeal Bill, the State-Owned Enterprises (Meteorological Service of New Zealand Limited and Vehicle Testing New Zealand Limited) Amendment Bill and the Accident Insurance Amendment Bill; and both urgency and extraordinary urgency was accorded to the Stamp Duty Abolition Bill: (20 May 1999) 577 NZPD 16618.
107 Urgency taken for the second reading of the Appropriation (2002/03 Estimates) Bill: (23 May 2002) 600 NZPD 16429. This was shortly after the Labour party's support partner, the Alliance Party, had split up, rendering the Government unstable. We understand from informal discussions with officials that the unusual inclusion of the Appropriation Bill itself in Budget Day urgency that year may have been driven by the Government's perception that an early election was likely.
108 Urgency taken for the passing of the Future Directions (Working for Families) Bill: (27 May 2004) 617 NZPD 13424.

2008,[109] 2009,[110] and 2010.[111] Although two pieces of legislation were accorded urgency on Budget day in 2007, both directly concerned taxation.[112]

The question remains: what are the reasons that underlie the use of urgency on Budget day? The deadlines contained in the Public Finance Act 1989 and the Standing Orders for the passage of the main Appropriation Bill are only peripherally relevant at best. These require the Appropriation Bill to be introduced by 31 July (that is, before the end of the first month after the start of the government financial year) and passed within three months.[113] This necessitates a degree of priority being given to the passage of the Appropriation Bill but does not necessitate Budget day urgency per se. In fact, in recent times, although Budget day urgency has generally been linked to Budget measures in the broader sense, very little Budget day urgency has concerned the Appropriation Bill itself.[114]

Where tax measures are concerned (as they often have been in recent times), informal deadlines created by the rhythm of the tax year may be at play. If the government wishes tax measures announced in the Budget to come into effect quickly, the first convenient date in the tax cycle will be 1 October, which is the half-way point in the tax year.[115] If that date is missed, practical reasons dictate that, in general, tax measures will not be brought into force until the start of the following tax year, that is, 1 April. We also understand from informal discussions with officials that, in order to provide for the necessary implementation arrangements, three months are required between the passage of legislation changing tax rates and its entry into force. This means that, if such legislation is to enter into force on 1 October, there is an effective enactment date of 1 July.

Ultimately, it seems to us that the Budget day is not a separate reason for taking urgency but, rather, an occasion on which a combination of the reasons

---

109 Urgency taken for the passing of the Taxation (Personal Tax Cuts, Annual Rates, and Remedial Matters) Bill: (22 May 2008) 647 NZPD 16251.
110 Urgency taken for the passing of the Taxation (Budget Tax Measures) Bill: (28 May 2009) 654 NZPD 3958.
111 Urgency taken for the passing of the Taxation (Budget Measures) Bill: (20 May 2010) 663 NZPD 11066.
112 See (17 May 2007) 639 NZPD 9379, according urgency to the passing of the Taxation (KiwiSaver and Company Tax Rate Amendments) Bill and the introduction and first reading of the Taxation (Annual Rates, Business Taxation, KiwiSaver, and Remedial Matters) Bill.
113 Public Finance Act 1989, s 12; Standing Orders (2008), SO 330(1). In the meantime, an imprest supply bill is invariably enacted towards the end of the government financial year in order to provide parliamentary authority for government spending in the interim.
114 See footnote 107, discussing a rare exception.
115 See Taxation (Personal Tax Cuts, Annual Rates, and Remedial Matters) Act 2008, s 2(4); Taxation (Budget Measures) Act 2010, s 2(2).

set out earlier in this chapter may (or may not) come into play. For example, although there is less evidence of this in recent times, it seems that in the years 1988–1991, urgency was being used simply to free up the order paper. On the other hand, as noted above, Budget day urgency may, in some cases, be linked to the "market distortion" justification, or to the related concern to provide certainty for financial markets. It may, in some cases, be driven by the informal deadlines created by the tax year – perhaps combined with the government's desire to be seen to implement Budget measures quickly. More generally, the special status of Budget measures – as defining policy issues for the government – may contribute to a political calculation that Budget day urgency will be tolerated by other political participants and approved of by the electorate. In this sense, Budget day urgency may perhaps be seen as an exemplar of the "tactical uses" category of urgency discussed above.

III *Conclusion*

As we have shown, a genuine need to expedite the passage of a specific piece of legislation is only one, and not even the dominant, reason why New Zealand governments use urgency. Urgency is used for a range of tactical reasons, including to send messages to voters that their governments are effective and responsive to their wishes. But urgency is also used to respond at a more generic level to the concern that Parliament's regular sitting hours are insufficient to enable the government of the day to make the progress that it would like with its legislative business.

In Chapter Six, we return to these motivations for using urgency and ask, in particular, whether urgency is a desirable or acceptable solution to the perceived problem of insufficient sitting hours. We conclude that urgency is a poorly designed mechanism to respond to that problem and that other more comprehensive solutions ought to be investigated.

First, though, we must examine how much urgency is used and what factors might control or inhibit its use. We do so in the next two chapters.

4

How Governments Use Urgency

In Chapter Three, we identified a range of interlocking motivations underlying the use of urgency by the New Zealand House of Representatives. In light of these multiple drivers, it is perhaps not surprising that, over time, urgency has been used a great deal. We did not collect data on the period prior to the 1985 reforms to the Standing Orders when, it will be remembered, the House used urgency routinely to sit through the night.[1] Even so, during the 24-year period of the study (1987–2010), urgency was taken on an impressive number of occasions and in relation to an even more impressive number of bills.

The use of urgency was not, though, distributed evenly across various parliaments and governments and there was a marked difference between the periods of highest and lowest use. In this chapter, we map the number of urgency motions taken and the number of bills accorded urgency, by year and by parliament, and we also calculate the proportions of House time spent under urgency in different parliaments. These data show that urgency was used substantially more, on average, by pre-MMP single-party majority governments than during subsequent periods of minority/coalition government under MMP. However, the pattern of use following the introduction of MMP was uneven. In particular, two post-MMP parliaments stand out for the comparatively high use of urgency motions: the forty-fifth Parliament (1996–1999) and forty-ninth Parliament (2008–2011).

As will, by now, be apparent, there are a number of distinct ways of using urgency that have different effects on the legislative process. Having mapped the overall use of urgency, we turn to consider how governments used these different types of urgency during the period of the study. We do this by unpicking the stages for which urgency was taken (in different years and by different parliaments) and by providing separate analysis of the use of extraordinary urgency. The most radical and democratically problematical uses of urgency are when it is taken for all stages of a bill's passage through Parliament or when it is otherwise taken in such a way as to eliminate the select committee stage. Although these uses of urgency were comparatively uncommon throughout the period of the study, again, we see the same two post-MMP parliaments – the forty-fifth Parliament (1996–1999) and forty-ninth Parliament (2008–2011) – relying on them with comparative frequency.

---

1   See Chapter Two, Part I.

Our analysis also reveals that, in many instances when urgency was relied on to bypass select committee scrutiny, there was no obvious rationale for expediting the legislation.

Finally, we turn in this chapter to document seasonal variations in the use of urgency (at different times of the year or different times of the electoral cycle) and to examine data on the policy areas to which urgency has been accorded.

The data presented in this chapter provide the foundations for a more extended analysis, to be found in Chapter Five, of the impact of proportional representation on the use of urgency by the New Zealand Parliament.

I Parliaments, Governments and the Use of Urgency

As noted in Chapter One, during the 1987–2010 period there were 222 urgency motions and eight extraordinary urgency motions. These motions collectively dealt with 1953 items of legislative business relating to 1608 bills.

The most popular day for moving urgency was Tuesday (the first sitting day in a sitting week). The greatest number of days during the period studied that the House sat continuously under urgency was five (Tuesday through to Saturday). Five day sittings were reasonably rare, comprising only 4 per cent of all urgency periods. The average length of urgency sittings during the period was 2.3 days, with no government exceeding a three day average. Although five day sittings were rare, Saturday sittings under urgency were less so.[2] They occurred 22 times during the period studied.

We assumed that urgency would be used by all governments, whatever their ideological perspectives. But what patterns of use are displayed by a more detailed breakdown of the data? Did some governments use urgency more than others? In sections A–C below, we address these questions by mapping data on the use of urgency motions, the number of bills accorded urgency and the percentage of sitting time taken under urgency. In section D, we identify some basic trends, which will be explored more fully in Chapter Five.

A Urgency Motions

Figure 4.1 shows the number of urgency motions moved by year. The multi-coloured bars indicate a change of government during the parliamentary term, with the top (crimson) stripe showing the urgency motions attributable to the later government. The average number of urgency motions for the period is 9.25 per calendar year.

---

2 The House might, for example, go into urgency on a Wednesday or Thursday and sit through the rest of the week.

Figure 4.2 attributes the 222 urgency motions to particular governments. The pale bars on the graph represent incomplete parliaments (as our data did not fully cover the years of those parliaments). Those bars do not, therefore, provide a fully comparable indication of the number of urgency motions moved in those terms.

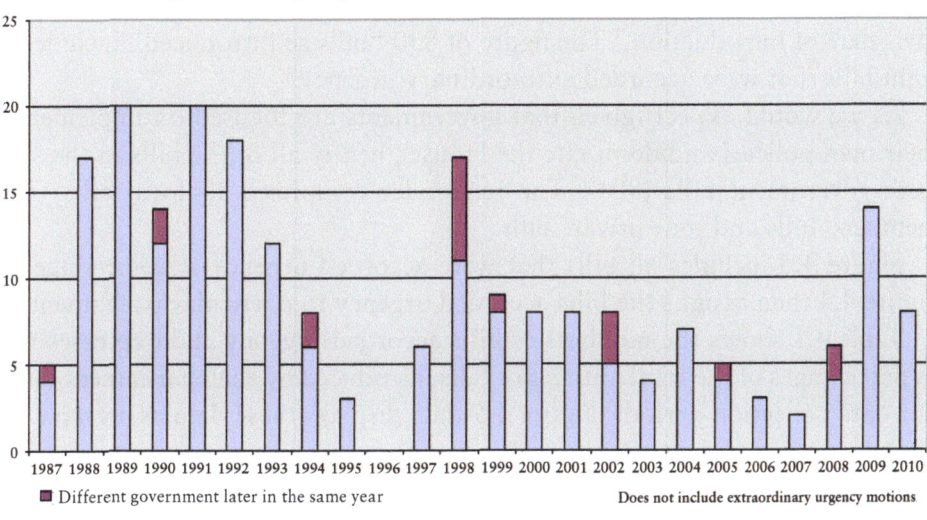

Figure 4.1: Urgency Motions Moved by Year 1987–2010

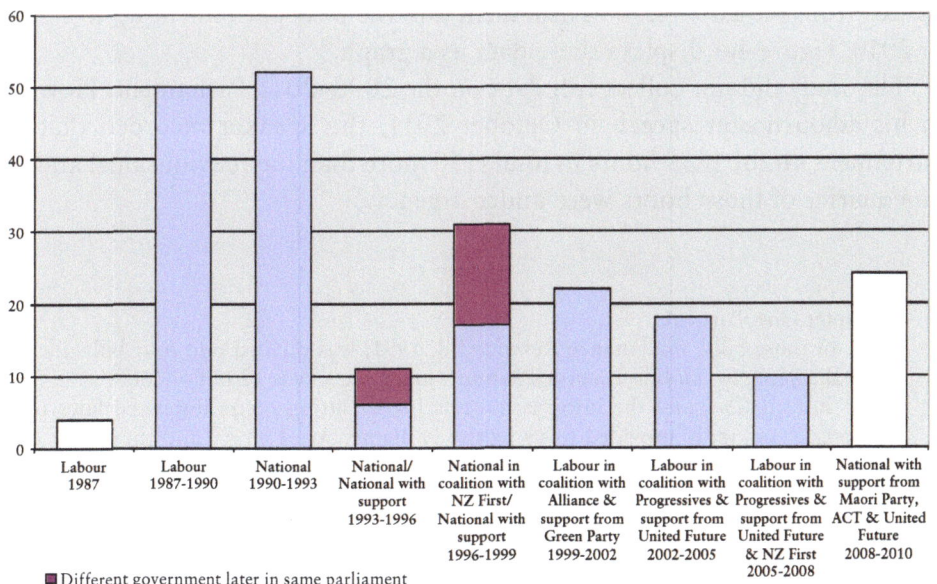

Figure 4.2: Urgency Motions Moved by Parliament 1987–2010

B Bills Accorded Urgency

It will be remembered that urgency motions can (and often do) include more than one bill. For that reason, analysis of the number of bills accorded urgency provides important additional data.

Although 1608 bills were accorded urgency between 1987 and 2010, the data and graphs set out below are based on the figure of 830 "bills as introduced" explained in Chapter One, with bills being assigned to a year on the basis of their date of introduction.[3] The figure of 830 "bills as introduced" includes the eight bills that were accorded extraordinary urgency.[4]

As we would expect (given that governments are focused on implementing their own policies and dominate the House), nearly all of the bills in the study were government bills (804). The remainder comprised 15 local bills, seven members' bills and four private bills.

Figure 4.3 includes all bills that were accorded urgency at some stage and Figure 4.4 then assigns the bills accorded urgency to particular parliaments.

Table 4.1 shows the numbers of bills accorded urgency and expresses them as percentages of the total number of bills introduced by each parliament during our data collection period.[5] Figure 4.5 then displays these data as a graph.

C Percentage of Sitting Time Taken under Urgency

In his 2008 study on government law-making under MMP, Ryan Malone provided data on the number of sitting hours taken under urgency during the period 1987–2005.[6] Table 4.2 reproduces this data and updates it to include the figures from the 2005–2008 Parliament and the next parliament up to the end of 2010. Figure 4.6 displays these data as a graph.

The study did not collect full data on the 2008–2011 Parliament. However, in his adjournment speech in October 2011, the Speaker recorded that this parliament sat for 1650 hours in total (150 more than the previous one) and that one quarter of those hours were under urgency.[7]

---

3   Chapter One, Part I.A.
4   One of those bills, the Finance Revenue Bill 1991, was divided into four bills, meaning that the figure for *all* bills accorded extraordinary urgency is 12 out of 1608.
5   This information, and the information relating to sitting hours discussed later in this chapter, was kindly provided to us by the Parliamentary Library and the Office of the Clerk. The information provided did not include data on the first part of the year 1987 (prior to the general election), and so the collection period is slightly shorter than the collection period for our own data on urgency, as reflected in other figures and tables.
6   Ryan Malone, *Rebalancing the Constitution: the Challenge of Government Law-Making under MMP* (Institute of Policy Studies, Wellington, 2008) at 211–212.
7   (6 October 2011) 676 NZPD 21855.

Figure 4.3: Bills Accorded Urgency (Attributed to Year of Introduction) 1987–2010

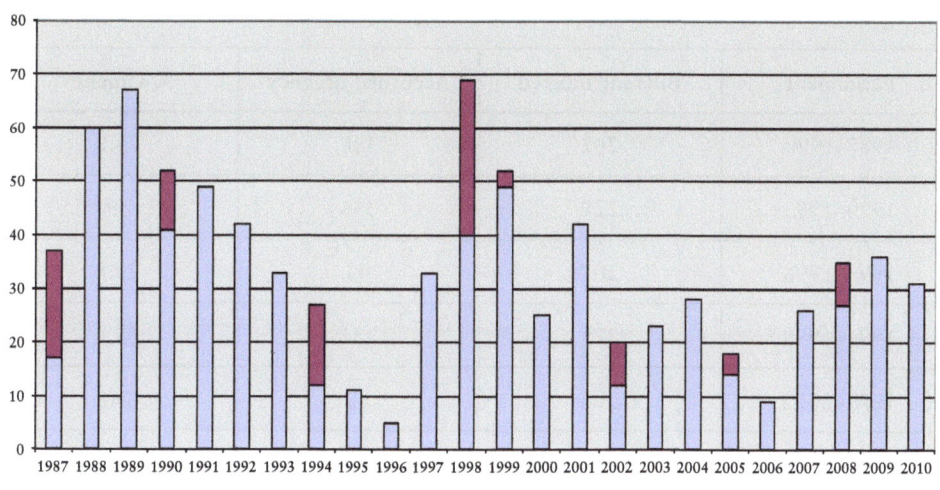

■ Different government later in the same year

Figure 4.4: Bills Accorded Urgency by Parliament 1987–2010

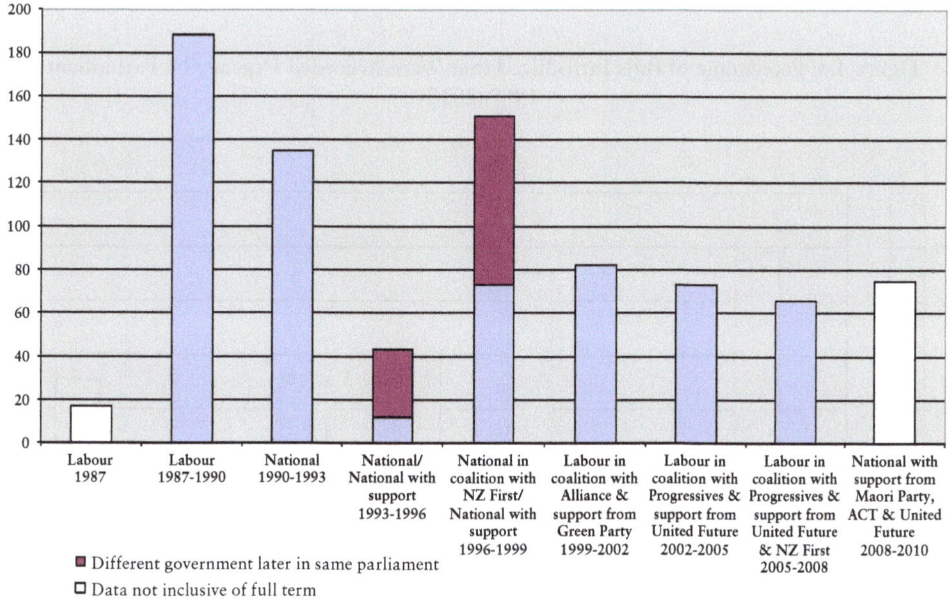

■ Different government later in same parliament
□ Data not inclusive of full term

Table 4.1: Percentage of Bills Introduced that Were Accorded Urgency by Parliament 1987–2010

Parliament	Bills introduced	Accorded urgency	% Urgency
1987–1990	262	188	71.8
1990–1993	229	135	59
1993–1996	207	43	20.8
1996–1999	273	151	55.3
1999–2002	206	82	39.8
2002–2005	202	73	36.1
2005–2008	238	66	27.7
2008–2010	211	75	35.5

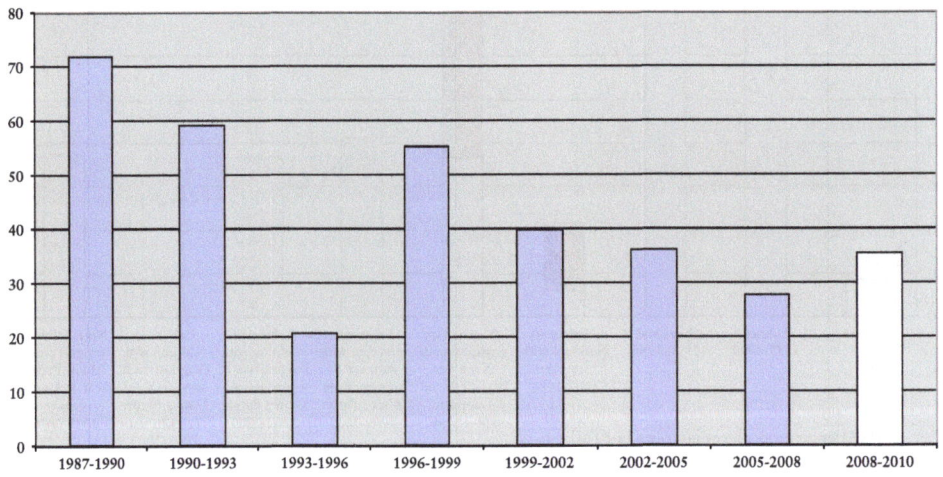

Figure 4.5: Percentage of Bills Introduced that Were Accorded Urgency by Parliament 1987–2010

Table 4.2: Percentage of Total Sitting Hours Taken under Urgency by Parliament
1987–2010

Parliament	Total	Urgency	% Urgency
1987–1990	2186	686	31.4
1990–1993	2082	630	30.3
1993–1996	1346	124	9.2
1996–1999	1773	545	30.7
1999–2002	1469	192	13.1
2002–2005	1801	384	21.3
2005–2008	1503	148	9.9
2008–2010	1254	354	28.2

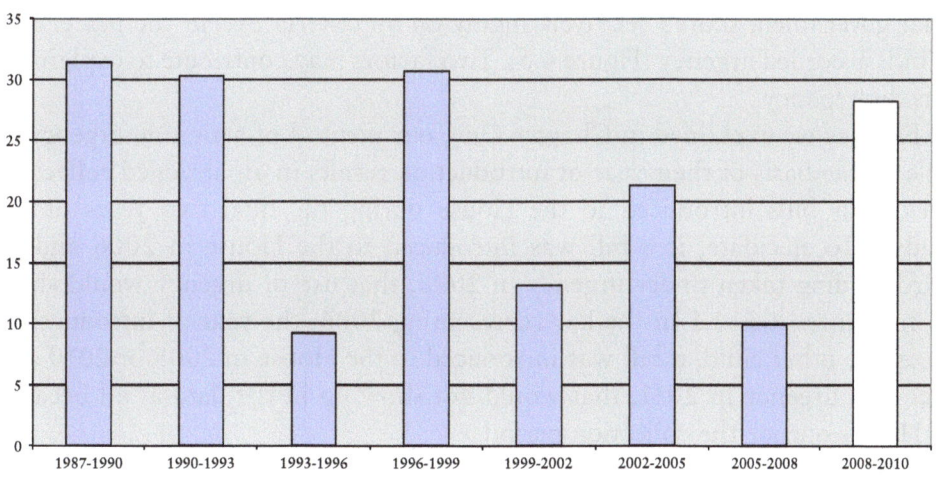

Figure 4.6: Percentage of Total Sitting Hours Taken under Urgency by Parliament
1987–2010

D Trends in the Data

The data displayed in Figures 4.1–4.6 and Tables 4.1–4.2 show that, indeed, governments of all colours put forward urgency motions. However, the use of urgency is not distributed evenly across various parliaments and governments. It will immediately be apparent that urgency was taken substantially more often by the single-party majority governments that typified government arrangements under the first-past-the-post electoral system than during subsequent periods of minority and/or coalition government under MMP.[8]

On the basis of our limited data sample, when in single-party majority government, both Labour and National were prolific users of urgency.[9] This suggests that, at least during that period, urgency was not ideologically driven. Rather, it was used liberally by governments on both sides of the House.

The data also show that Labour and Labour-led governments behaved very differently before 1996 and the first MMP parliament than after it, when they no longer commanded the majority of parliamentary votes without support from other political parties. National and National-led governments also used urgency less frequently after MMP than before it. However, National's use of urgency after 1996, was, on the whole, more frequent than was Labour's.

These issues are examined fully in the next chapter, where we explore in depth the extent to which the use of urgency was constrained by the implementation of proportional representation. However, one aspect of the data that warrants immediate explanation relates to the 2008–2010 National-led Government. That government scored relatively highly on all criteria *except* the percentage of bills accorded urgency (Figure 4.5). Two factors may contribute to explaining this discrepancy.

First, as we explained in Chapter One, our method of assigning urgency to bills on the basis of their year of introduction results in an abridged collection period for bills introduced to the House during the final two years of the study.[10] To elucidate, if a bill was introduced to the House in 2006 and its third reading taken under urgency in 2008, that use of urgency would show up in Figures 4.3–4.5 in the bar representing 2006: the year of introduction. If, on the other hand, a bill was introduced to the House in 2009 or 2010 and accorded urgency in 2011, that would not show up in the data at all because 2011 falls outside the collection period.

For this reason, we can assume that Figures 4.3–4.5 all under-represent the number of bills introduced in 2009 and 2010 that will ultimately have been

---

8   See Chapter One, Table 1.1 for a list of government formations throughout the period of study and Chapter Five, Part III for deeper analysis of the impact of MMP. The era of coalition and minority governments in fact began in 1994, in the lead-up to MMP.
9   The study only comprehends one full term single-party majority government of each stripe: Labour (1987–1990) and National (1990–1993).
10 Chapter 1, Part I.A.

accorded urgency by the National-led Government.

Secondly, this government was an active legislator overall. As can be seen from Table 4.1, in its first two years in office, it introduced almost as many bills to Parliament as had the previous three Labour-led governments, on average, during their full three-year terms. That may be part of the reason why this government scored comparatively highly on percentage of sitting hours spent in urgency but less highly on percentage of overall bills accorded urgency.[11]

II Different Types of Urgency

As we explained in Chapter Two, urgency motions can be deployed in different ways and to different effect. Understanding precisely how urgency motions have been deployed over time is important because some uses are much more controversial, and more democratically worrying, than are others. Compare a controversial bill passed through all its stages in one sitting under urgency, for example, with a bill taken through only one stage, as part of an urgency motion intended to clear the order paper prior to a parliamentary recess.

Table 4.3 sets out, year by year, five of the common ways in which urgency motions are deployed: to take only one stage at a time under urgency (column C); to take the introduction and initial debate together (column E); to take all remaining stages after the bill is reported back from select committee under urgency (column G); to take the Committee of the whole House and third reading stage together (column I); and to take all stages of a bill under urgency (column K). The table shows the number of times that each usage was deployed in each year and then reflects that figure as a percentage of all items of legislative business considered under urgency (see Column B). Where there was a change of government during the course of the year, that year appears twice (see column A).

In interpreting Table 4.3, two points should be borne in mind. First, the table is not exhaustive of all usages of urgency. It does not show occasions, for example, on which urgency was taken for the second reading and the Committee of the whole House but not the third reading. Secondly, some bills will have been put into urgency more than once during their passage through the House so will have been double or triple counted on the table. That is why the uses are shown as a percentage of items of legislative business accorded urgency rather than as a percentage of bills accorded urgency.

Table 4.3 includes bills accorded extraordinary urgency during the period of the study. All extraordinary urgency bills went through all stages under urgency apart from one (in 1991) which was divided at the Committee of the whole House stage.

---

11 See, also, the statistics on total sitting hours given by the Speaker in the October 2011 adjournment debate: (6 October 2011) 676 NZPD 21855.

Table 4.3: Stages Taken under Urgency by Year

A	B	C	D	E	F	G	H	I	J	K	L
Year introduced	Legislative business considered under urgency	Only one stage	%	Only introduction and initial debate	%	Remaining stages	%	Committee of the whole House and third reading	%	All stages	%
1987/1	23	10	43.5	2	8.7	3	13	3	13	1	4.3
1987/2	32	6	18.8	11	34.4	8	25	5	15.6	0	0
1988	100	33	33	28	28	10	10	10	10	5	5
1989	118	29	24.6	30	25.4	19	16.1	11	9.3	5	4.2
1990/1	65	20	30.8	25	38.5	7	10.8	4	6.2	4	6.2
1990/2	19	2	10.5	6	31.6	1	5.3	5	26.3	1	5.3
1991	77	23	29.9	29	37.7	6	7.8	8	10.4	1	1.3
1992	66	20	30.3	21	31.8	10	15.2	4	6.1	3	4.5
1993/1	45	13	28.9	8	17.8	8	17.8	6	13.3	5	11.1
1993/2	0	0	0	0	0	0	0	0	0	0	0
1994/1	17	2	11.8	8	47.1	1	5.9	1	5.9	1	5.9
1994/2	17	0	0	13	76.5	0	0	1	5.9	2	11.8
1995	11	4	36.4	6	54.5	1	9.1	0	0	0	0
1996/1	6	0	0	0	0	4	80	N/A	N/A	0	0
1996/2	0	0	0	0	0	0	0	N/A	N/A	0	0
1997	41	25	61	1	2.4	13	31.7	N/A	N/A	1	2.4
1998/1	52	18	34.6	13	25	10	19.2	N/A	N/A	10	19.2
1998/2	38	16	42.1	9	23.7	10	26.3	N/A	N/A	3	7.9
1999/1	66	17	25.1	23	34.8	16	24.2	N/A	N/A	8	12.1
1999/2	4	0	0	2	50	1	25	0	0	1	25
2000	33	22	66.6	0	0	1	3	5	15.2	2	6.1
2001	54	33	61.1	2	3.7	10	18.5	6	11.1	1	1.9
2002/1	12	5	41.7	0	0	5	41.7	0	0	1	8.3
2002/2	12	6	50	0	0	5	41.7	1	8.3	0	0
2003	24	5	20.8	1	4.2	10	41.7	2	8.3	3	12.5
2004	36	15	41.7	2	5.6	13	36.1	1	2.8	1	2.8
2005/1	14	8	57.1	0	0	3	21.4	1	7.1	1	7.1
2005/2	4	2	50	0	0	0	0	1	25	1	25
2006	9	4	44.4	0	0	3	33.3	0	0	1	11.1
2007	36	23	63.9	1	2.8	9	25	1	2.8	1	2.8
2008/1	30	13	43.3	1	3.3	7	23.3	4	13.3	1	3.3
2008/2	9	1	11.1	1	11.1	0	0	0	0	7	77.8
2009	54	16	29.6	11	20.4	9	16.7	10	18.5	4	7.4
2010	33	15	45.5	0	0	4	12.1	3	9.1	6	18.2
Totals	1157	406	34.8	254	22	207	17.9	93	8	81	7

A Taking Only One Stage under Urgency

Column C shows occasions on which urgency has been used for only one stage at time. This might be regarded as the most benign use of urgency because it does not interfere with select committee consideration and does not involve removal of the stand-down periods between the different stages. Notably, this was the most dominant use of urgency throughout all periods of the study (see column D).

B Removing the Stand-Down Period between Introduction and Initial Debate

Column E of Table 4.3 shows the occasions on which urgency was used to take together the introduction and the first substantive debate on a bill. When this occurs, the point at which an urgency motion is moved may be the first time at which many members of the House have heard of a bill (although informal notice may, in some cases, have been given). This use of urgency also results in the elimination of the stand-down period between the introduction and initial debate, meaning that members will have little, if any, time to prepare for the initial debate. This use of urgency does not, though, interfere with the select committee process.[12]

Prior to 1996 the introduction of a bill and initial debate were "taken together" as a matter of course and so there was no stand-down period in any event. During this period, therefore, the figures in column E are of less significance and are probably best thought of as a variation on urgency for one stage.

Between 1996 and 1999 the initial debate was the second reading debate. For this period, therefore, column E counts bills which had their introduction, first reading and second reading taken together.

Since 1999 the initial debate has been the first reading debate and so, for that period, column E shows bills that had their introduction and first reading taken together.

C Urgency for Remaining Stages

Column G of Table 4.3 shows occasions on which urgency was used to take together all the stages remaining after a bill returned from select committee (currently second reading, Committee of the whole House and third reading).[13]

---

12 Column E does not include bills that remained under urgency beyond the initial debate, thus interfering with select committee consideration.
13 When a bill is accorded urgency for its "remaining stages" in an urgency motion, the term "remaining stages" may have a variety of meanings, depending on which stages have already been completed. For the purposes of Table 4.3, however, we use "remaining stages" to mean *all* stages following select committee consideration.

This includes bills that had either their remaining legislative stages taken under one urgency motion or their select committee report debate and remaining legislative stages taken under one urgency motion.[14]

D Taking Committee of the Whole House and Third Reading Together

Column I shows occasions on which urgency was not used for all remaining stages but was used to take Committee of the whole House and third reading together. This category is not applicable between 1996 and 1999 because, during those years, the second reading stage was taken before a bill was sent to select committee. During that period, therefore, this category of use of urgency is identical to the "remaining stages" category.

E Bills Taken Through All Stages and/or Bills Not Sent to Select Committee

Column K shows bills taken through all their stages under an urgency motion. This means that the bills were introduced, read a first and second time, debated in the Committee of the whole House and then read a third time in the same "sitting day".[15]

Figures 4.7 and 4.8 show (by year and parliament respectively) any bills introduced during the period of study that were subject to an urgency motion that had the effect of denying the opportunity for select committee scrutiny.[16] As explained in Chapter Two, since 2003, that has occurred when urgency is accorded in one motion to *at least* the first and second reading of the bill.[17]

There is a substantial overlap between the bills not sent to select committee and the bills put through all stages under urgency. Apart from one bill (in 1994),[18] none of the bills put through all stages under urgency went to select committee. With that exception, where the figure for bills put through all stages

---

14   It also includes occasions where the House skipped a stage (for example by giving leave not to have a Committee of the whole House stage but to proceed with the second and third readings under urgency).

15   The Standing Orders provide that imprest supply bills can be put through all stages in one sitting without urgency being taken: see Standing Orders (2008), SO 321. However, if there are not enough hours remaining in the sitting day to do so, urgency will need to be taken to extend the sitting day: see David McGee QC, *Parliamentary Practice in New Zealand* (3rd ed, Dunmore, Wellington, 2005) at 476. Accordingly, Column K includes imprest supply bills where they were put through all stages with the benefit of an urgency motion (but not where they were put through all stages without urgency being taken).

16   As this is a composite category, it is not helpful to show it as a percentage of items of legislative business accorded urgency and so it is not included in Table 4.3.

17   See Chapter Two, Part III.D.

18   The Health Amendment Bill (No 2) 1994 went briefly to a select committee during the three-day urgency period in which it was passed.

under urgency (Table 4.3, Column K) is higher than the figure for bills not subject to select committee scrutiny (Figure 4.7), that is because Figure 4.7 does not include money bills (1987–1992),[19] nor appropriation and imprest supply bills. These follow their own special procedures, which do not involve select committee scrutiny even in the ordinary course of events.[20]

Conversely, the majority of bills that skipped the select committee stage went through all stages under urgency. That said, in around half the years in the study, at least one bill skipped the select committee stage but did not go through all stages under urgency. In some cases, urgency was lifted after the first and second reading,[21] or after the Committee of the whole House stage.[22] In others, urgency was not taken for the bill's introduction but was taken for all later stages.[23] In yet others, the explanation was more complex. For example, in 2009, the House took urgency for the introduction and first reading of the Electoral Amendment Bill but the Leader of the House, Gerry Brownlee, mistakenly omitted to include the second reading of the Bill in the urgency motion. Realising his mistake, he adjourned the debate and immediately moved a fresh urgency motion (this time seeking urgency for the first and second reading) but the Assistant Speaker ruled that, for reasons relating to the effect of the adjournment, the Bill could not be included in the new urgency motion.[24] When the House resumed the following week, Brownlee moved (this time successfully) that urgency be accorded to the adjourned first reading debate and all subsequent stages.[25]

---

19 For the purposes of the database, bills are deemed money bills if Hansard has recorded the Speaker declaring them as such. There is a small chance that the Speaker may have made the decision outside the debating chamber and that it is not recorded in Hansard. In particular it is difficult to tell whether three bills that dealt with excise tax were treated as money bills: the Customs Amendment Bill (No 2) 1988; the Finance (Revenue) Bill 1991; and the Transit New Zealand Amendment Bill (No 4) 1992. This is only relevant to data before 1992, when the money bill exclusion for select committee referral was removed (leaving only imprest supply and appropriation bills excluded from the ordinary select committee process).
20 See Standing Orders (2008), SOs 321–332. Although appropriation bills are not themselves subject to select committee scrutiny, the estimates prepared in association with them are subject to a special (and abbreviated) select committee process.
21 For example, Road User Charges Amendment Bill 2000; Tariff (Zero Duty Removal) Amendment Bill 2002.
22 For example, Conservation Amendment Bill (No 2) 1988; Taxation Reform Bill (No 3) 1988.
23 For example, Civil Aviation (Cape Town Convention and Other Matters) Amendment Bill 2010; Policing (Involvement in Local Authority Elections) Amendment Bill 2010.
24 (12 February 2009) 652 NZPD 1258–1273.
25 (17 February 2009) 652 NZPD 1318.

Figure 4.7: Bills not Sent to Select Committee by Year 1987–2010

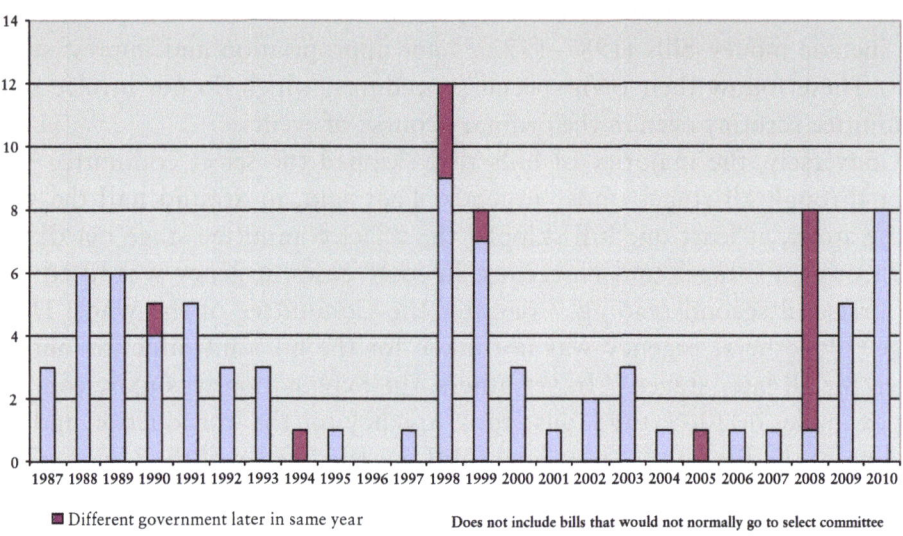

■ Different government later in same year   Does not include bills that would not normally go to select committee

Figure 4.8: Bills Accorded Urgency with No Select Committee Stage by Parliament 1987–2010

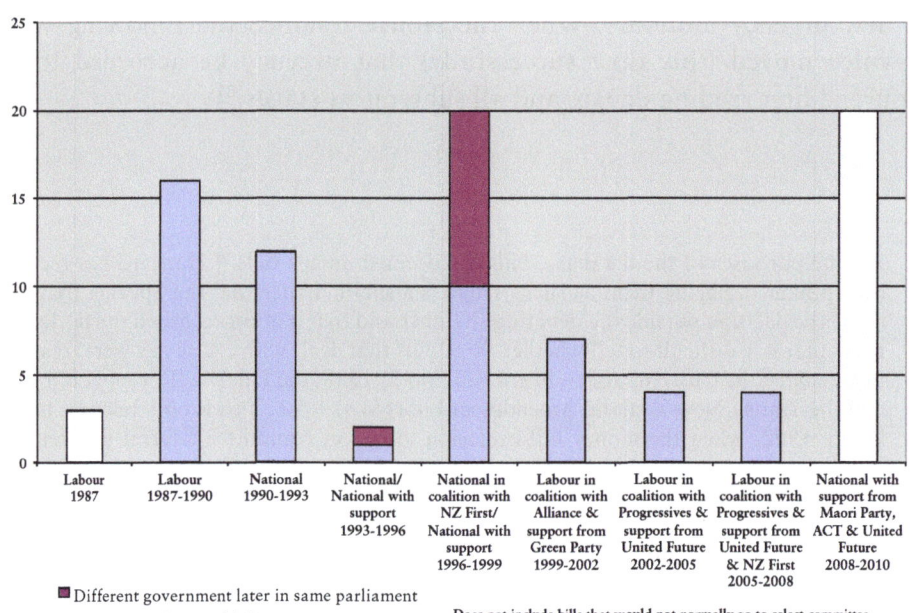

■ Different government later in same parliament
□ Data not inclusive of full term   Does not include bills that would not normally go to select committee

In Chapter Five, we return to these data on urgency for all stages (or otherwise to eliminate select committee scrutiny) and we provide further analysis of the behaviour of different parliaments across time. However, some brief preliminary analysis is appropriate here. First, it is important to acknowledge at the outset that, throughout the period under study, these uses of urgency (for all stages or otherwise to eliminate select committee scrutiny) were, in fact, relatively uncommon. The total number of bills put through all stages under urgency was 81 and the total number of occasions on which urgency was used to avoid select committee scrutiny was 88 (being an average of 3.7 occasions per calendar year).

However, as with urgency per se, these uses of urgency were not distributed evenly across different years and governments. As might be expected, the single-party majority governments that characterised the pre-MMP parliamentary environment were comparatively high users of urgency to take all stages (or otherwise to avoid select committee scrutiny). Additionally, the two periods of post-MMP National-led government (1996–1999 and 2008–2010) were characterised by a high incidence of this type of urgency. Indeed, urgency to take all stages (or otherwise to avoid select committee scrutiny) was used by these two post-MMP governments *even more* than by the pre-MMP single-party majority governments in the study.[26]

For reasons that are explored in Chapter Six, these extreme versions of fast-tracking the legislative process are by far the most troubling from a democratic legitimacy perspective. Resort to them ought to be rare, and justified by a genuine need for haste in relation to the particular measure.[27] In order to probe more deeply into these uses of urgency, we examined the parliamentary debates in relation to all 55 bills that had been enacted under urgency without select committee scrutiny since the introduction of MMP in 1996. Our goal was to shed further light on the circumstances in which this type of urgency was resorted to. To that purpose, we categorised all 55 bills, dividing them into three broad groups. The 55 bills and their categorisations, organised by parliamentary term, are listed in Appendix B so that readers can make their own assessments of our (necessarily subjective) judgements on each bill.

The first category, "A", includes all bills where an identifiable rationale for expediting the legislation was evident from the record. In order to receive an "A" nomination, bills had to comply with at least one of the following characteristics.

- (A1), there was an identifiable justification for urgency in relation to the particular measure. Thus, as we explained in Chapter Three, the bill might be intended to reduce the potential for speculative behaviour, to respond to an unexpected event or court decision, to remedy an anomaly, oversight or uncertainty in existing legislation, or to respond to external factors creating a deadline for the proposed legislative change.

26 1998, 1999, 2008 and 2010.
27 Chapter Six, Part II.

- (A2), the bill was accorded extraordinary urgency (and therefore its fast-tracking was approved by the Speaker).
- (A3), the bill both received unanimous support in the House, as indicated by voting at the third reading, and the omission of the select committee stage was not criticised by MPs.
- (A4), the bill repealed an act that itself went through select committee scrutiny and the repealing legislation received widespread (if not complete) parliamentary support.

The second category of bills, "B", includes all bills that proposed substantial policy (including constitutional) change where we could identify no obvious rationale for expediting the legislation. Obviously this is the group that is most democratically and constitutionally worrying.

The third category, "C", includes tax measures. We list these separately as we accept that the rhythm of the tax year, as well as the time that it takes to implement changes to tax rates, may sometimes create particular time pressures in relation to tax measures.[28] It does not, though, necessarily follow that tax measures are never suitable for select committee scrutiny. Where tax legislation embodies a major change in policy direction, a lag in the implementation timeframe may well be preferable to eliminating meaningful parliamentary scrutiny. That said, given the specific considerations that apply to tax measures, we decided to place them in a separate category and leave readers to form their own judgements on them.

In Appendix B, we also identify (by asterisks) which bills were included in Budget day urgency motions. However, for the reasons explained in Chapter Three, we do not consider that the Budget day is, itself, a freestanding reason for using urgency. For that reason, we subjected bills denied select committee scrutiny as a result of Budget day urgency motions to the same categorisation process as other bills.

These categorisations are necessarily somewhat subjective and, given the volume of bills considered, approximate. In particular, it does not necessarily follow from the allocation of a particular bill to category "A" that the justifications relied on in the particular case genuinely demanded the elimination of the select committee stage. Just because there is a legitimate reason to expedite legislation, it does not necessarily follow that the timeframe is so tight as to demand the complete elimination of the select committee stage. For example, referral to select committee for a truncated time period is always an option – a point that was stressed by the Standing Orders Committee in its report into the 2011 review of the Standing Orders.[29] It should be noted that some of the bills

---

28   See Chapter Three, Part II.D.
29   Standing Orders Committee, "Review of Standing Orders" [2011] AJHR I.18B at 18–19.

in category A, and the processes that were followed in relation to them, were highly contested in the House.

Nevertheless, the categorisation exercise is helpful in casting further light on the extent to which this usage of urgency is democratically troubling. Table 4.4 summarises our findings.

Table 4.4: Bills Not Sent to Select Committee by Parliament and Category 1996–2010

Parliament	"A" Bills with Identifiable Rationale for the Use of Urgency	"B" Bills without Identifiable Rationale for the Use of Urgency	"C" Tax Measures	Totals
1996–1999 National-NZ First Coalition: National-led Minority	7	12	1	20
1999–2002 Labour-Alliance Minority	4	2	1	7
2002–2005 Labour-Progressive Minority	1	2	1	4
2005–2008 Labour-Progressive Minority	1	1	2	4
2008–2010 National Minority (incomplete term)	7	10	3	20
Totals	19	27	9	55

The data in Table 4.4 demonstrate that, although many bills that passed through the House between 1996 and 2010 had some kind of identifiable rationale for being expedited, just less than half – 27 out of 55 – did not. This suggests that a worrying number of bills were passed through the legislative process without there being any good reason for the reduction in legislative scrutiny and public engagement that occurs when the select committee stage is bypassed. The data also show a sharp distinction between different parliaments and governments, an issue that is discussed further in the next chapter.

As we have shown, the most radical and democratically problematical fast-tracking of legislation – passing a bill through all its stages in one sitting day or otherwise using urgency to eliminate the select committee stage – has occurred less often than other forms of urgency. Nevertheless, the high occurrence of this form of urgency during the forty-fifth and forty-ninth parliaments in particular is a matter of real concern.

III Extraordinary Urgency

As noted above, there were only eight extraordinary urgency motions over the entire period. These were moved in 1988, 1991, 1998, 1999, 2000, 2002, 2003 and 2010. Each extraordinary urgency motion related to only one bill. However, as one of these bills was later divided into four,[30] the figure for *all* bills accorded extraordinary urgency is 12 out of 1608.

There was never more than one extraordinary urgency motion in any one year. There was one extraordinary urgency motion in the final term of the fourth Labour Government (1987–1990), three during the nine years of National and National-led governments in the 1990s, three during the nine years of post-MMP Labour-led governments, and one by the 2008–2011 National-led Government (as at the end of 2010). It is not possible to draw conclusions as to trends in the use of extraordinary urgency from such a small sample except to note that this procedure was used sparingly and that, as compared with (ordinary) urgency, it appears to have been used more evenly.

IV Seasonal Patterns in the Use of Urgency

In Chapter Three, we noted that our interviewees had identified certain pressure points in the parliamentary calendar where a desire to extend the House's sitting hours is particularly likely to arise. We also noted that some of these seasonal motivations for the use of urgency were borne out on occasion in the formal reasons given in Hansard for moving urgency.[31] To what extent are any of these seasonal motivations so pronounced in practice that their incidence shows up in our statistical data? The results are interesting but inconclusive.

Figure 4.9 divides the electoral cycle into four periods: the immediate months after an election to the end of the calendar year (light yellow); the first full year

---

30   Finance Revenue Bill 1991.
31   Chapter Three, Part II.B.

of the electoral cycle (light blue); the second full year (mid blue); and then the final year up to the date of the election (dark blue).

In the majority of full electoral cycles represented, urgency was in fact used the most during the second full year of the electoral cycle. The exceptions were the 1990–1993 Parliament and the 1993–1996 Parliament. In both those cases, more urgency was used during the first full year of the electoral cycle. In 1993–1996, this was no doubt because of the precarious nature of the National party's support arrangements following its loss of a majority in September 1994.[32] On the other hand, the 1990–1993 case can perhaps be explained by the fact that this was a first-term government, newly elected with a fresh electoral mandate. On the partial data available, it appears that the 2008–2011 Parliament is likely to follow the same pattern, perhaps for the same reason.

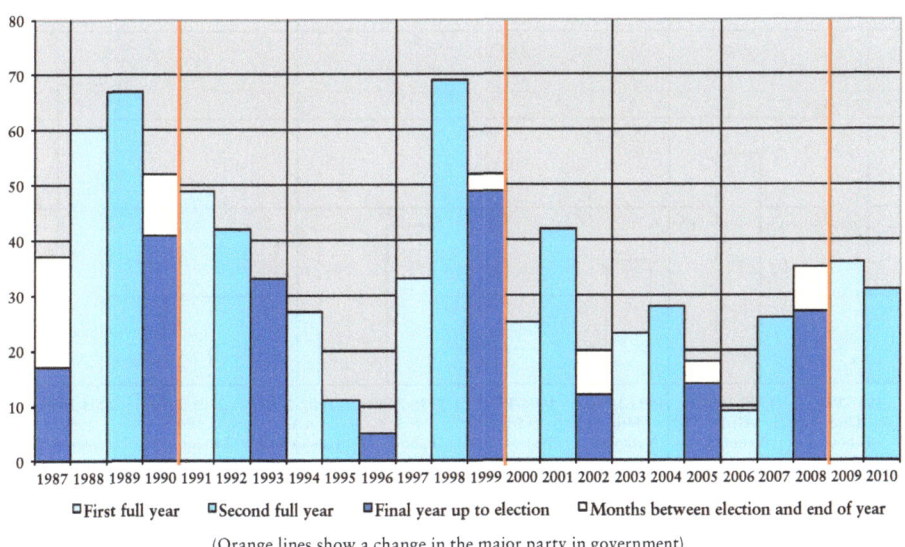

Figure 4.9: Bills Accorded Urgency by Year of Electoral Cycle 1987–2010

□First full year □Second full year ■Final year up to election □Months between election and end of year

(Orange lines show a change in the major party in government)

The same pattern was not, however, reflected in the use of urgency by the first term Labour-led government in 1999–2002. This is likely to be because of the tempering influence of Labour's support partners (a constraint examined in depth in Chapter Five). Relevantly, Labour's support partners appear to have been particularly resistant to urgency being used to take together the introduction and first reading stage of legislation (which is the most likely use of urgency during a government's first few months in office).[33]

---

32 See Chapter One, Table 1.1 and Chapter Five, Part III.A.
33 See Chapter Five, Part III.C.

The pattern of high use of urgency in the first year of first term governments is reinforced by the yellow bars, reflecting the use of urgency in the months between a general election and the end of the calendar year. These data must be treated with care as the date of the general election varies from cycle to cycle.[34] For example, the apparently high numbers of urgency motions following the elections in 1987 and 2002 reflect the early election date in each of those years. In 1990 and 2008, though, general elections were held late in the year – in late October and early November respectively. The comparatively high number of urgency motions following the general elections in those years, therefore, tends to confirm the impression that these first term governments used urgency comparatively aggressively in their first year or so in office.

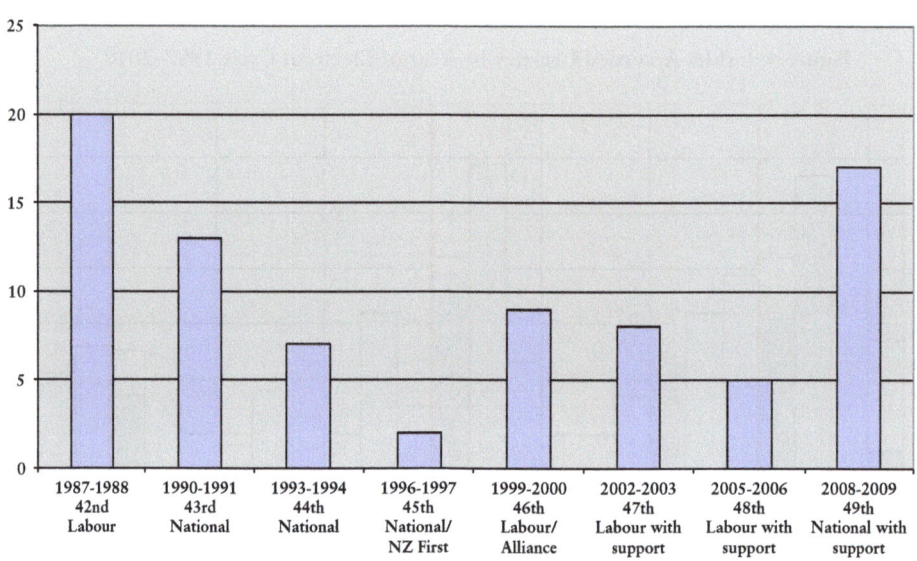

Figure 4.10: Bills Accorded Urgency First Six Months of New Parliament 1987–2010

The possibility that first term governments may be particularly motivated to use urgency aggressively during their first few months in government is further reinforced by Figure 4.10, which compares the use of urgency during the first six months after each election that fell within the period of our study. The 1987–1988 period under Labour and the 2008–2009 period under National and its support parties both stand out for the number of bills accorded urgency during these six-month periods. More generally, though, the graph indicates that the impetus to push through legislation immediately

---

34   During the period of the study, general elections fell on the following dates: 1987 – 15 August; 1990 – 27 October; 1993 – 6 November; 1996 – 12 October; 1999 – 27 November; 2002 – 27 July; 2005 – 17 September; 2008 – 8 November.

following an election is strongest following a change in major party power (1990 from Labour to National, 1999 from National to Labour and 2008 back from Labour to National again) and then subsides with each consecutive term in office.

Interestingly, Figure 4.9 does not reflect a particularly high use of urgency motions in the year leading up to a general election as compared with other years in the electoral cycle. That is, in part, because an election year is not a full sitting year. Nevertheless, it is worth noting that those election years before changes in major party power (1990, 1999 and 2008) had significantly higher proportions of bills being accorded urgency than the prior election years. This may perhaps confirm the suggestion of some interviewees that governments that are contemplating being voted out of office are more likely to use urgency.[35]

Turning to annual patterns in the use of urgency, Figure 4.11 shows the average number of urgency motions moved each month over the 24 years of the study. The December bulge clearly reflects the phenomenon of pre-Christmas urgency discussed in Chapter Two, and the May/June bulge most likely reflects the prevalence of Budget day urgency. What is particularly interesting, though, is the increase in the number of urgency motions after Parliament returned from the summer recess. The years 1988, 1989, 1990 and 1998 made particular use of March for urgency motions (with four passed in March in each of those years). In 2009, no urgency motions were passed in March but five urgency motions were passed in February.

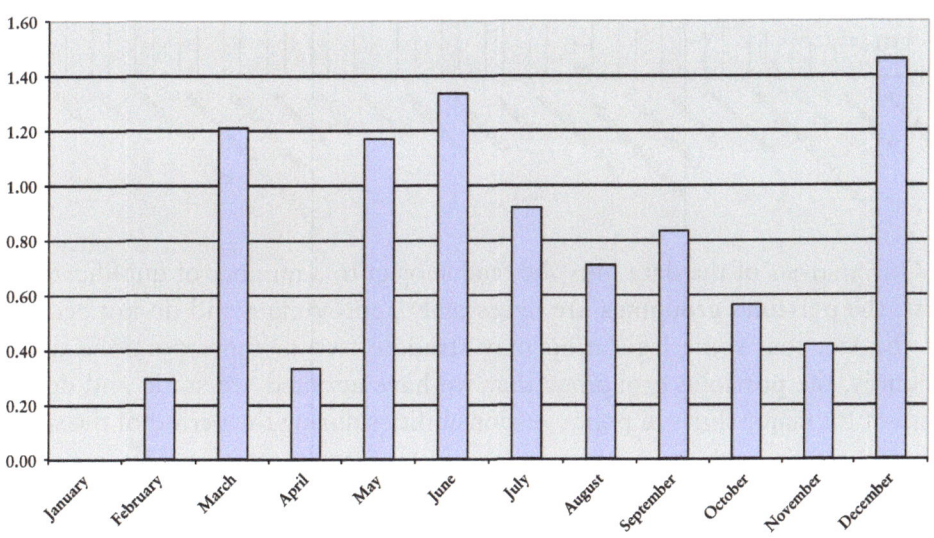

Figure 4.11: Average Number of Urgency Motions by Month 1987–2010

---

35   See Chapter Three, Part II.B.

88 ♦ What's the Hurry?

V Policy Areas of Bills Accorded Urgency

The final question that we address in this chapter is whether legislation is more likely to be accorded urgency in some policy areas than in others. This deepens our understanding of the use of urgency and links the quantitative data in this chapter with our qualitative findings on the motivations for using urgency discussed in Chapter Three.

Figure 4.12 groups the bills accorded urgency during the period of the study according to the portfolio area of the minister responsible for introducing the bill and shepherding it through the legislative process.[36] The content of the portfolio groupings that we adopted are set out in Appendix C.[37]

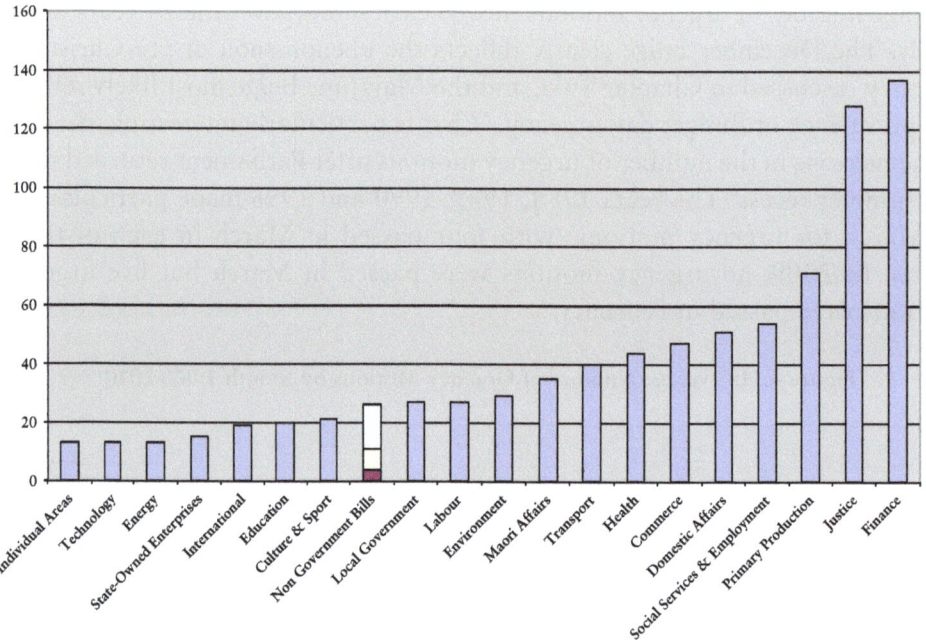

Figure 4.12: Bills Accorded Urgency by Portfolio Areas 1987–2010

Our analysis of the data must be read subject to a number of qualifications. First, the portfolio groupings are necessarily approximate and do not account for the fact that some legislation may straddle two or more portfolio areas. Secondly, the portfolio groupings that we have adopted are static and do not account for major shifts in policy responsibilities during the period of the study.

---

36 In the column for non-government bills, eggshell blue represents local bills, pale yellow represents members' bills and maroon represents private bills.

37 The ministerial portfolio is taken from the ministerial title noted in Hansard when a reading of the bill is moved. The Journals of the House of Representatives do not specify the ministerial title of the member in charge of the bill.

Finally, we have been unable to obtain data on the extent to which particular policy areas are responsible for a high proportion of Parliament's legislative output overall. That means that we are unable to account for the possibility that patterns of high use of urgency associated with a particular policy area, in fact, reflect a high overall legislative output in that policy area.

Putting to one side these qualifications, Figure 4.12 nevertheless reveals some interesting patterns. It is hardly surprising that financial policy (including the portfolio areas of finance, inland revenue and the treasury) is responsible for more urgency bills than any other portfolio area (16.5 per cent of the total 830 bills introduced between 1987 and 2010). Factors that would account for this would include the tradition of the Budget day urgency motion (which, in recent times at least, has tended to be dominated by financial legislation), the fact that financial legislation is most likely to attract the "pre-emptive behaviour" justification for urgency discussed in Chapter Three, and the time pressures created by the rhythm of the tax year.[38]

Also unsurprisingly, a high proportion of bills relating to social services and employment (including 10 housing bills), and health (which includes bills relating to accident compensation), were put through the urgency process. These social issues are highly contested policy areas, dividing the parties along philosophical grounds according to the extent to which they favour State involvement on such aspects as income redistribution and welfare. This may explain why parties have tended to push these sorts of core policy changes through the legislative process using urgency. Labour bills – a highly salient policy area and one where major lobby groups have close links with the two main parties – are not as high in number as might be expected, but this might reflect the fact that this sort of legislation goes through the House relatively infrequently and involves large bills that cover much regulatory detail.

The real surprise is the number of justice bills: 128 in the 1987–2010 period. We can only conjecture about why this is so. There are probably several interlocking explanations. First, New Zealand politicians are forever tinkering with the justice system, in part responding to perceived popular concerns. This delivers a large number of ad hoc, often small, bills that are promoted as "urgent" and therefore are viewed by governments as requiring hasty implementation. Secondly, many bills that emanate from justice ministers are, on the contrary, non-contested, perhaps clarifying or correcting existing laws. As such, they might well have been included in mid-year and end-of-year sittings where urgency is taken to clean up the backlog of bills. Further analysis might reveal that some justice bills are dealt with differently than others. The regulatory areas included in the justice portfolios – courts, corrections,

---

38   See Chapter Three, Part II.D.

police and justice – cover a wide range of bills from electoral to sentencing law, some highly contestable and the rest uncontroversial, at least in the eyes of the politicians. Finally, although we have been unable to obtain data, we understand from informal conversations with officials that the justice sector generates a high proportion of Parliament's overall legislative output. The high number of justice bills accorded urgency may, therefore, simply reflect a high proportion of justice bills overall.

VI Conclusion

The data set out in this chapter show that, despite the resilience and durability of the mechanism of parliamentary urgency, the way in which urgency has been used and the extent of its use has not been constant across time. What this chapter has not sought to address is why that might be so. What are the reasons why some governments used more urgency than others? We address that question in the next chapter in the context of a broad examination of the factors that inhibit or constrain New Zealand governments in the use of urgency.

5

The Constraints on the Use of Urgency

We have established that, despite the resilience and durability of the mechanism of parliamentary urgency, the way in which it has been used and the extent of its use has not been constant over time. In this chapter, we develop insights into the reasons for these changing patterns of use by focusing on the factors that constrain governments from taking urgency.

We begin by discussing the special case of extraordinary urgency, which was used on only eight occasions during the full 24-year period of the study. We then explore some practical constraints – whether internal or external to Parliament – that can sometimes work to limit the extent to which, and the way in which, urgency is taken. These include the possibility of hostile reactions from other players in the parliamentary system, the competing demands on parliamentary time and the role played by the media and public opinion.

We then turn to one of the key questions for our study: the impact of MMP on the use of urgency. We saw from the data presented in the preceding chapter that the introduction of MMP led to a significant reduction in the use of urgency. However, we also saw that the impact of MMP on the use of urgency has not been consistent. In this chapter, we consider the reasons why that might be so by examining, in detail, the behaviour of the various major and minor parties that participated in governing arrangements following the advent of multi-party parliaments. We conclude that, in order to account for the impact of multi-party governance on the use of urgency, it is necessary to look to a complex list of factors, including the particular makeup of the governing majority, the ideological perspectives of support parties and the people who comprise them, and the overarching support arrangements that have been entered into.

Not only did MMP impact on the extent to which urgency (or particular types of urgency) are taken, it also impacted on evolving cultural norms concerning how parliamentary actors behave when urgency is taken, and concerning the extent to which urgency is allowed to disrupt MPs' other activities – whether inside or outside the House. In this chapter, we explore those cultural changes, with particular reference to the transparency (or lack thereof) that surrounds the urgency process, the length of continuous sittings under urgency and the impact of urgency on question time.

The chapter concludes with a brief discussion of the extent to which internalised factors such as ideology and personality constrain the taking of urgency.

I *Extraordinary Urgency*

Extraordinary urgency motions differ from (ordinary) urgency motions in that the Standing Orders of the House of Representatives place a substantive limit on the circumstances in which extraordinary urgency can be taken. Standing Order 56 requires the minister moving a motion for extraordinary urgency to inform the House of the "circumstances that warrant the claim for extraordinary urgency" and to win the agreement of the Speaker that "the business to be taken justifies it." Hansard does not record any instances in which extraordinary urgency was sought by a government and turned down by the Speaker. Those negotiations happen behind closed doors in three-way discussions between the Leader of the House, the Clerk and the Speaker.[1] There is also no record of the occasions, if any, on which the Speaker has refused to follow the advice of the Clerk on whether extraordinary urgency is justified.

Interviewees tended to stress the infrequency of extraordinary urgency motions and saw the Standing Orders as placing tight constraints on their use – limiting them to circumstances where there is, as one interviewee put it, a "financial or life-threatening type of issue."[2] The infrequency with which extraordinary urgency has in fact been used during the 24-year period of the study tends to confirm this perception. Nevertheless, the former Clerk of the House, David McGee QC, told us that the Office of the Clerk has had to be vigilant in holding the line in the face of governments that are initially minded to use extraordinary urgency more broadly. In McGee's view, the Clerk's office has, so far, been successful but he observed in his interview:

> . . . That wasn't a given. It could have got out of hand and it could have been pushed a little bit further than it's gone. Fortunately it hasn't.

The Standing Orders do not specify a substantive criterion or standard for when extraordinary urgency would be "justified" or "warranted". It seems now to be generally accepted that its use is only appropriate where there is both a need for an immediate law change and where the new law will come into immediate effect.[3] However, on two occasions of which we are aware, discrete aspects of legislation accorded extraordinary urgency did not, in fact, come into immediate effect. First, the Customs and Excise Amendment Act 2000 (which increased the excise duty on tobacco) included one provision with a

---

1   McGee, Harris and Hunt interviews.
2   Sowry interview. Interviewees that expressed similar sentiments included Hunt, Cullen, Smith, Harris, Turei, Hughes and Kidd.
3   See Standing Orders Committee, "Review of Standing Orders" [1995] AJHR I.18A at 20; David McGee QC, *Parliamentary Practice in New Zealand* (3rd ed, Dunmore, Wellington, 2005) at 155 [*Parliamentary Practice*]; McGee, Harris and Smith interviews.

commencement date four weeks after the date of royal assent.[4] The provision exempted tobacco products from a regulation specifying a minimum amount below which duty did not need to be collected. When moving the extraordinary urgency motion, the Leader of the House, Dr Michael Cullen, expressed the view that this clause needed to be passed along with the rest of the bill "so that no uncertainty arises out of the passage of the remainder of the bill as to its impact on the *de minimis* provision."[5]

Secondly, the Excise and Excise-equivalent Duties Table (Tobacco Products) Amendment Act 2010 provided for three cumulative increases of 10 per cent to the duties on tobacco products. Although the first increase was to come into effect immediately, the second and third increases were signalled in advance by around eight months and 20 months respectively.

There might be legitimate differences of opinion on whether, and in what circumstances, it is appropriate for legislation enacted under extraordinary urgency to contain subsidiary provisions that do not themselves come into immediate effect. What can perhaps be said is that these two examples underline the former Clerk's view that continued vigilance is required to ensure that measures enacted under extraordinary urgency are, indeed, truly urgent.

The second of these examples surely also calls into question the continued validity of the "pre-emptive behaviour" justification for urgency.[6] If the Government perceived no difficulty in alerting the public many months in advance to the second and third projected increases to the excise duty, how can it follow that the first increase needed to be enacted in the dead of night to prevent speculative market behaviour?

On the whole, though, the infrequency of extraordinary urgency motions during the period of the study suggests that Standing Order 56 is working well and that it has created a culture of considerable restraint around the use of extraordinary urgency.

II *(Ordinary) Urgency*

In the case of (ordinary) urgency, the only explicit constraint is the need to get the support of the House for the urgency motion. The impact of multi-party parliaments on the ability of major parties to get that support is explored in Part III below. First, though, we explore some practical constraints that can sometimes work to limit the extent to which, and the way in which, urgency is taken. Some of these practical constraints are internal to Parliament: the

---

4   Customs and Excise Amendment Act 2000, s 4, amending the Customs and Excise Regulations 1996, r 70.
5   (9 May 2000) 583 NZPD 1983.
6   See Chapter Three, Part II.A.1.

possibility of hostile reactions from other players in the parliamentary system, for example, and the competing demands on parliamentary time. Others are external to Parliament: most importantly, the role played by the media and public opinion.

A *Internal Factors that Can Constrain Urgency*

Within Parliament itself, there are undoubtedly a range of considerations that can impact on a government's decision whether (and if so, how) to take urgency. One of the most interesting is the power of the opposition to deploy delaying tactics in the House in order to "punish" a government that is seen to be abusing the use of urgency.

To explain, the main purpose of urgency motions (as discussed above) is to free up more parliamentary time for disposing of the government's business in the House. That purpose can be significantly undermined by an opposition that has withdrawn its cooperation and is deploying every delaying tactic at its disposal. As Geoffrey Palmer quipped to the House when debating the abandonment of all-night sittings under urgency in 1985: "In the end, parliament, like prison, can only be run with the goodwill of its inmates."[7]

A number of our interviewees stressed the role of the opposition in inhibiting the excessive use of urgency powers.[8] For example, Jonathan Hunt, when questioned by us about the constraints on urgency, referred to "the fact that if they overdo it, they're going to end up having a lot of rows in Parliament". Similarly, Ken Shirley suggested to us that "there are instances where it actually would have been quicker and easier, more expedient, to have done it *not* in urgency."

Perhaps the most notorious example of the opposition withdrawing its cooperation in response to the perceived irresponsible use of urgency powers was the "Mother of All Budgets" in 1991, when the Government bundled up a number of unrelated pieces of legislation in a Budget day urgency motion.[9] Richard Prebble led the debate at the time for the Labour Party in opposition. He recalled:[10]

> All the MPs who moaned I sent home and then said to the team who were left "let's dig in". We caught the Government by surprise. When the MPs who had gone home switched on to Morning Report they discovered Parliament was still meeting and had made virtually no progress. Public opinion swung behind the opposition. The whole parliamentary party decided to fight and had caught the

---

7   (23 July 1985) 464 NZPD 5853.
8   For example, Hunt, Shirley, Sowry and Cullen interviews.
9   See Chapter Three, Part II.D.
10 Prebble email exchange (underlining retained from original).

public mood. <u>Better to fight in Parliament than in the streets.</u> National misread the situation.

This was one of the rare occasions in modern times when the House sat on a Monday. Even so, the Government could not get through all the business that it had scheduled and some bills for which urgency had been accorded were not finally enacted until months later. The former Clerk of the House, David McGee QC, suggested to us in his interview that the backlash from this incident may well have contributed to a change in the culture around the use of urgency after that time. Certainly, Budget day urgency motions were never used in quite the same way again.[11]

Other notorious examples of the opposition "digging in" in response to perceived unfair uses of urgency include the debates on the Maritime Transport Bill in 1994 (when, as a result of opposition delaying tactics, the House sat under urgency for eight non-consecutive sitting days for the second reading and Committee of the whole House stages),[12] and the debates on the Employment Relations Bill in 2000 (when Labour was forced to move a motion for the House to sit on a Monday after the Committee of the whole House stage continued until 11.30pm on the Saturday night without resolution due to "filibustering" from the opposition).[13] More recently again, in one of the debates on the Auckland super-city legislation, enacted in May 2009, the opposition, with the assistance of computer generation, put up over 30,000 amendments.[14] Darren Hughes, a Labour MP and senior whip at the time, stated in his interview with us that Labour believed the Bill was too important to be put through under urgency and so used parliamentary procedures to drag out its passage, to provide scrutiny and to "try and embarrass the Government into not using that kind of procedure repeatedly." Hughes also described to us an occasion in 2010 when the opposition withdrew cooperation because it objected to the Government taking urgency without preserving question time.[15] He noted:

> I think that was another reminder that, . . . [while the opposition] . . . can't necessarily prevent things becoming law, you do have to have some degree

---

11 See Chapter Three, Part II.D.
12 Sowry interview; (22 June 1994) 541 NZPD 1966; (5 July 1994) 541 NZPD 2597; (12 July 1994) 541 NZPD 2772.
13 Sowry and Harris interviews; (9 August 2000) 586 NZPD 4570.
14 Smith, Harris and Hughes interviews. See, also, Lindsay Tisch and Mary Harris, "Committee of the Whole House Consideration, 30,000 Amendments: What are the Implications for the Chair?" (paper presented to 40th Commonwealth Parliamentary Association Australian and Pacific Regions Presiding Officers and Clerks Conference, Kiribati, July 2009), reproduced in "Reports of the Official Inter-Parliamentary Relations Programme, 1 January-31 December 2009" [2009] AJHR J.21 at 61.
15 The changing cultural expectations around the preservation of question time are discussed further below: Chapter Five, Part IV.

of cooperation in order to make Parliament run effectively. Otherwise the opposition can slow things right down to the point of preposterousness and the government recognises that.

On the other hand, a prudent opposition will deploy obstructionist tactics of this kind sparingly and with some care. That is because the opposition runs the risk of a public backlash if it has misjudged public sentiment and is seen to be unnecessarily obstructing the legitimate agenda of a democratically elected government.[16] It is interesting to note in this respect that the extreme delaying tactics utilised by the opposition, in particular, in response to the Auckland super-city legislation, attracted criticism from some senior parliamentary officials and parliamentarians. In a 2009 conference paper, the Deputy Speaker and the Clerk of the House noted that:[17]

> Debate is an acceptable delay tactic, particularly where a bill has not gone to a select committee and is being considered under urgency. Members and the public understand that Oppositions have few options available to them other than delay. However, in these circumstances the amount of time spent voting was seen as an abuse of process. The lodging of thousands of computer-generated amendments just at the conclusion of each debate in the Committee of the whole House was a smart political tactic, but one that may ultimately bring the House into disrepute.

In its 2011 review of the Standing Orders, the Standing Orders Committee recommended enhancements to the chairperson's powers to deal with proposed amendments at the Committee of the whole House stage (for example, by grouping amendments to be taken as one question), and these have now been adopted by the House.[18] The Committee noted that procedural delaying tactics are "legitimate" and will always be part of the parliamentary environment but that:[19]

> They can have an adverse effect on the quality of debate and legislative outcomes, and the progression of legislative initiatives to improve the statute book. The reputation of Parliament as an effective institution is not enhanced by such outcomes.

Two further internal parliamentary factors that may impact on the use of urgency from time to time are worthy of brief comment. The first is the

---

16   This is discussed further in the next section: Chapter Five, Part II.B.
17   Tisch and Harris, above n 14, at 66.
18   Standing Orders Committee, "Review of Standing Orders" [2011] AJHR I.18B at 45, 47 ["Standing Orders Review 2011"]. For further discussion, see Chapter Six, Part I.B.2.
19   "Standing Orders Review 2011", above n 18, at 14. The Committee extended this critique to the government using urgency to make progress, as well as to opposition delaying tactics: see Chapter Seven, Part II.

government's own backbenchers.[20] That is because of the highly disruptive effects of urgency – particularly on out-of-town members and particularly when, as was common during the early part of our study, no advance notice is given. Nevertheless, backbenchers who want to advance their political careers are unlikely to be openly obstructive of the government's procedural motions. For that reason, the government caucus is likely to be a weak constraint, at best, on the use of urgency. Examples that were given to us by interviewees of government backbenchers acting to frustrate the use of urgency all related to the Fourth Labour Government (1984–1990), at a period when there were substantial ideological divisions more generally within the Labour caucus.[21]

Additionally, the introduction of the party voting system following the 1995 review of the Standing Orders meant that it was no longer necessary to maintain the presence of the entire caucus in the Chamber during periods of urgency.[22] This further weakened the potential for the government caucus to act as a constraint on the use of urgency.[23]

Another practical constraint on the use of urgency is its disruptive effect on the completion of other parliamentary business. For example, when urgency is taken, select committees do not generally meet.[24] For that reason, a government considering whether to take urgency will need to balance its desire to advance its legislative business in the House with its need to advance other forms of business, including the progression of legislation through select committees.[25]

B *External Factors that Can Constrain Urgency*

The ultimate constraint on the actions of politicians in a democratic system is, of course, the ballot box.[26] Accordingly, one would expect the media and public opinion to have a role in constraining the use of urgency. To what extent is that so?

Certainly, they do play some role. Media coverage of urgency tends to intensify around periods of high usage (such as during the latter years of the 1996–1999 Parliament and during the 2008–2011 Parliament).[27] As one interviewee said to

---

20   Sowry, Wilson, Dunne, McGee and East interviews.
21   Shirley and McGee interviews.
22   See Chapter Two, Part V.C.
23   Shirley interview.
24   For an explanation of the limited circumstances in which select committees can meet while urgency is being taken, see Chapter Two, Part III.B.
25   Sowry interview.
26   See, for example, Philip A Joseph, *Constitutional and Administrative Law in New Zealand* (3rd ed, Thomson Brookers, Wellington, 2007) at [14.6.2].
27   See, for example, "MPs Feel the Strain in Parliament 'Bear Pit'" in *The Waikato Times* (16 May 1998); Helen Bain, "It's a Hard Day's Night in Parliament" in *The Dominion* (2 July 1998); "Bulldozed Rush of Legislation Makes Mockery of Democracy" in *The New*

us, a government that is seen to be "ramming legislation through Parliament endlessly using urgency" runs the risk of a public backlash.[28]

However, media coverage of (and therefore public awareness of) the use of urgency is somewhat irregular and unpredictable. On some occasions during the period of our study, the phenomenon of urgency attracted high quality coverage from experienced parliamentary journalists.[29] Even at its best, though, media coverage of urgency almost never bothered to distinguish between the different ways in which urgency was used (the difference, for example, between urgency for one stage and urgency for all stages). Further, on many other occasions, media coverage of urgency was cursory, or non-existent, or fell back on emotive language about politicians "ramming" legislation through the House without careful analysis of what was actually at stake on the particular occasion.

Almost universally, parliamentarians whom we interviewed were highly sceptical about the quality of media scrutiny of parliamentary procedure in general and of urgency in particular. They regarded it as erratic, often ignorant and, at times, sensationalist. Their view was that the media and, therefore, the public has a limited interest in and an even more limited understanding of parliamentary procedure.[30]

In our view, a significant additional factor contributing to the poor levels of public understanding of urgency is the confusing regulatory framework in which urgency operates. The hybrid role played by urgency – as both a device for fast-tracking particular bills (by removing stand-down periods and/or select committee scrutiny) and a widely deployed mechanism for achieving an ad hoc extension to the House's sitting hours – is baffling to all but those deeply versed in parliamentary procedure. The very terminology of "urgency" sends out a false signal to the electorate and therefore generates confusion as to the constitutional ramifications of what is occurring. We return to consider this problem more fully in the next two chapters, where we also discuss recent changes to the Standing Orders that may go some way to addressing this problem.

It seems, therefore, that the media act as a blunt constraint at best on the use of urgency. While, on occasion, the media may take an interest in the fact, or perceived fact, that Parliament is "ramming through" legislation, those occasions

---

Zealand Herald (14 December 2008); Tracy Watkins, "Urgency Erodes Right of Scrutiny" in *The Dominion Post* (16 April 2011).

28   Smith interview. Sowry, Dunne and Shirley made similar comments in their interviews.

29   For example, Helen Bain, "It's a Hard Day's Night in Parliament" in *The Dominion* (2 July 1998); Joanne Black, "News – Parliament" in *The Dominion Post* (23 November 2002); "Bulldozed Rush of Legislation Makes Mockery of Democracy" in *The New Zealand Herald* (14 December 2008).

30   For example, Turei, Sowry, Kidd, Wilson, Hughes, Katene, Brownlee, Hide and East interviews. Current and former clerks of the House, Mary Harris and David McGee QC, had similar perceptions of the media and the public.

are irregular and are not always well-informed. At the time of writing, there is evidence of informed discussion of urgency appearing in the "blogosphere".[31] However that development is at an early stage.

It is also important to note that, when the media and public opinion do have an impact on urgency, it is not necessarily a negative impact. The public's desire to see the policies for which they voted put in place may, in fact, encourage governments to use urgency. Certainly, that is the view of politicians themselves, as we discussed in Chapter Three.[32]

Further, as suggested above, an opposition that deploys obstructionist tactics in response to an urgency motion may risk a public backlash.[33] Some of the media coverage that urgency attracted over the years of our study was certainly highly derisive of the "filibustering" that sometimes occurs when the House goes into urgency.[34]

III Getting the Numbers – The Impact of Multi-Party Parliaments on the Use of Urgency

Ultimately, the only explicit constraint on (ordinary) urgency is the need to get sufficient votes for the urgency motion.[35]

Since 1994, no single party has held a majority in the New Zealand Parliament. One of the key questions for this study was whether the presence of smaller parties in governing arrangements limits the extent to which the larger parties, National and Labour, use urgency. Certainly, the expectation of many electoral reformers and commentators when MMP was introduced was that the more diverse parliaments produced by MMP would help prevent hasty legislation.[36] Has that happened in practice?

---

31 See, for example, David Farrar, "Use of Urgency" (2011) <www.kiwiblog.co.nz>; Grant Robertson, "Urgency – Some Real Information" (2011) <www. grantrobertson.co.nz >.
32 Chapter Three, Part II.C.1.
33 See Chapter Five, Part II.A. This point was also made to us in interviews by Sowry, Harris and Creech.
34 See "Political Review: Strange Politics or Urgency" in *The New Zealand Herald* (12 October 2002); Joanne Black, "News – Parliament" in *The Dominion Post* (23 November 2002). "Filibustering" has a specific technical meaning in, for example, United States legislative practice but is used loosely in New Zealand public discourse to refer to opposition delaying tactics in the House.
35 On the importance of this constraint see, for example, Sowry, Wilson, Smith, Hughes, Kidd, Dunne, McGee and Harris interviews.
36 For example, an elite survey of 1145 MPs, academics, media commentators, interest group leaders and senior public servants, conducted before the first MMP election, found that 79 per cent of the respondents agreed with the statement that "the passage of legislation through the Parliament will be slower than in the past": Jonathan Boston and others, *New Zealand Under MMP* (Auckland University Press/Bridget Williams Books, Auckland, 1996) at 33.

MMP still operates within a Westminster system that requires a government to command a parliamentary majority. This underlying characteristic means that governments typically do not "lose" – whether that be a vote on a bill or a vote on a procedural motion. No government in the period studied lost an urgency motion. Even when their support parties would not support them, they ensured they had support elsewhere before putting the motion to the House.

Table 5.1 shows the ways in which minor parties with more than one member voted on urgency motions during any period since 1996 in which they had an agreement to support the governing party (or at least not actively to oppose it) on confidence and supply.[37] It is interesting to note that, during the entire period of the study, minor parties that entered into support arrangements of this kind were only rarely prepared to vote against the government on an urgency motion.

What this table cannot tell us is the number of occasions on which the refusal of a support party or parties to support a proposed urgency motion stymied the government's intention to seek urgency. The majority of politicians whom we interviewed were of the view that the need to negotiate support for urgency motions with minor parties placed a significant constraint on the extent of, and manner of, the use of urgency motions in the MMP Parliament.[38] This is borne out by the data that we set out in Chapter Four. First, the overall number of times that Parliament went into urgency decreased significantly once more parties were represented in Parliament and in governing arrangements (see Figures 4.1 and 4.2). The two single-party majority governments for which this study has full data (Labour 1987–1990 and National 1990–1993) moved a very large number of urgency motions (50 and 52 respectively) compared to later parliaments. The highest number of urgency motions moved after 1993 by any one parliament is 31.[39]

---

[37] The table does not include the individual-by-individual agreements made between the Shipley Government and independents or the Shipley Government and Peter Dunne (United New Zealand) during 1998–1999. Nor does it include the written "cooperation" agreement between Labour and the Greens in place during 2002–2005, when the Greens reserved their position on confidence and supply. During that period, the Greens supported the Government on urgency motions on five occasions and opposed the Government on 13.

[38] For example, Wilson, Dunne and Shirley interviews; Prebble email exchange. For academic commentary suggesting that MMP has decreased the House's reliance on urgency see, for example, David McGee QC, "Concerning Legislative Process" (2007) 11 Otago Law Review 417 at 420; Ryan Malone, *Rebalancing the Constitution: The Challenge of Government Law-Making under MMP* (Institute of Policy Studies, Wellington 2008) at 205–212.

[39] This was for the 1996–1999 Parliament.

Table 5.1: Support Parties' Voting Patterns on Urgency Motions after 1996

	Voted Yes	Voted No	Abstained	No vote cast	Total
New Zealand First					
National coalition 1996–1998 (until demise of coalition)	17	0	0	0	17
Labour confidence and supply 2005–2008	8	0	0	0	8
Alliance					
Labour coalition 1999–2002	21	0	0	0	21
Greens					
Labour confidence and supply 1999–2002[40]	17	3	1	0	21
Labour agreement not to "oppose" on confidence and supply 2005–2008[41]	4	2	2	0	8
Progressives					
Labour coalition 2002–2005	15	0	0	3	18
Labour coalition 2005–2008	8	0	0	0	8
United Future					
Labour confidence and supply 2002–2005	14	4	0	0	18
Labour confidence and supply 2005–2008	6	2	0	0	8
National confidence and supply 2008–2010	23	0	0	0	23
ACT Party					
National confidence and supply August 1998–1999 (unwritten)	12	1	0	0	13
National confidence and supply 2008–2010	22	0	0	1	23
Māori Party					
National confidence and supply 2008–2010	20	0	2	1	23

40 A written agreement was drafted but never signed: Green Party of Aotearoa New Zealand, "The History of the Green Party" (2011) <www.greens.org.nz>; Jonathan Boston and Stephen Church, "Government Formation after the 2002 General Election" in Jonathan Boston and others (eds), *New Zealand Votes: The General Election of 2002* (Victoria University Press, Wellington, 2003) 333 at 343.

41 "The Green Party agrees to provide stability to a Labour/Progressive coalition government by cooperating on agreed policy and budget initiatives and not opposing confidence or supply for the term of this Parliament": Green Party of Aotearoa New Zealand, "Labour-led Government Cooperation Agreement with Greens" (press release, 17 October 2005) <www.greens.org.nz>.

Secondly, the average number of bills accorded urgency also decreased significantly after the advent of multi-party parliaments (Figures 4.3 and 4.4). During the parliamentary terms of the two single-party majority governments on which we have full data, the average number of bills accorded urgency was 161.5. The average for the later multi-party parliaments on which we have full data was 82.2.

The same pattern is evident from Figure 4.5, showing the bills accorded urgency as a percentage of all legislation introduced. During the 1987–1990 and 1990–1993 parliaments, an average of 65.4 per cent of all bills introduced were accorded urgency at some stage. The average for all subsequent parliaments in our sample is 35.9 per cent (roughly speaking, a reduction from two thirds to one third).[42] The sitting hours of the House conducted under urgency have also decreased: for the two single-party parliaments (1987–1990 and 1990–1993), the average percentage of sitting hours conducted under urgency was 31 per cent; for the later multi-party parliaments the average was 18.7 per cent.[43]

Finally, the way in which urgency was used also changed following the advent of multi-party parliaments. It is fair to note that the use of urgency to put a bill through all its stages or to avoid select committee scrutiny was low (compared with other uses) throughout the period of study. Further, our data do not reflect a decrease in these usages of urgency when taken as a percentage of overall use (see Column L of Table 4.3). There is, though, a significant decrease in these uses of urgency in absolute terms (see Column K of Table 4.3, and Figures 4.7 and 4.8). For example, under the two single-party majority governments for which this study has full data (Labour 1987–1990 and National 1990–1993), bills were accorded urgency with no select committee stage on 16 and 12 occasions respectively (Figure 4.8). In contrast, the average number of bills to have been accorded urgency with no select committee scrutiny by subsequent parliaments on which we have full data is 7.4.

On the other hand, as we noted in Chapter Four, the pattern of decline in the use of urgency since the advent of multi-party parliaments is uneven. In particular, there are two apparent exceptions: the forty-fifth Parliament (1996–1999) and the forty-ninth Parliament (2008–2010). This raises an important question as to how to explain the uneven impact of multi-party governing arrangements on the use of urgency. This question is explored below by examining in turn each of the parliaments during the period of the study in which there was not a single-party majority government. A full account of the changing governance arrangements that existed over the relevant period was set out in Chapter One as Table 1.1.

---

42 This includes data on the forty-ninth Parliament up until 31 December 2010.
43 This includes data on the forty-ninth Parliament up until 31 December 2010.

A The Lead-Up to MMP (1993–1996)

The era of multi-party governance arrangements in New Zealand in fact began two years prior to the first MMP election, in September 1994. In the lead-up to MMP, the two larger parties began to fragment as MPs positioned themselves for the different electoral system. The National Party, which had started in 1993 with a bare majority of 50 out of 99 MPs, ended in 1996 with 41 MPs, relying on a range of support from independents and small parties. Technically speaking, National transitioned through a number of different governance arrangements during this parliament, including single-party majority government, coalition majority government, coalition minority government and single-party minority government.[44]

The precarious nature of National's support arrangements no doubt explains the low use of urgency during this period, whether calculated as an absolute figure, as a percentage of all bills introduced or as a percentage of sitting hours taken under urgency (Figures 4.1–4.6). Two of the three urgency motions passed in 1995 had the support of both National and Labour as the smaller parties and independents refused to vote for them.

B The First MMP Government (1996–1999)

The first governing arrangement in the forty-fifth Parliament (1996–1999) was a formal majority coalition between the National Party and New Zealand First. After the breakdown of that coalition in August 1998, the National Party relied on a combination of support from independent MP, Alamein Kopu, the ACT Party, the United Party and some of the New Zealand First MPs.[45] Individual agreements were drawn up for a number of independents which stipulated that the independent "agrees to support the legislative and policy programme of the Government" in return for becoming a member of the executive.[46]

In his 2008 study, Ryan Malone contrasted the use of urgency during a period of 109 sitting days under the National–New Zealand First coalition majority Government with similar periods under FPP majority government and MMP minority government. On the basis of this data, he concluded that MMP coalition majority governments are in a similar position to FPP majority

---

44 Jonathan Boston and others, "Experimenting with Coalition Government: Preparing to Manage Under Proportional Representation in New Zealand" (1997) 35 Journal of Commonwealth and Comparative Politics 108 at 110.

45 See "Prebble in Threat to Sink Govt" in *The Waikato Times* (17 August 1998). A confidence motion was moved and won on 8 September 1998.

46 "Agreement Between the New Zealand National Party and Independent Members of Parliament (August 1998)" in Jonathan Boston and others (eds), *Electoral and Constitutional Change in New Zealand: An MMP Source Book* (Dunmore, Palmerston North, 1999) at 363–365.

governments with respect to their ability to dictate when urgency is to be taken. In contrast, in his view, MMP minority governments find it significantly more difficult to use urgency.[47]

Our more extensive data on the use of urgency over the full term of the forty-fifth Parliament does not entirely support this conclusion. As Figure 4.1 shows, the number of urgency motions moved by the forty-fifth Parliament was in fact relatively low during 1997 – the period of most stable government – but was relatively high during the second and third years of the parliamentary session. The same is true of the number of bills accorded urgency (Figure 4.3). Indeed, the years 1998 and 1999 stand out as two of the highest in the entire period of the study. Significantly, the number of bills accorded urgency remained high even after the breakdown of the National–New Zealand First majority coalition.

Even more strikingly, this parliament stands out for the number of bills in respect of which urgency was used to avoid select committee scrutiny – a total of 20, divided equally between the period before and after the breakdown of the National–New Zealand First majority coalition (Figure 4.8). The year 1998 was the highest year in the study overall on this criterion (with 12 uses of urgency to deny select committee scrutiny). Overall, the forty-fifth Parliament ranked highest equal on this criterion, alongside the 2008–2010 Parliament (although our data on that parliament was, admittedly, incomplete).

What, then, can account for the high use of urgency during this period? It is not hard to account for the reasons why the National party might have *wished* to use urgency. This was a third term government with low prospects of re-election and therefore an incentive to realise outstanding policy goals while it was still in a position to do so. It is interesting to note that the last full year in office of the previous Labour Government – 1989 – was also characterised by a particularly high number of bills accorded urgency (see Figure 4.3). Further, the period of heightened use of urgency coincides with the stewardship of Jenny Shipley, who took over as Prime Minister and leader of the National Party in December 1997. As Roger Sowry, the Leader of the House during Shipley's period at the helm, suggested to us in his interview:[48]

> . . . [Shipley] wanted to stamp her mark on the Government. We had a majority with some of the people that had been chucked off the edges of New Zealand First, and so there was a view that you just go in and ram this stuff through . . . so you can actually go into the election and say look, we passed this, this and this.

---

47 Malone, above n 38, at 205–212.
48 Rodney Hide made a similar suggestion in his interview. For media coverage of the National–New Zealand First coalition's use of urgency, see Helen Bain, "It's a Hard Day's Night in Parliament" in *The Dominion* (2 July 1998).

But given the precarious nature of the National Party's support arrangements after August 1998, what was it that made it *possible* for the high use of urgency to continue? The answer is necessarily speculative. It is perhaps relevant that a number of National's support partners from this time were one-term MPs with little sophistication about or interest in parliamentary procedure and little prospect of re-election (and, therefore, no incentive to invite an early return to the polls).[49] More generally, in this early period of MMP government, there may have been a general lack of sophistication from minor parties as to their negotiations over support arrangements. So, for example, Ken Shirley, who was an ACT Party member at this time, observed to us:[50]

> [W]e actually offered supply and confidence, as ACT Party, cheaply, we had the numbers, and we could have actually got a lot more than we did. We were more worried about the disintegration of the Centre Right . . . and we gave our eight or nine votes at no price.

This is consistent with the memory of Gerry Brownlee, a National Party junior whip at this time, who recollected in his interview that the confidence and supply arrangements entered into by National during this era included an understanding and expectation that National's support partners would support it on procedural motions.[51] On the other hand, Roger Sowry's memory was somewhat different. He recalled support for urgency motions being negotiated on the floor of the House with support partners sometimes holding out on procedural motions as a bargaining tool. Even during this period, therefore, the multi-party parliamentary environment may have posed distinctive challenges for the Leader of the House in negotiating support for urgency motions.

C *The Labour-led Governments (1999–2008)*

Over the period 1999–2008, the Labour party led three relatively stable minority coalition governments. Despite that stability, Figures 4.1 to 4.6 show that the use of urgency declined substantially and remained relatively low throughout the period. This was so even during the final term, when both New Zealand First and the United Future Party had ministers outside Cabinet and so the governance arrangements closely resembled a majority

---

49   East interview.
50   Note, though, that the ACT party did vote against the Government on an urgency motion on one occasion during this period: see Table 5.1.
51   The wording of the confidence and supply agreements referred to support for "the legislative and policy programme" of the Government, including issues "nominated by the Prime Minister as ones of confidence", but was no more explicit: see "Agreement Between the New Zealand National Party and Independent Members of Parliament (August 1998)", above n 46, at 364.

coalition government.⁵² The type of urgency used also followed distinctive patterns during this period. Urgency for all stages of a bill, or otherwise to avoid select committee scrutiny, was extremely low throughout the period. As Figure 4.7 shows, urgency was used to avoid select committee scrutiny an average of 1.4 times per year during the 10 years or partial years of this government (as compared with 6.66 times per year or partial year during the previous parliamentary term). Interestingly, the use of urgency to take together the introduction and first reading stage was even lower – an average of less than one time per year (Table 4.3, Column E). In contrast, urgency for all remaining stages of a bill (once it had been reported back from select committee) was far more common (Table 4.3, Column C).

The low use of urgency by the post-MMP Labour-led governments, and the distinctive patterns of use, must in large part be accounted for by the attitude of its various support partners. Labour Party MPs from around this time whom we interviewed saw the need to negotiate support for an urgency motion with their several legislative partners as a significant constraint on the use of urgency.⁵³

Most notable in this respect was the impact of the Green Party. The Greens had a series of interesting arrangements with the Labour-led governments between 1999 and 2008: informal support on confidence and supply between 1999 and 2002 (seven MPs);⁵⁴ a "cooperation agreement" with confidence and supply on case-by-case terms between 2002 and 2005 (nine MPs); and, between 2005 and 2008, agreement on certain policy issues in return for abstaining on confidence and supply motions (six MPs). The Green Party was well known to oppose urgency on principle and the evidence from the interviews is that this party, more than any other, constrained the Labour-led Government from taking urgency – either by refusing support altogether for an urgency motion or by demanding a price for support that the major party regarded as too high.⁵⁵ As Margaret Wilson observed in her interview, under MMP, "nothing comes without a price" and "the Greens were appropriately . . . quite good at extracting the price".

52   Figure 4.6 (percentage of sitting hours taken under urgency) shows a bulge (compared with the other graphs) during the 2002–2005 parliamentary term. This discrepancy may suggest that a number of bills that have been "assigned" by us to the 1999–2002 Parliament (on the basis of the year of introduction) were, in fact, considered under urgency during the following term.
53   Wilson, Cullen and Hughes interviews.
54   In the period 1999–2002, the Green Party granted confidence and supply to the Labour Government, although the draft written agreement was never signed: Green Party of Aotearoa New Zealand, above n 40; Boston and Church, above n 40, at 343. See, also, (21 December 1999) 481 NZPD 25–26.
55   Turei, Wilson, Hughes, Cullen, Kidd, Dunne, Shirley, McGee, Harris, Creech and East interviews.

More than one interviewee suggested to us that the Greens would not support urgency unless it was only taken for one stage at a time.[56] Although this was certainly the predominant use of urgency throughout their period of influence, the data show that the Greens would, on occasion, support urgency for more than one stage. Indeed, they would even support urgency for all stages if they could be convinced there was a genuine reason to expedite the passage of the legislation. On the other hand, the data indicate a very strong resistance from the Greens to the use of urgency to take together the introduction and first reading of a bill. Throughout the three terms of Labour-led government, the Greens were never recorded as supporting an urgency motion that included this form of urgency.[57]

The Greens, therefore, appear to have had an important role in inhibiting the use of urgency by the three Labour-led post-MMP governments. That said, in evaluating their role, it is important to bear in mind that the Greens were only necessary for the governing majority in the 1999–2002 period, when the Labour Party was in a minority coalition with the Alliance Party. It is, therefore, interesting to note that the number of urgency motions and bills accorded urgency in fact decreased further during each of Labour's subsequent terms (Figures 4.2 and 4.4).

This could be explained by a number of factors. First, and speculatively, it is possible that, when a major party is in power for multiple terms, its use of urgency tends to decrease in each parliamentary term – reflecting the party's greater legislative momentum following a period in opposition.[58] However, a longer data collection period would be needed to test this hypothesis. It is not supported by the data on the use of urgency by the National-led Government in 1998/1999 but, as discussed above, this may be explained by the fact that the National Party had a new leader at the helm at that time.

Secondly, the Greens' impact on the use of urgency may well have permeated beyond the first term, when its bargaining power was at its peak, to influence the culture in which decisions on whether to take urgency were made, and the actions and expectations of Labour itself and its support parties more generally. Thirdly, it seems that United Future may also have played a significant role in tempering Labour's use of urgency in the second and third Labour-led

---

56 Cullen, Hunt and Dunne interviews.

57 The Greens abstained on one occasion: (17 May 2007) 639 NZPD 9379, according urgency to the introduction and first reading of the Taxation (Annual Rates, Business Taxation, KiwiSaver, and Remedial Matters) Bill. On a further occasion, the matter was decided on a voice vote so the Greens' stance was not recorded: (20 September 2001) 595 NZPD 11897, according urgency to the introduction and first reading of the Commerce (Clearance Validation) Amendment Bill 2001.

58 See Chapter Four, Part IV, Figure 4.10, suggesting that this may, at least, be true of the use of urgency in the first few months following each election.

governments. As Table 5.1 shows, United Future is the other party that has opposed urgency motions on occasion while in a support arrangement with a governing party. Peter Dunne told us that, when in a support arrangement with Labour, he was "critical and wary of . . . the excessive use of urgency". He claimed to have used what influence was possible to reduce the use of urgency for "non-urgent purposes". This was corroborated by David McGee QC, who recalled in his interview that United Future was demanding as to the conditions under which it would support urgency.

On the other hand, other interviewees saw Peter Dunne's attitude to the use of urgency as pragmatic rather than principled.[59] No clear pattern emerges from the data as to the nature of United Future's opposition to urgency and it seems likely that its support (or not) for urgency motions was often tied to its stance on the substance of the relevant legislation, rather than to a principled stance on urgency itself.

Generally, though, our interviews suggest that throughout its nine years in government, Labour's support partners behaved in a more sophisticated way than had earlier (and indeed subsequent) support parties, refusing blanket support for urgency motions and negotiating their "price" on a case-by-case basis.[60] It is not clear from the record what that price might have been on each occasion, but presumably it would have included anything from policy trade-offs, to placing conditions around the way in which urgency was used and the length of time the House sat under urgency, to negotiating extra speaking time for the support party in the House.[61]

If Labour wanted to use urgency in the face of opposition from its support partners, it needed to rely on (and pay a price for) support from other parties in the House. For example, during the 1999–2002 term, New Zealand First abstained on one, then voted for another, urgency motion in relation to the Electoral Integrity Amendment Bill. The stated "price" for the abstention was "a commitment to implement . . . the reinstatement of the superannuation payment to the elderly at the rate of 65%."[62] The price for New Zealand First's support for the second urgency motion appears to have been the Government's agreement to include in the motion a member's bill of Winston Peters.[63] This is a good indication of the bargaining that takes place in the MMP environment.

59 Cullen, Wilson and Creech interviews.
60 There was, though, no suggestion in our interviews that New Zealand First, while supporting Labour on confidence and supply (2005–2008) played a similar role with respect to the use of urgency: Wilson, Hughes, McGee, Creech and East interviews.
61 Jonathan Hunt suggested to us in his interview that this latter trade-off was common.
62 Winston Peters, "Winston Peter's Letter to Cullen on Urgency" (press release, 20 December 1999).
63 Local Government (Prohibition of Alcohol in Public Places) Bill (accorded urgency for all stages). This was the only bill accorded urgency for all stages in the year 2001.

D The National-led Government (2008–2010)

We do not have full data for the forty-ninth Parliament. Nevertheless, the available data are revealing. The number of urgency motions moved during the first full year of this parliament – 2009 – was the second highest since the advent of multi-party parliaments, topped only by the year 1998 (Figure 4.1). Figure 4.2 shows that, as at the end of 2010, this parliament had already moved more urgency motions during its term than were moved during any of the three full terms of Labour-led MMP governments. It was comfortably on track to top all multi-party governments on this criterion by the end of its term.

On the criterion of the number of bills accorded urgency (Figures 4.3 and 4.4), this parliament also scored relatively highly. As at the end of 2010, it was on track to rank second of all multi-party parliaments by the end of its term (behind the 1996–1999 Parliament). Indeed, this may understate the position given the point made in foregoing chapters: that our method of assigning urgency to bills on the basis of their year of introduction results in an abridged collection period for bills introduced to the House during the final two years of the study.

Figure 4.6 shows that this government also scores highly on the percentage of total sitting hours taken under urgency. Interestingly, though, the one criterion on which this government scores less highly is the percentage of bills accorded urgency (Figure 4.5). As noted in Chapter Four, two factors may contribute to explaining this. The first is the matter of the abridged collection period already mentioned. The second is that, as is clear from Table 4.1, this government was an extremely active legislator overall. As at the end of 2010, with almost a full year of its term to go, it had already introduced to the House 211 bills (compared with 273 in the highest full three-year term of the study – 1996–1999). As mentioned in Chapter Four, in his adjournment speech in October 2011 (just as this book was going to press), the Speaker recorded that this parliament sat for 150 more hours than the previous one overall.[64]

The data on the way urgency was used by the forty-ninth Parliament is also striking. Between its election in November 2008 and the end of that parliamentary year, the National-led Government put seven bills through all their stages under urgency (Table 4.3). This was the third highest number by one government in any one year in the study – behind 1998 (13) and 1999 (8). And, of course, this government achieved the feat in the nine calendar days that Parliament sat after the 2008 general election. Expressed as a percentage, this figure is even more staggering – it represents 78 per cent of the total number of items of legislative business considered under urgency by that government that year – more than three times more than the next highest percentage score (Table 4.3, Column L).

---

64 (6 October 2011) 676 NZPD 21855.

The use of urgency for all stages, or to avoid select committee scrutiny, remained high during 2009 and 2010, particularly when contrasted with other governments since the advent of multi-party parliaments. To illustrate, the top five post-1993 years in the study for these uses of urgency are reflected in the following table:

Table 5.2: Bills Passed Through All Stages and Bills Not Sent to Select Committee (Highest Post-1993 Years)

Year	Government	All stages	Not sent to select committee
1998	National/NZ First	10	9
1999	National with support	8	7
2008	National with support	7	7
2010	National with support	6	8
2009	National with support	4	5

The first four of these years were the highest in the study overall, even taking into account the single-party majority parliaments.

Figure 4.8 shows that, by the end of 2010, this parliament already ranked the highest equal of all parliaments during the period of the study in its use of urgency to avoid select committee scrutiny. Further, Table 4.4 shows that, on around half the occasions when this government used urgency to bypass select committee scrutiny, there was no legitimate reason for urgency in relation to the particular measure (let alone a reason sufficient to justify eliminating select committee scrutiny).

There may have been a number of interlocking reasons why this government was freer in the extent to which, and the way in which, it used urgency than the previous post-MMP Labour-led governments. Two such reasons were, undoubtedly, the size of the major party (National) in Parliament vis-à-vis its support parties, and its governing arrangements, which allowed it to choose between either the ACT Party or the Māori Party for support.[65] This combination of factors seems to have put it in a stronger bargaining position than was Labour at any time during the 1999–2008 period.[66]

---

65   United Future also had a confidence and supply agreement with the National Party but its vote was neither required (nor sufficient) to create a majority. Peter Dunne told us in his interview that his more cooperative stance on urgency with this government related, in large part, to the small size of his parliamentary party in that parliament.
66   See Harris and Cullen interviews.

The perception of a number of interviewees was that another important factor was the existence of clauses relating to procedural support in the confidence and supply agreements that National entered into with its support parties.[67] Darren Hughes suggested to us in his interview that one of the key differences between this government and the former Labour-led governments in this regard was Labour's inability to get a similar understanding reflected in its support agreements (though, he observed, "not for want of trying").

On closer analysis, however, the position turns out to be a little more complicated. It is true that National's support agreements with United Future, ACT and the Māori Party made specific reference to procedural support. However, the precise wording of the relevant clauses only went so far as to require those parties to support the Government on procedural motions "unless [the support party] has previously advised that such support is not forthcoming".[68] Labour's support agreement with United Future during the 2005–2008 term, in fact, contained an identically worded provision, yet United Future did not regard it as an obstacle to taking an independent stance on urgency motions on occasion.[69] In contrast, National, ACT and the Māori Party shared a common understanding that the effect of the 2008 support agreements was to require ACT and the Māori Party to support procedural motions as a matter of confidence.[70] The Māori Party abstained twice on urgency motions at the start of their support agreement with National in 2008 but interviewees from both parties told us that this stemmed from early confusion over the nature of the party's obligations.[71]

There was a perception from some interviewees (not involved in the 2008–2011 National-led Government) that National's support partners had given away their support on procedural issues too lightly and that this reflected a lack of sophistication about parliamentary process.[72] As Margaret Wilson suggested to us: "if you're a minority party worth your salt, you will extract a price for it."

Before leaving the use of urgency during the forty-ninth Parliament, it is only fair to note some trends that suggest an evolution towards a more restrained approach to urgency, at least in some respects. Table 4.3 (Columns E and F)

---

67 Katene, Hide, Brownlee, Turei and Hughes interviews; Prebble email exchange.
68 For example, New Zealand National Party "Relationship and Confidence and Supply Agreement between the National Party and the Māori Party" (2008) <www.national.org.nz>.
69 Labour's agreement with New Zealand First went even further, requiring New Zealand First to "vote with the government on procedural motions in the House . . . unless they relate to a bill on which the party has specifically registered their opposition": New Zealand Government, "Confidence and Supply Agreement with New Zealand First" (2005) <www.beehive.govt.nz>.
70 Katene, Hide and Brownlee interviews.
71 Katene and Brownlee interviews.
72 Wilson and Cullen interviews.

shows that, during 2009, the National-led Government placed comparatively high reliance on the use of urgency to take together the introduction and initial debate, using urgency in this way in relation to 11 bills. This amounted to more than the sum total of all such uses by the post-MMP Labour-led governments during their nine years in office.

It seems that the National party may have attracted criticism for this approach, including from its own support partners.[73] It is interesting to note, therefore, that this usage dropped away entirely. During 2010, the National-led Government accorded no bills urgency for the introduction and initial debate stages alone (although, as noted above, it continued to use urgency on occasion for all stages).

It is also worth noting that this government's use of urgency for remaining stages (Table 4.3, Columns G and H) and to take the Committee of the whole House stage and third reading together (Table 4.3, Columns I and J) both trended downwards during its term in office. Conversely, its use of urgency to take one stage alone trended upwards (to 45.5 per cent of all items of legislative business considered under urgency in 2010: Table 4.3, Columns C and D).

E *Conclusions on the Impact of Multi-Party Parliaments*

In conclusion, the introduction of proportional representation profoundly affected the practice of taking bills under urgency. MMP provided the opportunity for legislative actors representing the smaller parties to constrain and influence the behaviour of major parties in relation to the use of urgency. Some of the occasions on which they did so are reflected in the official record, showing minor parties voting against their major party allies on urgency motions. However, the formal record is incomplete as we can only document numerically the occasions when minor parties formally opposed urgency in the House. We cannot document numerically the occasions on which major parties did not ultimately seek urgency in the House because they could not guarantee majority support for the procedural motion. Our interviews with participants in the parliamentary system, reinforced by data suggesting a sharp decline in the use of urgency since 1994, suggest that the presence of minor parties in governing arrangements sometimes acts as a significant constraint on the use of urgency.

Evidently, not all minor parties have availed themselves of their potential bargaining power in relation to the use of urgency. However, it is important to remember that under majoritarian electoral rules, the option to influence the governing party's domination of the legislative process (and, hence, the use of urgency) seldom existed at all. Under majoritarian electoral rules, smaller

---

73 Katene interview, complaining of the extent to which this required MPs to debate legislation that they had not had the opportunity to look at in advance.

parties have to await the infrequent advent of a "hung" parliament (when neither main party had an absolute majority in the House) in order to influence the legislative process.

In the MMP Parliament, a number of factors may influence whether or not smaller parties avail themselves of their potential bargaining power in relation to the use of urgency. On the one hand, there may be strong reasons why they choose not to do so. For example:

(a) When parties agree to support the government on confidence they are committing themselves to supporting it, at minimum, on bills granting supply and on those tax bills that set the annual tax rates.[74] Additionally, there may be considerable pressure to support the government on major policy issues (such as Budget announcements) that may be regarded as matters going to "confidence".

(b) More generally, there may be considerable pressure from major parties to treat support for procedural motions as matters of "confidence".

(c) All parties, large or small, have an interest in keeping their MPs in office and so may not wish to risk early general elections by upsetting government stability.[75]

(d) Smaller parties may be able to use their support on urgency motions to bargain with their larger partners for substantive policy gains.

(e) Smaller parties may risk public backlash if they are seen to be holding the government to ransom on procedural issues.

On the other hand, urgency is particularly onerous on parties with a small parliamentary membership as the Standing Orders place restrictions on the extent to which they can participate in the vote if they do not have members present in the House or, in some circumstances, within the parliamentary precincts.[76] These strictures were relaxed somewhat by 2011 amendments to the Standing Orders, adopted by the House as this book was going to press.[77]

---

74 McGee, *Parliamentary Practice*, above n 3, at 98.
75 The histories of New Zealand First in 1998 and the Alliance in 2001/2002, however, tend to show the weakness of this incentive when minor parties feel that they are not achieving their policy goals.
76 Katene and Sowry interviews. Specifically, under the 2008 edition of the Standing Orders, any party with more than three members was required to have one member in the House in order to vote: Standing Orders (2008), SO 139(4). A party with two or three members was required to have one person within the parliamentary precincts in order for a proxy vote to be cast: SO 151(3). A party with one member (or an independent) was required either to be in the precincts or away on approved business (or approved leave) in order for a proxy vote to be cast: SO 151(2).
77 Parties with five or fewer members will now be excused from the requirement in the Standing Orders (2008), SO 139(4) to have one member in the House in order to vote and will, instead, be subject to the requirement in SO 151(3) to have one person within

Even so, minor parties still need to have members present in the House if they want to participate meaningfully in the debate.

Further, there may be a number of reasons why minor parties might wish to take an individual line on urgency issues. They may disapprove of the legislation itself.[78] They may have a principled objection to the use of urgency per se (or to particular ways of using urgency). They may see refusal to support urgency motions as a way to distinguish themselves in the eyes of the electorate. Or they may attempt to extract a higher price than the governing party is prepared to pay.[79] In some cases, attempting to negotiate agreement for urgency with reluctant allies might simply not be worth the effort involved. For example, Margaret Wilson told us that urgency was not necessarily a good idea for controversial legislation because it increased the pressure and tensions around getting support for the policy proposal itself.

One important consideration seems to be whether or not support for procedural motions, including urgency, was negotiated at the beginning of the relationship. However, our research indicates that unwritten understandings as to what was agreed may be as or more important than the formal document itself – as evidenced by the different attitudes taken by United Future, ACT and the Māori Party to identically worded documents.

There is also the institutional culture to be considered. It must not be forgotten that ACT, the Alliance, New Zealand First, the Progressive Party and United Future all came from the pre-MMP days and have been led by politicians who had their formative experiences under the adversarial two-party politics of that era. The Green Party and the Māori Party were parties that developed as parliamentary parties after MMP and their leaders were politicians who came from that environment.

If institutional socialisation and expectations are important, however, it makes the behaviour of the Māori Party in the forty-ninth Parliament somewhat puzzling. Its support for urgency motions might, as one of our interviewees suggested, reflect a lack of parliamentary experience and therefore lack of sophistication in its ongoing negotiations with the National Party.[80] Alternatively, though, it could perhaps be interpreted as a strategic stance that permits it to pursue its policy goals – not an easy task for a relatively new small party in a four-party legislative support group.

What is clear is that in order to account for the impact of multi-party parliaments on the use of urgency, we must look beyond the formal designation of the governance arrangements (majority coalition versus minority) to a

---

the parliamentary precincts for a proxy vote to be cast: "Standing Orders Review 2011", above n 18, at 29 and 72.
78 Dunne interview.
79 Wilson interview.
80 Wilson interview.

complex list of factors, including the particular makeup of the governing majority, the ideological perspectives of support parties and the people who comprise them, and the overarching support arrangements that have been entered into.

IV Urgency and Evolving Parliamentary Culture

Not only has MMP impacted on the extent to which urgency is taken and the stages for which it is taken, it has also impacted on evolving cultural norms concerning how parliamentary actors behave when urgency is taken, and concerning the extent to which urgency is allowed to disrupt MPs' other activities – both inside and outside the House.

Most obviously, MMP has impacted on the degree of openness or transparency surrounding a government's decision to take urgency. In the 1970s and 1980s, the government's intention to take urgency was generally swathed in secrecy and sprung on the opposition without notice. Indeed, Roger Sowry told us in his interview that, when he was a National Government whip between 1993 and 1996, even Cabinet was left in the dark as to when urgency would be taken. Ken Shirley (a Labour MP during the 1980s) had this to say to us of the culture surrounding urgency during that period:

> Often the caucus wouldn't be advised. Sometimes they would be. Sometimes you got a hint from the whip – "don't book an early plane on Thursday home" sort of thing. And "nod, nod, wink, wink", and you knew why ... And smart people very quickly learnt to go to the Travel Office and found whether Government MPs were doing their normal bookings or not, and if not, you knew that there was urgency coming.

That degree of secrecy would simply not be possible in the context of multi-party governance as the major party must, at minimum, discuss its intentions with its support partners. The creation of the Business Committee, which is a forum in which information about parliamentary procedure (including urgency) can be exchanged and discussed, may have also contributed to a change in culture around the use of urgency.

Whether for these reasons or others, increased transparency of the government's plans, and increased negotiation inside and outside the Business Committee, became features of urgency in the post-MMP House. The fact that urgency is to be taken is generally now notified to all parties in advance, even if the precise content of the urgency motion is not always known.[81]

---

81 This point was made by many of our interviewees, for example, Hughes, Dunne, Sowry, Brownlee and Smith. It is also evident from the Business Committee Agendas and Minutes, August 1997–August 2008 (being the dates to which we had access). For reflections in urgency motions themselves of this emerging practice of giving notice, see: (9 August 2000) 586 NZPD 4043; (28 May 2009) 654 NZPD 3959.

Amendments to the Standing Orders that are shortly to come into effect as a result of the 2011 review of the Standing Orders seek to enhance the role of the Business Committee in relation to negotiations over the allocation of parliamentary time.[82] These amendments (which are discussed at length in Chapters Six and Seven) will, if anything, strengthen the emerging culture of transparency and negotiation surrounding the taking of urgency in the post-MMP House.

Another potential area of emerging cultural change relates to the length of time for which the House sits continuously under urgency and the extent to which it sits under urgency on Fridays and Saturdays. Our data and interviews suggest that, since the advent of multi-party parliaments, urgency has been taken for shorter periods and weekend sittings are much less common. For example, five-day sittings (from Tuesday through to Saturday) have become a rarity. During the eight years or partial years of single-party majority government that fell within our study (1987–1994), the House held six five-day sittings (with the majority – four – falling during the 1987–1990 Labour term). During the 17 years or partial years of multi-party government (1994–2010), the House held two five-day sittings – one each during the 1996–1999 term and during the partial 2008–2010 term.

A breakdown of the 22 occasions on which the House sat on a Saturday during our study reveals a similar pattern. During the eight years or partial years of single-party majority government, the House sat on a Saturday on 13 occasions (the bulk of which – eight – fell during the 1987–1990 term). During the 17 years or partial years of multi-party government (1994–2010), the House sat on a Saturday on nine occasions. Five of these fell during the 1996–1999 term and three during the partial 2008–2010 term. During nine years of post-MMP Labour-led governments, the House sat on a Saturday on one occasion.

A number of our interviewees commented on the practice of the post-MMP Labour-led governments of lifting urgency at 6pm on a Friday night.[83] The Clerk of the House, Mary Harris, put this down to the tempering influence of the Greens, noting their preference for family-friendly sitting hours. Peter Dunne, on the other hand, was inclined to take some of the credit for this development on his own shoulders:

> In the previous Labour-led government where our numbers were greater [than during the 2008–2011 term] and therefore I had correspondingly more influence, we agreed to what we regarded as the judicious use of urgency, and essentially that was that we never went past six o'clock on a Friday evening. So in other words, people could get home Friday night, they weren't going to be disrupted for their weekend.

---

82   See "Standing Orders Review 2011", above n 18.
83   For example, Harris, Dunne, McGee, and Sowry interviews. Roger Sowry described this as urgency "for softies".

Dunne contrasted this with the situation in the late 1980s when, in the lead-up to Christmas in particular, the House would regularly go into urgency on Tuesday and not rise until Saturday evening. Dunne noted: "It was just soul-destroying. You couldn't do that today, because you wouldn't get the support of support partners".

Parliament sat on a Saturday three times during the partial 2008–2010 term of National-led Government. On the other hand, although we were not able to test this assertion numerically, a number of interviewees referred to an emerging pattern during that term whereby the House would sit under urgency from Tuesday through to Thursday morning but would adjourn at the usual time of 6pm on Thursday. This allowed members to return to their constituencies as per usual on Thursday night.[84]

This emerging practice of periodic bouts of "short, sharp burst urgency"[85] in order to make progress with the order paper has been formalised, following the 2011 review of the Standing Orders, through the addition to the Standing Orders of a separate "extended sitting" power. That development is discussed at length in Chapters Six and Seven.

A third (and final) area of emerging cultural change concerns the relationship between urgency and question time. One of the most important roles of the House is to hold governments accountable, and one of the most public and effective ways of doing this is through members' lively daily questioning of ministers. When the House is in urgency, the afternoon question time does not take place unless by leave of the House (that is, if no member present dissents). In practice, this means that there will be question time if the government agrees to it (as opposition parties are highly unlikely to oppose a request for leave for question time to be preserved). As we noted in Chapter Three, urgency can be used as a deliberate tactic to avoid question time, and this appears to have been a common tactic during the pre-MMP era.[86]

Some interviewees suggested to us that there is now a tendency to preserve question time when urgency is taken.[87] We used our data to test this suggestion. Figure 5.1 divides the urgency motions into those where, at the time the urgency motion was moved, leave was sought to retain question time during the urgency period, and those where it was not. In assessing the significance of this graph, it is important to bear in mind several factors. First, as urgency motions are moved after question time, if the House sits for only one day under urgency, then no loss of question time will arise. Secondly, if the House sits for only two days, it may end its sitting under urgency in time for question time on the second day (although it certainly does not have to do so).

84 For example, Brownlee, Hughes and Dunne interviews.
85 This expression was used by Peter Dunne in his interview.
86 Chapter Three, Part II.C.2.
87 Brownlee and Hughes interviews.

Figure 5.1: Question Time Provided for at the Time of Urgency Motion 1987–2010

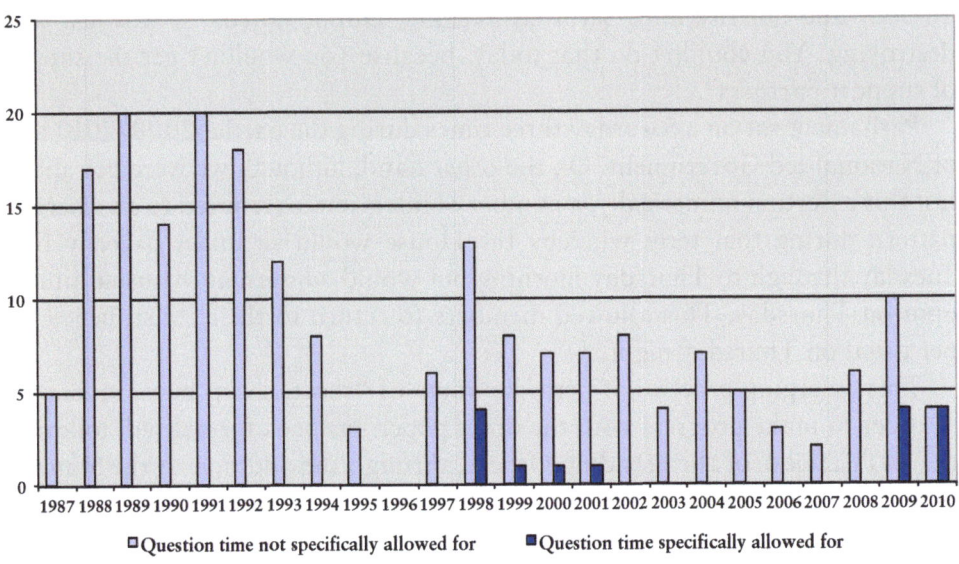

For these reasons, a failure to seek leave to retain question time when moving an urgency motion is most likely to be significant when the House sits under urgency for three or more days. Accordingly, Figure 5.2 shows the number of occasions each year on which the House sat for three or more days under urgency but made no provision for question time when the urgency motion was moved. Even here, though, it is important to bear in mind the possibility that opposition parties may have succeeded in negotiating question time with the government during the course of the urgency period.[88] This would usually be on the basis of a guarantee of "reasonable progress" by the opposition or some other quid pro quo.[89]

Three points can perhaps be made in respect of the data in Figures 5.1 and 5.2. The first is that, whereas there is not a single example in the pre-MMP period of a minister, when moving an urgency motion, seeking leave for question time to be retained, there were a number of such examples in the post-MMP period. Nevertheless, retention of question time remained the exception rather than the rule.

---

88 Even if leave to have question time is not sought at the time that urgency is moved, it may nevertheless be sought at some later point during the urgency period.
89 See, for example, the urgency motion moved on 21 August 1990 by Jonathan Hunt: "I have said, and I have already approached the shadow Leader of the House about the matter, that if he gives a guarantee of reasonable progress the Government will provide time for questions and the general debate tomorrow": (21 August 1990) 510 NZPD 3630.

Figure 5.2: Leave Not Sought for Question Time when Urgency Motion Moved (Urgency for Three Days or More)

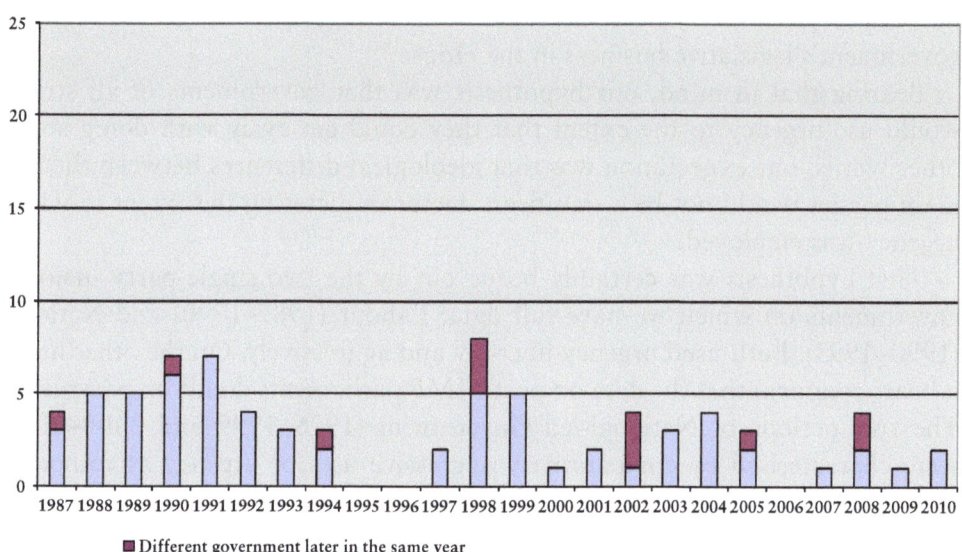

■ Different government later in the same year

Secondly, it is interesting to note that the only three years in which leave was sought in this manner on more than one occasion were 1998, 2009 and 2010 – three of the post-MMP years that stand out for the relatively high number of urgency motions overall. In other words, there was a correlation between periods of particularly high reliance on urgency in the MMP Parliament and governments seeking leave for question time to be retained. This may suggest that, at least post-MMP, governments that seek to rely heavily on urgency feel the need to appease oppositions, or perhaps their support partners, by making concessions in relation to the process that is followed.

Thirdly, it is significant to note that, in the final year of the study, 2010, the Government sought leave to preserve question time under urgency as often as it did not. It is too early to tell whether this is an aberration or whether it may signal a more permanent culture shift.

V *Ideology, Personality and Internalised Constraints*

Finally, to what extent do ideology, personality or an internalised sense of illegitimacy play a part in constraining the use of urgency?[90]

Our interviews revealed that participants in the political system do not, on the whole, regard urgency as an illegitimate or democratically suspect activity.

---

90 See A V Dicey, *Introduction to the Study of the Law of the Constitution* (8th ed, Liberty Fund, Indianapolis, 1982 reprint) at 32, stressing the importance of internalised morality as a limit on legislative power.

The dominant perspective expressed to us by politicians whom we interviewed was that urgency is a legitimate (if grossly misunderstood) tool for mitigating the serious problem of insufficient scheduled sitting hours to get through the government's legislative business in the House.[91]

Bearing that in mind, our hypothesis was that governments of all stripes would use urgency to the extent that they could get away with doing so. In other words, our expectation was that ideological differences between the two main parties would not be a significant factor in dictating the extent to which urgency was employed.

That hypothesis was certainly borne out by the two single-party majority governments on which we have full data: Labour (1987–1990) and National (1990–1993). Both used urgency liberally and aggressively. On the other hand, it bears comment that the data on post-MMP parliaments divide on party lines. The two periods of National-led Government (1996–1999 and 2008–2010) were characterised by comparatively aggressive uses of urgency as compared with the three terms of Labour-led Government (1999–2008).

We have suggested above that a significant reason for that disparity is the varying attitudes of particular support parties to the use of urgency. In the case of the Greens at least, that attitude was clearly grounded in an ideological objection to urgency – a view that urgency is democratically suspect. But is there any evidence of an ideological divide over the use of urgency emerging between the two main parties?

As we have already noted, the influence of the Greens cannot provide the complete explanation for the low reliance on urgency throughout the three terms of Labour-led post-MMP Government as the Greens were only a part of the governing majority during the first of those terms. We suggested above that one possible explanation for the fact that urgency continued to decline throughout Labour's three terms in office is that the Greens' stance may have begun to influence cultural expectations and assumptions around urgency within Labour itself. For example, our interview with one key Labour politician from that era, Margaret Wilson, disclosed a rather more ambivalent attitude to the use of urgency than was evident from our interviews with National politicians. She said that urgency was not generally seen, in the government that she was part of, as a "normal or quasi-normal mechanism" or as "the proper way to act" but that it was "a mechanism that was available if all else failed."

However, our dataset is simply not sufficient to enable us to conclude that a durable ideological divide between the two main parties over the use of urgency has emerged. It bears reminding that the 1993–1996 Parliament (comprised

---

91 For example, Sowry, Hunt, Cullen and Smith interviews. For further discussion, see Chapter Three, Part II.B.

of a succession of National and National-led governance arrangements) was the lowest user of urgency in the entire study. Further, as we were reminded by interviewees, the impact of individual personality is also "part of the mix and fabric of it all".[92] For example, more than one interviewee suggested to us that the personality of the new Prime Minister, Jenny Shipley, and her desire to stamp her mark quickly on government, was a factor explaining the high use of urgency in 1998/1999.[93]

Before leaving the topic of internalised constraints, it is worth recording here recognition in the report of the Standing Orders Committee on the 2011 review of the Standing Orders that, although it is a "legitimate" parliamentary tactic, the use of urgency "to make progress" can nevertheless have an "adverse effect on the quality of debate and legislative outcomes" and that it does not enhance "the reputation of Parliament as an effective institution".[94] This may signal an emerging sea change with respect to the attitudes of parliamentarians to urgency – a possibility that is discussed in Chapter Seven.[95]

We also note that, whereas our interviewees did not generally regard urgency *per se* as an illegitimate or democratically suspect activity, many expressed reservations about particular kinds of urgency – most particularly, using urgency to avoid select committee scrutiny.[96] It may well be the case that an internalised constitutional morality has contributed to the relatively low use of this type of urgency throughout most of the period of the study.

VI *Conclusion*

MMP has had a profound impact on the use of urgency. However, any assessment of the efficacy of MMP as a check on the use of urgency must account for the fact that its impact has not been consistent. In essence, MMP provided informal constraints through bringing new parties into the House. Thus, its effects have been contingent on the attitudes and strategic votes held by those small parties. MMP did not, and could not, provide formal constraints on the use of urgency. For that reason, the constraint imposed on urgency by the multi-party environment is sometimes weak or even absent.

The other factors examined in this chapter can and, on occasion, do constrain excessive uses of urgency. But here, too, the effect of these constraints is somewhat erratic and unpredictable. Importantly, the ultimate constraint on political behaviour – the ballot box – does not always operate effectively in

---

92   East interview.
93   Sowry and Hide interviews.
94   "Standing Orders Review 2011", above n 18, at 14. The Committee offered the same critique of opposition procedural tactics to delay or extend the House's consideration of matters.
95   See Chapter Seven, Part II.
96   For example, Sowry and Smith interviews.

the case of urgency. The media may sometimes take an interest in the fact, or perceived fact, that Parliament is "ramming through" legislation but the occasions on which it does so are irregular and are not always well-informed. The public has a limited interest in, and an even more limited understanding of, parliamentary procedure – a matter that is not assisted by the confusing regulatory framework in which urgency operates.

All of this raises the question whether the current constraints on urgency are inadequate and, if so, what can be done about that. These questions are addressed in the final two chapters.

6

Urgency, Time and Democratic Legitimacy

It is clear from the preceding chapters that the use of urgency motions to extend the House's sitting hours and to fast-track particular items of legislative business is a prevalent feature of New Zealand parliamentary practice, employed by governments on both sides of the House over the course of many decades. Our interviews indicate that many politicians do not see urgency as a problem. They see urgency as a valid procedural device for extending the House's sitting hours and pushing forward with the government's legislative programme. Their concern is that there are insufficient scheduled sitting hours for the House to get through government business and they view urgency as a legitimate device for ameliorating this problem. Are they right?

In this chapter, we consider whether we should be worried about the use of urgency. We begin by tackling the perceived problem of insufficient legislative capacity, which is a significant driver for the use of urgency. The wide-ranging and multi-faceted debate that underlies this perceived problem demands far more comprehensive examination than this focused study on the use of urgency can provide and so we do not seek to provide definitive answers. Nevertheless, it is important to understand the general contours of the debate over parliamentary time so as to be able to locate the problem of urgency within it. In this chapter, we sketch in more detail the dimensions of that debate and we also consider a package of relevant recommendations made by the Standing Orders Committee in its 2011 review of the Standing Orders (released shortly before this book went to press).[1] This package of reforms was adopted by the House and will be in force when Parliament meets following the November 2011 election.[2]

We then turn to consider the democratic and constitutional implications of the use of urgency. We suggest that any use of urgency comes at a cost to the principles of good law-making that were set out in Chapter One. That is so even in the case of relatively "benign" uses of urgency (for one stage of legislation at a time) because the use of urgency contributes to a public perception – whether fair or not – that Parliament is not following its own rules and that legislation is being "rammed through" the House. For these reasons, reliance on urgency as a mechanism to address the perceived problem of insufficient legislative capacity is, in our view, undesirable.

---

1   Standing Orders Committee, "Review of Standing Orders" [2011] AJHR I.18B ["Standing Orders Review 2011"].
2   (5 October 2011) 676 NZPD 21758–21765.

We certainly do not suggest that the use of urgency is always inappropriate. There will always be situations in which the benefits outweigh the disadvantages. There is, however, a need for effective disincentives to be put in place to ensure that it is not used too frequently or in the absence of appropriate justification.

I Time and the Legislative Process

A major subject of concern for many of those we interviewed, and a driving force behind the use of urgency, is the perception of many participants in the political system that the House has insufficient regular sitting hours to deal with the government's legislative business. It is clear from the analysis conducted in Chapter Three (of the reasons why New Zealand governments take urgency) that many politicians perceive the House's sitting schedule as posing severe restrictions on their ability, when in government, to advance their legislative programmes. It is also apparent that they see urgency as a legitimate means to ameliorate that problem.

This gives rise to a number of questions. Is there, in fact, a problem in New Zealand with insufficient legislative capacity to process government business? If so, what are the various options for dealing with that problem and which are to be preferred? More specifically, ought the House to sit for longer hours? Alternatively, would it be better to make further efficiencies in the way the House divides up the hours that it already has? What role, if any, should urgency play in responding to the perceived problem of insufficient legislative capacity?

Only the last of these questions falls directly within the ambit of this study. Nevertheless, as we noted above, it is important to understand the general contours of the debate over parliamentary time so as to be able properly to locate the problem of urgency within it.

A Does the House Have Insufficient Capacity to Process Government Business?

The first question, then, is whether one should accept the premise that the House has insufficient regular sitting hours to process government business? At the outset, it is important to lay bare an unstated assumption that underlies the concerns expressed to us by parliamentarians about the insufficiency of the House's sitting hours. This is that more capacity to legislate is better than less. Yet is that necessarily so?

It was (then Professor) Geoffrey Palmer who famously described the pre-MMP New Zealand Parliament as "the fastest law-maker in the west".[3] There

---

3   Geoffrey Palmer, *Unbridled Power: An Interpretation of New Zealand's Constitution and Government* (Oxford University Press, Wellington, 1979) at 77.

is a conflict in academic opinion as to whether the introduction of MMP slowed the pace of legislating.[4] Regardless of who is right, some academics and commentators continue to criticise the New Zealand Parliament for legislating too much – for seeking to use legislation as a tool for solving social problems that are not amenable to legislative solutions or as a technique to signal to the public that the government of the day is responding firmly to perceived problems.[5] If that is so, the question might be whether governments should be given incentives to prioritise their legislative business more effectively rather than extending the hours available to them.

Further, even assuming that, in principle, more legislative capacity would be a good thing, any decision to extend the House's sitting hours involves difficult trade-offs between the perceived advantages of more legislative time, the non-legislative functions of the House (such as the scrutiny of executive action) and competing demands on the time of MPs – a particular problem for smaller parties with limited party membership. Sitting in plenary sessions forms only part of the role of an MP, albeit its most visible and newsworthy one. Members have additional parliamentary responsibilities, such as select committee membership. Additionally, MPs in all democracies spend time in party meetings, both in and outside Parliament, and in their constituencies where, especially in New Zealand, they are expected to be available for consultation and to attend community functions. On top of this, in New Zealand's system of responsible government, senior government MPs are also government ministers, charged with the substantial responsibilities that this entails.

There is also the question of fairness to MPs and their families. For example, when the Procedures Committee of the Scottish Parliament undertook a review of parliamentary time in 2006, it took as a governing principle of its review, the principle of "family friendly" hours.[6] Parliamentarians with young children, especially women, can find the demands of late night sittings and travel from their homes to the location of the parliament very difficult.[7] All these competing pressures – for time to complete the House's non-legislative business, for time to meet in committee, for time to meet with parties and

---

4   Contrast David McGee QC, "Concerning Legislative Process" (2007) 11 Otago Law Review 417 at 418, 429 and 431 ["Concerning Legislative Process"] with Ryan Malone, *Rebalancing the Constitution: The Challenge of Government Law-Making Under MMP* (Institute of Policy Studies, Wellington, 2008) at 223–225.

5   For example, Geoffrey Palmer and Matthew Palmer, *Bridled Power: New Zealand's Constitution and Government* (4th ed, Oxford University Press, Melbourne, 2004) at 183–188. See, also, McGee, "Concerning Legislative Process", above n 4, at 429–430.

6   Procedures Committee, "Review of Parliamentary Time" (2006) at [4] <www.scottish.parliament.uk>.

7   Joanna McKay, "'Having it All?' Women MPs and Motherhood in Germany and the UK" (2011) 64 Parliamentary Affairs 714.

constituents, for time to undertake ministerial duties and for sitting hours that are at least a little compatible with family life – constrain the hours spent in plenary sessions.

On the other hand, a number of commentators and senior officials have expressed concern over the years about the House's lack of legislative capacity.[8] A factor that particularly drives this concern is that, when governments feel the squeeze from insufficient legislative capacity in the House, they tend to de-prioritise important technical bills in order to make room for more politically saleable legislation.[9] For example, in its submission to the 2008 review of the Standing Orders, the Legislation Advisory Committee worried about: "the current scarcity of available legislative time in the House of Representatives and the impacts that this scarcity is having on governments' ability and inclination to progress technical, administrative or uncontroversial Bills through the legislative process."[10] Similarly, in its submission to the 2011 review, the Parliamentary Counsel Office noted as relevant to the scarcity of available legislative time:[11]

> Parliament continues to be unable to process Bills introduced by the Government in a sufficiently efficient, effective, and timely way, as shown clearly by the Order Paper which, at any time, generally includes 40–55 Bills, many of which have been waiting several months to progress, and a large number of which make largely technical uncontroversial amendments to remedy existing problems, or to otherwise maintain and enhance our legislative infrastructure.

In terms of the raw data on sitting hours, a case can be made to support the proposition that the sitting hours of the New Zealand Parliament are on the low side. In the decade from mid-1999 to mid-2009, the House sat for between 59 (in an election year) and 96 sitting days – an average of 79.3 sitting days per year. Bearing in mind that the use of urgency can artificially extend a "sitting day" over several days, the figure for calendar days during the same period is slightly different: between 62 and 100. The House's annual sitting hours ranged from 357 to 601 – an average of 531 sitting hours per year.[12]

---

8   For example, David McGee QC, "Review of Standing Orders: Submission of the Clerk of the House of Representatives" (2003) ["2003 Submission"].
9   See Sascha Mueller, "The Busy House: Alternatives to the Urgency Motion" (2011) 9 NZJPIL (forthcoming).
10 Quoted in Standing Orders Committee, "Review of Standing Orders" [2008] AJHR I.18B at 23 ["Standing Orders Review 2008"]. See, also, "Standing Orders Review 2011", above n 1, at 14.
11 Parliamentary Counsel Office, "Review of Standing Orders: Submission of Parliamentary Counsel Office" (2011) at 4.
12 These figures are taken from the annual reports of the Office of the Clerk of the House of Representatives 2000–2009 (found in the Appendices to the Journal of the House of Representatives at A.8 and reported according to the financial years ending 30 June).

It is interesting to consider how this compares with other legislatures in similar systems of parliamentary government, although any such comparison must be treated with great care. The United Kingdom House of Commons sits for more days per year than does the New Zealand House. Again taking the 1999–2009 decade as a comparison, the House of Commons sat for between 65 sitting days (in an election year) and 208 sitting days.[13] The average number of sitting days during that decade was 149.3.

The data represented in Table 6.1 are extracted from a comparative survey of parliamentary sitting days and hours in 2008 conducted by the Australian Parliamentary Library[14] and supplemented by data on the Scottish Parliament for the year 9 May 2008 to 8 May 2009.[15] Even allowing for the fact that 2008 was an election year for New Zealand (which substantially deflates the total number of sitting days and hours), the sitting hours for the New Zealand Parliament were at the lower end of the range.

These figures must, however, be interpreted in the light of the different contexts, norms and legal traditions of the respective jurisdictions. For example, one important contextual factor is the proportion of the overall workload performed in the particular jurisdiction by parliamentary committees rather than the plenary body. In some houses (such as the German Bundestag, the Scottish Parliament and, indeed, the New Zealand Parliament) parliamentary committees have wide and powerful terms of remit and sit for substantial amounts of time. In others, the role of parliamentary committees is more constrained. For example, the Australian House of Representatives only refers some bills to committee for scrutiny (although more are examined by Senate committees). In New Zealand, members of Parliament can spend many hours each year attending select committees. By way of example, in the year ended 30 June 2008, the House of Representatives sat for 89 days (and 86 sitting days), a total of 511.39 hours. During that same year, the Office of the Clerk serviced 389 meetings of select committees (including sub-committees) which, among their other functions, considered 92 bills.[16]

---

13 House of Commons Information Office, "Sittings of the House" (Factsheet P4, Revised June 2010) Appendix A at 13 <www.parliament.uk>. Unfortunately this document does not report sitting hours.
14 Nicholas Horne, "Background Note: Parliamentary Sitting Days and Hours 2008" (Parliament of Australia Parliamentary Library, 2009) <www.aph.gov.au>. Because the sitting hours provide more accurate data than sitting days, we include only those countries which provided the former figure.
15 Scottish Parliament, "Scottish Parliament Statistics 2008–2009" (2009) at 18 <www.scottish.parliament.uk>. This figure was for the year 9 May 2008 to 8 May 2009. The figure for the preceding year, 2007–2008, was 358 hours: Scottish Parliament, "Scottish Parliament Statistics 2007–2008" (2008) at 16 <www.scottish.parliament.uk>.
16 Office of the Clerk of the House of Representatives, "Annual Report of the Office of the Clerk of the House of Representatives" [2009] AJHR A.8 at 35–36.

Table 6.1: Parliamentary Sitting Hours 2008

Country	Chamber	Sitting Hours (rounded up)
Australia	House of Representatives	639
	Senate	482
New Zealand	House of Representatives	486
Republic of Ireland	Dáil Éireann (House of Representatives)	795
	Seanad Éireann (Senate)	551
Scotland	Parliament	364
South Africa	National Assembly	141
	National Council of Provinces	91
United Kingdom	House of Commons	1188
	House of Lords	1010
Average	**Lower houses and unicameral houses only**	**602**

Another contextual factor affecting the workload of particular legislatures is the extent of their law-making authority. New Zealand's unicameral legislature operates within a unitary system of government and has plenary authority to make laws. In contrast, in a federal system such as Australia, legislative authority is shared horizontally between the federal and state legislatures (as well, of course, as vertically between the two houses of Parliament). A similar point can be made of the devolved Scottish Parliament. Although it has a similar number of MPs to the New Zealand Parliament (129) and is elected under a similar mixed member proportional system, it has only limited legislative competence conferred on it by Act of the United Kingdom Parliament.[17] In the five years from 2005 to 2010, it never enacted more than 29 bills in any one year and, more typically, around half that.[18]

A third factor relates to varying norms and traditions regarding the division between primary legislation (made by the legislature) and delegated legislation (made by the executive under statutory authority). For example, the United Kingdom House of Commons passes fewer bills each year than does the New Zealand House of Representatives, despite the disparities in the sizes of the

---

17 Scotland Act 1998 (UK).
18 This data is extracted from the annual reports on "Scottish Parliament Statistics" found on the Scottish Parliament website: <www.scottish.parliament.uk>.

two countries, but relies far more heavily on delegated legislation. To illustrate, in the year ending 30 June 2010, the Office of the Clerk of the New Zealand House of Representatives prepared 95 bills for royal assent.[19] The United Kingdom government website lists only 41 public general acts and five local acts enacted by the United Kingdom Parliament that year.[20] On the other hand, the New Zealand government website lists 223 new pieces of delegated legislation published in the Statutory Regulations Series in 2010.[21] In contrast, the United Kingdom government website lists 2,801 statutory instruments for that year.[22] Based on these figures, the ratio of primary to secondary legislation was approximately 1:2 in New Zealand and 1:70 in the United Kingdom. Even allowing for the differences in what may have been counted as delegated legislation for the purposes of this calculation, this suggests a significant difference in operating norms between the two jurisdictions.

The above factors suggest that one should be slow to draw definitive conclusions from a bare comparison of sitting hours across different jurisdictions. The most that can be said is that, on its face, this dataset tends to reinforce the widespread perception of our interviewees, as well as of some commentators and senior officials, that the sitting hours of the New Zealand Parliament are somewhat low.

In 2006, the Procedures Committee of the Scottish Parliament conducted a major and wide-ranging review of the question of parliamentary time.[23] Its remit empowered it to look, for example, at options for different sitting patterns in different parts of the parliamentary session, at different ways of using time each week, at how much time is allocated to different types of business, at how topics for debate are chosen and at how speaking time is allocated amongst those wishing to contribute.

In a submission to the 2011 review of the Standing Orders, the authors of this study recommended that the Standing Orders Committee consider whether New Zealand would benefit from a similar wide-ranging review.[24] The Committee did not take up that recommendation for a free-standing inquiry. On the other hand, the question of parliamentary time formed a major preoccupation of the Committee's report and recommendations on the 2011 review itself. While acknowledging that the limited time available to the House to conduct its business may, in fact, provide "a safeguard against unfettered legislative

---

19   Office of the Clerk of the House of Representatives, "Annual Report of the Office of the Clerk of the House of Representatives" [2010] AJHR A.8 at 25.
20   <www.legislation.gov.uk>.
21   <www.legislation.govt.nz>. This does not include deemed regulations.
22   <www.legislation.gov.uk>.
23   Procedures Committee, above n 6.
24   Claudia Geiringer, Polly Higbee and Elizabeth McLeay, "The Urgency Project: Revised Submission to Standing Orders Committee" (2011).

activity", the Committee concluded that "the balance is not right at present" and put forward a wide-ranging package of reforms designed to ameliorate the problem of limited legislative capacity.[25] This package of reforms is explored below. It was adopted by the House and will be in force when Parliament meets following the November 2011 election.[26]

B Possible Solutions

Assuming that we accept the proposition that the House has insufficient capacity to process the government's legislative business, what are the various options for dealing with that problem and which of these options is to be preferred? Again, in the context of this study, our intention is not to provide answers to these questions but to outline the contours of the debate.

As we explained in Chapter Two, the options available to the House to increase the House's legislative capacity fall into two broad categories: on the one hand, extending the House's sitting hours; on the other, streamlining the House's business within the hours that are available. These are discussed in turn.

1 Extending the House's sitting hours

If the answer lies in the House sitting for more hours, there are a number of potential methods for achieving that result. For example, a regularised extension to the House's sitting hours might involve:

- sitting on a Friday;
- sitting for longer hours on its current sitting days (for example, into the evening on a Thursday); or
- sitting for more weeks during the year.

The point has already been made but it is worth restating that any of these options involve difficult trade-offs between MPs' activities in the House and the competing demands on their time, whether inside or outside Parliament. For example, from 1996–1998, the House's regular sitting hours included Thursday mornings (but not Tuesday evenings). The Standing Orders Committee found that this "caused significant problems on Thursday mornings when members may need to be both in the House and at a committee meeting." Consequently, the current sitting pattern was established by sessional order in 1998.[27]

Concurrent sittings of the House and select committees are a particular problem for small parties with limited parliamentary membership – a point

---

25 "Standing Orders Review 2011", above n 1, at 14.
26 (5 October 2011) 676 NZPD 21758–21765.
27 Standing Orders Committee, "Interim Report: Sitting Hours of the House and the Time Limits on Speeches and Debates in the House" [1998] AJHR I.18A at 3.

made to the Standing Orders Committee by the Green Party in the course of the 2011 review of the Standing Orders.[28]

The same tension arises in relation to another reform proposal made to us by more than one of our interviewees: that the House should introduce a system analogous to the Australian "Main Committee".[29] As noted in Chapter Two, the "Main Committee" system enables the Committee of the whole House to sit concurrently with the House itself in order to debate uncontroversial legislation. This frees up additional legislative capacity – by relieving some of the time pressure in the House itself – but creates the same dilemma for small parties as concurrent select committee sittings.

Thursday evening or Friday sittings, on the other hand, may accentuate a different set of tensions by disrupting the ability of MPs to return to their electorates to fulfil constituency duties and, indeed, family responsibilities.

Another option for increasing the time MPs spend in the House is to leave the House's regular sitting hours intact but to expand the tools available to the House to extend its sitting hours on an ad hoc basis. Up to this point, urgency motions have been the principal means available to the House for doing this. Interestingly, though, an alternative means of providing for ad hoc extensions to the House's sitting hours formed one of the recommendations of the 2011 review of the Standing Orders, now adopted by the House. Having given formal notice at the Business Committee the previous week (and subsequently in the House), the government will be able to move to extend one sitting per week – either the Tuesday or the Wednesday sitting – across to the next day. The sitting will still be suspended at the usual time on the Tuesday or Wednesday evening (10pm) but will resume at 9am the next morning and continue until 1pm. The Business Committee will be able to authorise further extensions – to more than one sitting a week or into Thursday evening or Friday morning. Select committees will not meet during extended sittings unless authorised to do so by the House or the Business Committee.[30]

For reasons discussed in the next chapter, we believe that this extended sittings provision is a valuable addition to the parliamentary armoury that will have the beneficial effect of reducing the use of urgency motions in the House of Representatives. The reform is, though, a cautious one that, at least in the absence

---

28 "Standing Orders Review 2011", above n 1, at 15–16.
29 For example, McGee and Harris interviews. This was proposed to the Standing Orders Committee in 2003 by the then Clerk of the House, David McGee QC: McGee, "2003 Submission", above n 8. McGee noted and documented the trend towards reduced hours between 1984 and 2002 (at 10–13) and made a number of suggestions, including the separate sitting (at 13–18).
30 For example, "Standing Orders Review 2011", above n 1, at 15–16. The new "extended sittings" provision drew heavily on (but is not identical to) a proposed sessional order put forward by Gerry Brownlee during the 2008–2011 Parliament but never adopted: Gerry Brownlee, "Extension of Wednesday Sitting", lodged 9 December 2009.

of the unanimity or near unanimity required for a determination of the Business Committee, will free up only a modest amount of additional legislative capacity. For that reason, it may not satisfy those who favour more radical reform.

On the other hand, the Standing Orders Committee's recommendation for extended sittings is part of a complex package of reforms, aimed to "promote constructive engagement between parties as to the arrangement of the House's business."[31] A number of those reforms are directed at the second category of options for increasing the House's legislative capacity: streamlining the House's business within the hours that are available. We turn now to trace the contours of the debate over that second category.

2 *Streamlining the House's business*

In Chapter Two, we detailed a number of ways in which, over the course of the last century, the House altered its procedures in order to free up additional legislative capacity: the move from clause-by-clause to part-by-part debates in the Committee of the whole House; the move from personal voting to party voting; the limits placed on the number and length of speeches and debates; and the various reductions made to the time spent on non-legislative business of the House. We also detailed a number of ad hoc techniques that the House has available to it for expediting the legislative process still further in particular cases: the powers of the Business Committee to streamline the passage of particular legislation; the use of closure motions; the House's power to reduce the period for which legislation is to be referred to select committee; and the House's power to vary its procedures by leave (that is, if no one dissents).[32]

Following the 2011 review of the Standing Orders, the House adopted a number of changes to the Standing Orders, designed to streamline the House's legislative business still further. It is impossible in this context to explain fully the entire package of reforms but some of the main ones are as follows:

- The Business Committee will now be able to group two or more bills together as "cognate bills", to be debated together (at the option of the member in charge) at their first, second and third readings.[33] This will offer an alternative to the introduction of "omnibus bills". Omnibus bills are bills that relate to more than one subject area. They speed up the legislative process because each omnibus bill is only subject to one sequence of legislative debates, even though it will ultimately be divided off into more than one enactment. Grouping bills as "cognate bills" will have a similar effect but will maintain more transparency (as each bill will retain its separate form throughout the legislative process).

---

31   "Standing Orders Review 2011", above n 1, at 15.
32   Chapter Two, Part VI.
33   "Standing Orders Review 2011", above n 1, at 35–36.

- The Business Committee will now be able to divide an omnibus bill off into its component legislation.[34] Ordinarily, this happens in the Committee of the whole House. This, though, has meant that omnibus bills must always be subject to a Committee stage. Following this amendment, the power to dispense with the Committee stage (which, as we noted in Chapter Two, can be exercised by leave of the House or by the Business Committee) will now also be able to be exercised in respect of omnibus bills.
- The Business Committee will be able to fix the time for select committees to report back on bills (and, therefore, to stipulate a reduction in the standard six-month report back period). The Business Committee will also be able to determine that a select committee may meet while the House is sitting, or on a Friday in a week where there has been a sitting of the House.[35]
- The Business Committee will be empowered (whether before or after a bill's introduction) to decide that a bill is suitable for some other method of consideration in the Committee of the whole House than part-by-part consideration. For example, it might decide that the legislation would suit consideration on an issues basis or through the grouping of parts.[36]
- The chairperson at the Committee of the whole House stage will have the power to group amendments to be taken as one question or, where there are numerous amendments to substantially the same effect, to select amendments on which questions are to be put.[37] Although unstated, this presumably constitutes a regulatory response to some of the more extreme delaying tactics employed by oppositions in recent times, for example, the 30,000 computer-generated amendments put up by the opposition at the Committee stage of the Auckland supercity legislation in May 2009.[38]
- The Business Committee will be empowered to determine that the new "extended sittings" provision can be utilised in particular cases to consider more than one stage of a bill at a time (thereby removing any relevant stand-down periods).[39]

Finally, the Standing Orders Committee also recommended a special streamlined procedure for the enactment of "revision bills", to be adopted

---

34 "Standing Orders Review 2011", above n 1, at 47–48.
35 "Standing Orders Review 2011", above n 1, at 41–42.
36 "Standing Orders Review 2011", above n 1, at 45–46.
37 "Standing Orders Review 2011", above n 1, at 45 and 47.
38 See Chapter Five, Part II.A.
39 "Standing Orders Review 2011", above n 1, at 15 and 17. See further discussion in Chapter Seven, Part II.

through a sessional order should the Legislation Bill 2010 be enacted. The Legislation Bill is before Parliament at the time of writing. If enacted, it will establish a three-yearly "revision programme" for the preparation of "revision bills", being bills that re-enact existing laws in an up-to-date and accessible form without changing their substance.[40]

In accordance with the procedure recommended by the Standing Orders Committee for the enactment of revision bills, there will be no debate on their first or third readings, and they will only be considered in the Committee of the whole House if the minister in charge puts up an amendment or if a member gives 24 hours' notice of an amendment. Select committee consideration will be limited. Further, the Business Committee will be required to ensure that, once a revision bill is reported back from select committee, it receives a prompt second reading and does not languish on the order paper. Revision bills will also be recognised as a permissible type of omnibus bill, enabling them to be combined together for the purposes of legislative deliberation.[41]

In summary, over the course of a century or more, the House has adopted a range of measures to streamline particular stages of legislative consideration and, indeed, to dispense with particular stages altogether in certain circumstances. The 2011 review of the Standing Orders resulted in a package of amendments designed to streamline the legislative process still further.

The question whether these various efficiency measures go too far, or not far enough, is at the heart of any serious debate over the problem of parliamentary time. Options have been mooted from time to time for more dramatic efficiencies. For example, some parliamentarians and senior officials have sought relaxations in the restrictions that the Standing Orders place on the use of omnibus bills. As noted above, omnibus bills enable amendments relating to more than one subject matter to be combined together into one bill for the purposes of legislative consideration but then divided off into component parts prior to enactment. In 1995, in order to curtail abuse of this practice, the Standing Orders placed significant constraints on the type of legislation that can be introduced as an omnibus bill and the circumstances in which such a bill can be introduced.[42]

Relaxation of these restrictions has been mooted as a means of further expediting the House's legislative business. For example, the then Attorney-

---

40 "Revision bills" will be able to "make minor amendments to clarify Parliament's intent, or reconcile inconsistencies between provisions" and to update monetary amounts, having regard to movements in the Consumers Price Index, but will not otherwise be entitled to "change the effect of the law": Legislation Bill 2010 (162-2), cl 31.
41 "Standing Orders Review 2011", above n 1, at 37–39.
42 See Standing Orders Committee, "Review of Standing Orders" [1995] AJHR I.18A at 49–51. See, now, Standing Orders (2008), SOs 256–259.

General and Minister for Treaty of Waitangi Negotiations Chris Finlayson suggested to the 2011 review of the Standing Orders that Treaty of Waitangi settlement legislation should be recognised as a permissible class of omnibus bill.[43] The Parliamentary Counsel Office supported this proposal and also proposed a more general clarification and simplification of the rules around omnibus bills.[44] In submissions to earlier Standing Orders reviews, both the Chief Parliamentary Counsel and the Legislation Advisory Committee had recommended an even more wide-ranging relaxation of the restrictions on omnibus bills: to allow the government to introduce omnibus bills that affect a particular sector.[45]

By way of a further example of proposals for greater efficiency, Canterbury academic Sascha Mueller proposes radical reforms to introduce greater flexibility into the House's legislative procedures. He proposes that the House (acting by broad agreement but not necessarily unanimity) should be able to ease the passage of uncontroversial legislation by dispensing with a general debate at any or all of the stages.[46]

By outlining the contours of this debate, we should not be taken to be suggesting that these, or any other proposals to streamline the legislative process further, are necessarily desirable. Efficiency comes with a trade-off in terms of the quality of legislative deliberation. As Ken Shirley put it to us in his interview:

> Democracy isn't meant to be efficient. And to try and make democracy efficient is actually almost a self-defeating concept. Part of its strength is its inefficiency.

A number of commentators (including Jeremy Waldron, in his 2008 critique of the New Zealand legislative process) have suggested that the Standing Orders have already gone too far in streamlining the legislative process,[47] and some of our interviewees expressed similar concerns about aspects of current procedure.[48]

Specifically in relation to the proposal to allow for single-sector omnibus

---

43 Chris Finlayson, "Submission: Procedures for Historical Treaty of Waitangi Settlement Bills" (2011).
44 Parliamentary Counsel Office, above n 11.
45 Chief Parliamentary Counsel, "Submission to the Standing Orders Committee" (2003), referred to in McGee, "Concerning Legislative Process", above n 4, at 429 footnote 23; Legislation Advisory Committee, "Submission to the Standing Orders Committee", referred to in "Standing Orders Review 2008", above n 10, at 24.
46 Mueller, above n 9.
47 Jeremy Waldron, "Parliamentary Recklessness: Why We Need to Legislate More Carefully" (Maxim Institute Annual John Graham Lecture, Auckland, 2008).
48 For example, Kidd interview (expressing concerns about the limits in the Standing Orders on the length of debates); Harris and Hughes interviews (expressing concerns about legislation being sent to select committee for severely contracted periods); McGee interview (expressing the view that the Standing Orders do not provide enough opportunity for filibustering).

bills, both the current and previous clerks of the House have expressed concerns about that proposal and the Standing Orders Committee has resisted it to date.[49] In its 2011 review, the Committee stressed that: "The rule [restricting omnibus bills] continues to meet its purpose, that is, preventing unacceptable truncation of the legislative process and reduced scrutiny of important stand-alone Acts."[50]

It is perhaps also important to note that not all of the changes adopted as a result of the 2011 review of the Standing Orders will promote greater legislative efficiency. Some, to the contrary, aim to balance out efficiency by incentivising robust legislative scrutiny at important points in the legislative process. Perhaps the most significant in this regard is an amendment to make instructions to select committees debatable. To explain, after a bill has been read a first time, it automatically stands referred to a select committee unless the House has otherwise accorded urgency to it.[51] The member in charge of the bill moves a motion nominating which committee is to consider the bill. Significantly, the member is entitled to include in that motion any special instructions in respect of the committee's consideration of the bill. The motion is not (or was not) debatable.[52]

One common use of this instruction power is to abbreviate the default six-month timeframe for committees to report back on legislation. During the course of our research, some interviewees suggested to us that a practice may be emerging of the government routinely imposing significantly abbreviated report back timeframes on select committees.[53] This was borne out by the 2011 review of the Standing Orders, which noted that instructions that shorten significantly the time available for select committees to consider bills had become common.[54]

Another widespread use of the instruction power is to permit select committees to meet during sittings of the House. This is generally to the advantage of the government, which can thereby advance its legislative proposals in the House without obstructing the progress of its legislation through select committees. On the other hand, as already noted above, it is of concern to smaller parties, which have difficulties in participating in House and committee business simultaneously.[55]

In order to curtail both these practices, the Standing Orders Committee recommended (and the House agreed) that instructions to select committees

---

49   See "Standing Orders Review 2008", above n 10, at 24; McGee, above n 4, at 429–430.
50   "Standing Orders Review 2011", above n 1, at 35.
51   Standing Orders (2008), SO 280.
52   Standing Orders (2008), SO 281.
53   Harris and Hughes interviews.
54   "Standing Orders Review 2011", above n 1, at 40–41.
55   "Standing Orders Review 2011", above n 1, at 15–16. Metiria Turei expressed particular concern about this practice in her interview with us.

should be debatable, except where the sole effect of the instruction is to reduce the time for reporting on a bill to between four and six months. This measure aims to provide a procedural disincentive to the frequent moving of instructions because the advantage to be gained by the instruction may be cancelled out by the disadvantage of lost time in the House while the motion is being debated. In explaining the rationale for this recommendation, the Committee emphasised the give-and-take of its proposals with respect to parliamentary time:[56]

> Reducing the number of bills that are subject to shorter deadlines for select committee consideration will be an effective way of enhancing legislative scrutiny and thus improving the quality of legislation in New Zealand. This recommendation is made in exchange for other proposals that will be of significant benefit to the Government's ability to progress its legislative programme, such as the provision for extended sittings.

For similar reasons, the Standing Orders Committee tempered the addition of a new power to facilitate extended sittings by providing that, during those sittings, select committees will not be able to sit unless authorised to do so by the House or Business Committee. The Committee anticipated that: "this should prevent the taking of extended hours as a matter of routine, and would provide a further incentive for the Government to work constructively in the Business Committee to arrange the House consideration of matters."[57]

This last comment reflects another significant theme underlying the Standing Orders Committee's package of recommendations: an emphasis on cross-party negotiation and consensus as a means to progress House business. By far the majority of the new measures for streamlining the House's legislative business rely on powers being accorded to the Business Committee. It will be remembered that the Business Committee is a cross-party committee that includes representatives from all, or almost all, the parliamentary parties and that makes its decisions on the basis of unanimity or "near unanimity". The thrust of the reforms, therefore, is towards stimulating cross-party cooperation rather than advancing the unilateral progression of the government's legislative agenda. The reforms focus on the way that House business is managed and timetabled and seek to encourage constructive engagement between the government and the opposition through the vehicle of the Business Committee.[58]

This focus on negotiation and consensus also responds to the concern of commentators and officials that pressures on House time result in important non-controversial technical legislation being de-prioritised at the expense of

---

56 "Standing Orders Review 2011", above n 1, at 41.
57 "Standing Orders Review 2011", above n 1, at 16.
58 "Standing Orders Review 2011", above n 1, at 8–9.

higher profile legislative proposals. Cross-party consensus to ease the passage of legislation is more likely to be forthcoming in relation to non-controversial legislation thereby, arguably, freeing up more House time to focus on matters of political importance or high public interest. Thus, the Standing Orders Committee described the purpose of the package of reforms as being to "make more effective use of sitting hours, while providing opportunities for members to debate matters that are important to them."[59] The Committee also encouraged members to be "imaginative" in their negotiations:[60]

> For example, the determination by the Business Committee of extra sitting hours for Government business, over and above the hours the Government could obtain through a motion for an extended sitting, might also include some time for a lengthened second reading debate on a bill that is of interest to Opposition parties, or for consideration of a significant select committee report.

The focus on negotiation and consensus may turn out to be the great strength of this new package of procedural reforms. On the other hand, it may also turn out to be its Achilles' heel. Opposition parties use non-cooperation over measures that are uncontroversial in themselves as a strategy to exert time pressure on more controversial proposals. Only time will tell whether the incentives for collaborative engagement created by this new package of reforms are sufficient to overcome, in an appreciable number of cases, the perceived advantages of a withdrawal of cooperation. In the end, much is likely to depend, as it always has done, on the management and negotiation skills of key parliamentary figures such as the Leader of the House and the whips. As Margaret Wilson said to us in her interview when asked what other processes or strategies (apart from urgency) a government can use to speed up the passage of legislation:

> ... making sure you've got your policy right to begin with ... Work out what [is] achievable and what [isn't]; know what you [are] going to have to trade because you always do ... know exactly what you want and then have your numbers tied in from the outset ... running an efficient administrative process. It's like your infrastructure: understanding the rules, the Standing Orders, what *is* the legislative process – when things are due and when they are not. It sounds boring and mundane but if you do that, you by and large will progress it.

If anything, the 2011 amendments to the Standing Orders will place an even greater premium on good management of the House as a means to advance the government's legislative programme. It remains to be seen whether future leaders of the House, and other key parliamentary figures, will have the wherewithal to take advantage of it.

---

59 "Standing Orders Review 2011", above n 1, at 8.
60 "Standing Orders Review 2011", above n 1, at 9.

C Urgency as a Tool for Making Progress

It will be apparent from the foregoing discussion that the problem of parliamentary time is a complex and multi-faceted one that is not amenable to easy solutions. As we suggested in Chapter One, it is also part of a wider narrative – the debate over parliamentary time is part of the terrain on which, throughout the history of the New Zealand Parliament, the political executive has fought to take and maintain control of the House.[61]

To repeat, we do not presume, in the context of this focused study on the use of urgency, to provide definitive answers to the range of questions raised by this debate. We do, though, offer a definitive answer to the final question posed at the beginning of this section: what role, if any, should urgency play in responding to the perceived problem of insufficient legislative capacity?

We have seen in preceding chapters that many New Zealand politicians see urgency as a legitimate procedural device for ameliorating the perceived problem of insufficient scheduled sitting hours in the House. Governments use urgency, in the absence of any specific need for haste relating to the particular legislation, in order to make faster progress overall with their legislative agendas. In our view, this reliance on urgency to "make progress" is undesirable. We turn in the next section to explore the reasons for that.

II Urgency and Democratic Legitimacy

In Chapter One, we identified 10 principles that are fundamental to a democratic legislative process and, against which, the democratic and constitutional legitimacy of urgency ought to be assessed. To recapitulate, these are:

1. Legislatures should allow time and opportunity for informed and open policy deliberation;
2. The legislative process should allow sufficient time and opportunity for the adequate scrutiny of bills;
3. Citizens should be able to participate in the legislative process;
4. The House ought to operate in a transparent manner;
5. The House ought to strive to produce high quality legislation;
6. Legislation should not jeopardise fundamental constitutional rights and principles;
7. Parliament should follow stable procedural rules;
8. Parliament should foster, not erode, respect for itself as an institution;

---

61 See, for example, John E Martin, "From Talking Shop to Party Government: Procedural Change in the New Zealand Parliament, 1854-1894" (2011) 26 Australasian Parliamentary Review 64; John E Martin, "A Shifting Balance: Parliament, the Executive and the Evolution of Politics in New Zealand" (2006) 21 Australasian Parliamentary Review 113.

9. The government has a right to govern, so long as it commands a majority in the House;
10. Parliament should be able to enact legislation quickly in (actual) emergency situations.

Urgency advances principles 9 and 10 by assisting governments to implement their legislative programmes in the face of finite regular sitting hours and by providing a mechanism for governments to respond expeditiously to unexpected events and contingencies.

Nevertheless, the use of urgency can run foul of a number of the other principles. That is most obviously so when urgency is used to bypass select committee scrutiny. Especially since 1985, the select committee system has played a pivotal role in the legislative process – one that has come to compensate, in many respects, for the absence of an upper house.[62] Sir Geoffrey Palmer made this point in successive editions of *(Un)bridled Power*. For example, in the 1987 edition, discussing the possibility of having a second house, he wrote that the tasks that it could undertake:[63]

> ... could just as effectively be carried out by an enlarged House of Representatives using the new select committee system. The effect of delay in the passage of legislation is incontestably beneficial, but a second chamber is not needed to do that.

He added that: "Now that all Bills go to select committees, they function in a manner somewhat akin to a second chamber."

In our view, principles 1–8 are all appreciably impacted upon when the select committee process is bypassed. That is because of the select committee system's important role in enhancing the House's deliberative and scrutiny functions, in

---

62 On the importance of the New Zealand select committee system, see Marcus Ganley, "Select Committees and their Role in Keeping Parliament Relevant: Do New Zealand Select Committees Make a Difference?" (2001) 16 Australasian Parliamentary Review 140; Liz Gordon, "Radical Democracy on Committees in an MMP Parliament" (2001) 16 Australasian Parliamentary Review 151; Elizabeth McLeay, "Scrutiny and Capacity: An Evaluation of the Parliamentary Committees in the New Zealand Parliament" (2006) 21 Australasian Parliamentary Review 158; Malone, above n 4, at 131–68; Austin Mitchell, "The New Zealand Way of Committee Power" (1993) 46 Parliamentary Affairs 91.

63 Geoffrey Palmer, *Unbridled Power: An Interpretation of New Zealand's Constitution and Government* (2nd ed, Oxford University Press, Auckland, 1987) at 236. Sir Geoffrey was referring to the 1985 select committee reforms, and the House was enlarged in 1996 with the implementation of MMP. See, also, Palmer and Palmer, above n 5, at 371. A similar view was expressed recently by the Committee System Review Committee of the Legislative Assembly of Queensland (the only unicameral State legislature in Australia) when recommending that Queensland move to a select committee system similar to the New Zealand one: Legislative Assembly of Queensland Committee System Review Committee, "Review of the Queensland Parliamentary Committee System" (Brisbane, December 2010) at vii.

providing opportunities for public participation and in thereby enhancing the quality of legislative output. It is for this reason that a number of commentators have greeted instances of the use of urgency to remove select committee scrutiny with dismay. For example, Lord Cooke of Thorndon wrote the following of the use of urgency, in 1998, to put the Social Welfare Amendment Act (No 5) 1998 and the Copyright (Removal of Prohibition on Parallel Importing) Act 1998 through all their stages under urgency:[64]

> To call what was enacted democratic in any true sense would seem inappropriate. The tyranny of an elected majority and party discipline are seen in practical operation. It is further to be noted that the two Acts of 1998 have been passed in this way notwithstanding that the House of Representatives is now elected by a system of proportional representation.

In our view, the use of urgency to bypass select committee consideration ought to be rare and justified by a genuine need for haste in relation to the particular measure. Despite the relatively low incidence of this use of urgency, the data discussed in previous chapters, particularly relating to the forty-fifth and forty-ninth parliaments (1996–1999 and 2008–2011), suggest that, even under MMP, there were periods when this form of urgency was used uncomfortably often. Further, when those uses of urgency are examined closely, the reasons given to justify urgency do not always withstand scrutiny. Too often when this occurred, the legislative process was, to put it simply, too hurried.

Although not directly relevant to the use of urgency, it is perhaps worth stressing that similar democratic concerns can arise from the frequent use of instructions to select committees to abbreviate significantly the timeframe for committees to report to the House. The Standing Orders Committee made that observation in the 2011 review of the Standing Orders, noting that:[65]

> The truncation of the select committee process can have serious implications for legislative quality and confidence in the legislative process. As we heard in submissions, it also affects the public perception of Parliament, especially when submitters are required to prepare submissions in a short time and hearings are compressed.

Returning, though, to the democratic and constitutional implications of the use of urgency, more commonly, urgency is accorded to one or more stages of legislative consideration of a bill but the select committee stage is preserved. In such cases, the extent to which the principles set out above are impacted will depend on a number of factors such as the subject matter and complexity of the legislation, the stage or stages of the legislative process at which urgency is

---

64 Robin Cooke, "Unicameralism in New Zealand: Some Lessons" (1999) 7 Canta LR 233 at 241.
65 "Standing Orders Review 2011", above n 1, at 40.

accorded, and the degree of scrutiny that the legislation has already received or is due to receive. Context and circumstance are important. However, we would make the following general points.

First, if urgency is taken for more than one stage at a time, the stand-down periods between the legislative stages are eliminated. Democratic deliberation needs time. Stand-down periods play an important role in allowing legislation to proceed through the House at a measured pace, and in providing opportunities both for members of the House and for interested members of the public to digest and respond to developments. For example, the stand-down period following presentation of a select committee report on a bill provides a valuable opportunity for members to digest the report and arm themselves for the second reading debate. We accept that the reasons that might justify elimination of a stand-down period might not necessarily be expected to be as compelling as the reasons that might justify elimination of the select committee stage. Nevertheless, there ought to be a good reason of some kind.

Secondly, when urgency is accorded to the introduction and first reading stage, there may not be any opportunity for opposition and support parties (as well as members of the public) to see and digest the legislation prior to the first reading debate. That is no doubt why this use of urgency has attracted particular criticism from minor parties.[66] One aspect of the Standing Orders that, it seems, may have been driving this use of urgency was addressed in the 2011 review. The Standing Orders provide that urgency can only be accorded to business that is before the House. This means that urgency cannot be accorded to legislation that is in the middle of a stand-down period. A submission to the 2011 review from blogger and Parliament-watcher, Graeme Edgeler, suggested that this was incentivising the use of urgency to take together the introduction and first reading. If the government introduced legislation without according urgency to the first reading at the same time, there would be no opportunity to debate the legislation until the stand-down period had elapsed. This all-or-nothing regime was, the submission suggested, driving the use of urgency to take the introduction and first reading stages together.[67]

The Standing Orders Committee accepted this submission and, as a result, the Standing Orders will be amended to enable the government to include a bill in an urgency motion even if the stand-down period between introduction and first reading has not elapsed.[68] The rationale for this amendment is that some gap between introduction and first reading is better than none, even if the full three-sitting-day stand-down period is not able to be achieved. This is

---

66   See discussion in Chapter Five, Part III.C and D.
67   Graeme Edgeler, "Review of the Standing Orders: Submission of Graeme Edgeler" (2011) at 4.
68   "Standing Orders Review 2011", above n 1, at 18.

no doubt true but should not be allowed to disguise the underlying point made above – that there ought to be a good reason to justify any interference with the prescribed stand-down periods.

Turning to the most benign use of urgency – for one stage at a time – with this use, the impact on principles 1–6 may be minimal. Nevertheless, even here, it is important to bear in mind that, by prioritising the government's legislative business in the House, urgency diverts members of the House from their other responsibilities. These potentially include select committee work, consideration of members' bills, and non-legislative functions such as scrutiny of government activities through the mechanism of question time.

Additionally, even where urgency is only taken for one stage at a time, there is a significant impact on principles 7 and 8. That is because the use of urgency contributes to a public perception – whether fair or not – that Parliament is not following its own rules, and that legislation is being "rammed through" the House.[69] In our view, a significant problem in this regard is the hybrid role played by urgency as both a device for fast-tracking particular bills in cases of genuine need and a widely deployed mechanism for extending the House's sitting hours to "make progress". As we suggested in Chapter Five, the very terminology of "urgency" sends out a false signal to the electorate and therefore confuses it as to the constitutional ramifications of what is occurring when urgency is taken. This means that "urgency" can, on occasion, attract negative public attention even when it is being utilised in relatively benign circumstances – without interfering with any stand-down periods.[70]

For all these reasons, we do not accept the view expressed to us by a number of former and current members of the House that urgency is an intrinsically benign mechanism for extending the House's sitting hours.[71] In our view, any use of urgency in its present form comes at a cost – albeit a varying one – to the integrity of New Zealand's constitutional and democratic system. That does not mean that its use is always inappropriate. There may be a range of circumstances in which the benefits to be gained by taking urgency outweigh the detriments. It does, however, mean that there should be effective disincentives to it being used too much, or in the absence of appropriate justification. It would be unwise to attempt an exhaustive account of what might amount to appropriate justification. As noted above, context and circumstance are

---

69 See, for example, Tracy Watkins, "Urgency Erodes Right of Scrutiny" in *The Dominion Post* (16 April 2011), suggesting that urgency can leave "a sour taste in the mouth" even when there has been plenty of public scrutiny of the relevant legislation.
70 For example, Colin Espiner, "Parliamentary Sitting" in *The Press* (14 December 2007), describing the Government trying to "ram through the first readings of 14 new bills under urgency".
71 See, especially, Chapter Three, Part II.B.

important. However, some general remarks are appropriate.

In Chapter Three, we divided the reasons governments use urgency into four categories: specific reasons to expedite the passage of particular legislation; freeing up the order paper; tactical reasons for using urgency; and Budget day urgency. Under the first head, we identified a broad range of situations in which governments in New Zealand and elsewhere have felt the need to expedite the passage of particular legislation. These include:

- where the announcement of an intended change to fiscal policy might create the potential for speculative behaviour from market participants and/or uncertainty for the business community and market participants if the legislation is not enacted immediately;
- where there has been an unexpected event such as a civil emergency, an economic crisis, the failure of a financial institution or an unexpected court decision;
- where an anomaly, oversight or uncertainty in existing legislation has been uncovered; and
- where external (or pre-set) factors such as a forthcoming event create an effective deadline for proposed legislative change.

We accept that any of these reasons may, on occasion, provide sufficient justification for using urgency. Whether or not the justification is sufficient in the particular case, though, will depend on a range of factors. These include the type of urgency that is to be taken, the strength of the underlying reason for expediting the legislation, the complexity and constitutional significance of the legislative proposal and the extent of any prior (or future) opportunities for public input and democratic deliberation. Even in relation to this category of urgency, the reasons that governments put forward to justify urgency sometimes bear careful scrutiny. For example, changes in consumer behaviour and expectations may well cast into question the continued validity of the "speculative behaviour" justification in some cases.[72]

We turn now to the second head – urgency to free up the order paper. Putting to one side the changes to be introduced as a result of the 2011 review of the Standing Orders, throughout the period of our study urgency was the principal mechanism by which governments achieved an ad hoc extension of the House's sitting hours, from time to time, in order to progress their legislative business generally. At least in the absence of fundamental reform to the House's sitting hours, we accept that some kind of ad hoc mechanism of this kind is an indispensible feature of modern parliamentary life. In our view, though, urgency is a badly designed mechanism for performing this function. The fact

---

72   See Chapter Three, Part II.A.1 and Chapter Five, Part I.

that the government wishes to make faster progress with its legislative agenda in general may well justify the House sitting for longer hours but it does not, on its own, justify reduced scrutiny of any particular piece of legislation. In other words, it may justify urgency for one stage of a bill but it does not justify the loss of stand-down periods that results when urgency is taken for more than one stage of a bill at a time, let alone the elimination of select committee scrutiny that results when the first and second stage of legislation are taken together under urgency. That can only be justified by reasons relating to the urgency of the particular legislation.

The problem with the urgency provisions in the Standing Orders is that they muddle together these different outcomes. This contributes to confusion in the community as to what urgency is and as to its constitutional and democratic implications. We suggested above that "urgency" can, on occasion, attract negative public attention even when it is being utilised in relatively benign circumstances. The flipside to this is that the frequency with which urgency is used, the sheer number of bills to which it is accorded and the very fact that many such uses are relatively benign, may serve to camouflage more troubling uses (for example, to eliminate select committee scrutiny).

For these reasons, the authors of this study were one of a number of submitters to the 2011 review of the Standing Orders to suggest that the Standing Orders ought to be amended so as to provide separately for an "extended hours" provision.[73] As discussed earlier in this chapter, that submission was taken up by the Standing Orders Committee and adopted by the House. We expand in Chapter Seven on its anticipated effect with regards to the use of urgency.

Turning to tactical reasons for using urgency, while some of these are doubtless more troubling than others, tactical considerations of the kind explored in Chapter Three are, in our view, never sufficient to justify the use of urgency. It is an inherent feature of political life that governments will engage in such tactical or strategic behaviour to the extent that they can get away with it. However, the underlying regulatory framework ought to disincentivise such behaviour as much as is possible.

It will be apparent from the very fact that we have categorised it as a "tactical" reason for using urgency, that the authors are unimpressed by the "first 100 days" justification relied on, for example, by the Leader of the House Gerry Brownlee, to justify the National-led Government's heavy reliance on urgency (including urgency for all stages) following the November 2008 election. Brownlee argued that urgency was justified by the election promises that had been made and by the fact that the policy intention behind the legislation was well canvassed

---

73   Geiringer, Higbee and McLeay, above n 24. See, also, Edgeler, above n 67.

and supported.[74] This argument misconceives the very nature of deliberative democracy. On election day, voters do not clearly signal their preference for any particular policy or policies but for one package of personalities and policies over another. Further, following the election, the generalised pre-election policy platform is transformed by the government into detailed legislative proposals. The deliberative, participatory and scrutinising functions of parliamentary institutions in relation to such legislation are no less important because the underlying policy happens to have been signalled prior to the election.[75]

Finally, we have already made the point in Chapter Three that the invocation of the "Budget day" as a reason for taking urgency bears careful scrutiny. In our view, the Budget day is not so much a reason of its own as an occasion on which a combination of the other reasons explored in Chapter Three may (or may not) come into play.

III Conclusion

To summarise, any use of urgency in its present form comes at a varying cost to the integrity of our constitutional and democratic system. Accordingly, there should be effective disincentives to prevent it being used too frequently.

In our view, the need to "make progress" with the order paper is not, in itself, an appropriate justification. We accept that governments need flexibility to advance their legislative programmes. However, urgency is an imperfect device for achieving that flexibility for two reasons. First, within the current regulatory framework, the pretext of insufficient sitting hours can provide the excuse for abbreviating opportunities for deliberation, consultation and scrutiny of legislation, in the absence of any justification relating to the urgency of the legislation itself.

This is most troubling when urgency results in the elimination of the select committee stage. Doubtless, governments need the flexibility to be able to expedite the passage of legislation in this manner in exceptional cases. In our view, however, they ought truly to be exceptional.

More generally, in our view, the stand-down periods between the different legislative stages play an important role in providing opportunities for scrutiny and deliberation. For that reason, a desire to make faster progress with the order paper ought not, on its own, to justify taking urgency for more than one stage of a bill at a time.

The second problem is that, even when urgency is used for relatively benign purposes (in relation to one stage of legislation at a time), its use contributes

---

74 See (10 February 2009) 652 NZPD 1075–1076; (12 February 2009) 652 NZPD 1258; (15 October 2009) 658 NZPD 7113; Brownlee interview.
75 For a contrary view from the Standing Orders Committee, see Chapter Seven, Part II.

to a public perception that Parliament is not following its own rules and that legislation is being "rammed through" the House. In such cases, the very terminology of "urgency" confuses the electorate as to the constitutional ramifications of what is occurring.

This raises the question whether the current constraints on the use of urgency are adequate? We think not and, in Chapter Seven, we consider how more effective disincentives might be able to be put in place.

7

Conclusion and Options for Reform

As we have argued in the preceding chapters of this book, any use of urgency comes at a varying cost to the integrity of our constitutional and democratic system. This does not mean that the use of urgency is always inappropriate but it does mean that there is a need for effective disincentives to stop it being used too frequently or in the absence of appropriate justification.

In Chapter Five, we explored various factors that have constrained governments over the years from excessive reliance on urgency. One of these is the multi-party make-up of the House that became the norm following the introduction of MMP. We saw that the advent of multi-party parliaments, providing new opportunities for smaller parties to influence the parliamentary process, slowed the use of urgency overall. Nevertheless, our data reveal that the impact of MMP on the use of urgency is uneven and that the constraint imposed by the multi-party environment is sometimes weak or even absent.

We also examined other factors that sometimes act to inhibit the excessive use of urgency but we suggested that all of these factors were somewhat erratic and unpredictable in their effects. In particular, we suggested that the ultimate constraint on political behaviour – the media and public opinion – is misfiring in the case of urgency due to poor levels of public understanding of what urgency is, and of its constitutional and democratic implications. We suggested that a problem in this regard is the hybrid role played by urgency as both a general "overtime" mechanism and as a device for fast-tracking particular bills. Just as this results in "urgency" sometimes attracting negative public attention in relatively benign circumstances so, too, can the frequent (and often relatively benign) deployment of urgency motions serve to camouflage their more democratically troubling uses. The former frustrates politicians, who consider themselves unfairly judged. The latter suggests that the constraints on the use of urgency are inadequate.

What, then, is to be done about this? In early 2011, the authors of this study made a submission to the Standing Orders Committee (as part of its tri-annual review of the Standing Orders).[1] We summarised our empirical data and put forward a package of proposed reforms, designed to prise apart "overtime"

---

1   Claudia Geiringer, Polly Higbee and Elizabeth McLeay, "The Urgency Project: Revised Submission to Standing Orders Committee" (2011). For an explanation of the composition of the Standing Orders Committee, with particular reference to the 2008–2011 term, see Chapter Two, Part V.E.

from "urgency" and to improve the incentives for governments to limit reliance on "urgency" to genuinely urgent situations. For the most part, our proposed reforms accepted as their underlying premise that the justifiability of urgency in any particular case is a political question and that the ultimate arbiters of political behaviour are the public. The proposed changes sought to enhance the political sanctions for the use of urgency. In the case of the use of urgency to eliminate the select committee stage, however, we went further. In our view, the time has come to accord a role to the Speaker in approving this form of urgency, similar to the role he or she plays in relation to extraordinary urgency.

In this chapter, we document our recommendations to the Standing Orders Committee and the Committee's response to them, as reflected in its report on the 2011 review of the Standing Orders.[2] It will be remembered that the House has now adopted the Committee's recommended changes to the Standing Orders and that these will be in force when Parliament meets following the November 2011 election.

The Committee made recommendations consistent with the general thrust (but not the detail) of two of our recommendations: the introduction of an "extended sitting" power; and a requirement of greater specificity in the reasons given in urgency motions. Both of these reforms are to be welcomed, as is broader acknowledgement in the Committee's report that the use of urgency can detract from the reputation of Parliament.

Nevertheless, the Committee's recommendations were, in other respects, disappointing. Most regrettably, the Committee resisted calls to place special controls around the most troubling use of urgency – to eliminate select committee scrutiny.

For this, and other reasons, a further round of reforms may need to be contemplated. In the final sections of this chapter, we make some suggestions for what these may be.

I A Review of Parliamentary Time?

Our first recommendation to the Standing Orders Committee was that it would be timely for the Committee to consider conducting a comprehensive review of the broader question of parliamentary time, similar to the one conducted in 2006 by the Procedures Committee of the Scottish Parliament.[3] As we stressed in Chapter Six, urgency is just one piece of a complex jigsaw puzzle relating to issues of parliamentary time and legislative capacity. This book focuses on one piece of that puzzle. Ultimately, however, the broader issues need to be examined methodically and comprehensively.

2   Standing Orders Committee, "Review of Standing Orders" [2011] AJHR I.18B ["Standing Orders Review 2011"].
3   Geiringer, Higbee and McLeay, above n 1, at 12.

The Committee did not take up this recommendation. On the other hand, as we noted in Chapter Six, the question of parliamentary time formed a major preoccupation of the Committee's report on the 2011 review itself. We can still see some value in a free-standing inquiry that seeks evidence and submissions from a range of interested sources. That said, in the light of the wide-ranging package of reforms adopted as a result of the 2011 review, the time is no longer ripe for such an examination. At least one parliamentary term will need to elapse before the impact of the new changes will be able to be assessed.

II Separate Provision for Extended Hours

Our second recommendation to the 2011 review of the Standing Orders was that the Standing Orders ought to deal separately with (and rename) the situation in which the House seeks to devote extra time to completing its legislative business but does not wish to interfere with select committee consideration and/or the stand-down periods between the legislative stages.[4] Our point was that the simple act of prising apart the more benign uses of urgency (for one stage) from those uses that interfere with the orderly and measured progression of legislation through the House might have a significant effect. It would enable governments to better explain and defend their actions to the electorate and it would enable the electorate to make more finely nuanced judgements about the behaviour of their elected representatives. When "urgency" was taken, the media would know that vigilance was required and that justification ought to be expected; when "extra time" was taken, the media would not necessarily need to be so concerned.

The Standing Orders Committee accepted the general thrust of this recommendation. The Committee stressed that urgency is a "legitimate" parliamentary tactic but nevertheless accepted that the use of urgency "to make progress" can have an "adverse effect on the quality of debate and legislative outcomes" and that it does not enhance "the reputation of Parliament as an effective institution".[5] It was against that background that the Committee introduced its recommendation for an "extended sitting" power, which we detailed in Chapter Six. The Standing Orders Committee was explicit in drawing the link between this new "extended sitting" power and the likely downstream impact on urgency, which "should then be confined to situations that genuinely require an urgent approach."[6]

---

4   Geiringer, Higbee and McLeay, above n 1, at 11–12. We were not the only submitters to make this recommendation: see Graeme Edgeler, "Review of the Standing Orders: Submission of Graeme Edgeler" (2011).
5   "Standing Orders Review 2011", above n 2, at 14. The Committee offered the same critique of opposition procedural tactics to delay or extend the House's consideration of matters.
6   "Standing Orders Review 2011", above n 2, at 17.

To recapitulate, the new Standing Order will empower the government, having given formal notice at the Business Committee the previous week (and subsequently in the House), to move to extend one sitting per week – either the Tuesday or the Wednesday sitting – across to the next morning. The Business Committee will be able to authorise further extensions (to more than one sitting a week or into Thursday evening or Friday morning). Importantly, in the absence of agreement from the Business Committee, the extended sitting will only be able to be utilised for "bills available for debate on the Order Paper" and "only for the stage set out in the Order Paper." This means that, in the absence of unanimity or near unanimity, extended sittings will only be able to be utilised to consider one stage of a bill at a time.[7]

The very fact that a cross-party parliamentary committee has recorded in a public document its concern that excessive reliance on urgency does not enhance the reputation of Parliament as an effective institution is, in our view, highly significant. Our interviews with experienced politicians from both the pre- and post-MMP era revealed that, in general, politicians were somewhat defensive about the use of urgency. They viewed it as a legitimate tactic that is sometimes subject to unfair attack from commentators with a weak grasp of parliamentary procedure.[8] The Standing Orders Committee's report suggests that, under pressure from a range of sources, this view may have subtly shifted, even during the lifetime of this project. Politicians are still anxious to stress that urgency is a legitimate parliamentary tactic but they are readier to concede that its use does not always enhance the reputation of Parliament as an institution. This is an important shift.

More specifically, the creation of an "extended sitting" power is a valuable addition to the parliamentary armoury that has the potential to diminish parliamentary reliance on urgency. It stands to reason that, if governments can avoid the stigma of "urgency" by relying on an extended sitting power, they will do so. As we noted in Chapter Two, there is some evidence that the creation of the Main Committee in Australia had a similar effect, reducing the number of bills subject to the "guillotine".[9] If, as a consequence, urgency is used more rarely and in relation to fewer bills, effective public scrutiny of urgency when it *is* deployed will be achieved more readily.

Nevertheless, in evaluating the operation of the new provision, one question that will require close attention during the course of the next parliamentary

---

7   "Standing Orders Review 2011", above n 2, at 15–16. Presumably, even the Business Committee will not be able to authorise the elimination of the select committee stage under the guise of an "extended sitting". That is because of Standing Order 280 (Standing Orders 2008), which stipulates that a bill stands referred to select committee after its first reading "unless the House has otherwise accorded urgency to it."
8   See, especially, Chapter Three, Part II.B.
9   Chapter Two, Part VII.

term is whether it is sufficiently flexible to act as a substitute for urgency to "make progress" in all or most cases. In our view, any new Standing Order to provide for "extra time" ought to be designed to replace (rather than merely supplement) urgency as the mechanism by which governments seek an ad hoc extension of the House's sitting hours to "make progress" (and in the absence of any genuine reason to expedite a particular piece of legislation).[10] It is not clear whether the provision that has, in fact, been adopted will be sufficiently flexible to do so. In the absence of agreement from the Business Committee, it will only be available for one extended sitting per week, earning the government only an additional four hours of sitting time in the House. The danger is that, at pressured times in the parliamentary calendar, governments may still be tempted to rely on urgency to "make progress" if they cannot get agreement from the Business Committee to take additional hours.

Indeed, the Standing Orders Committee actually anticipated that this may be so. Its view was that urgency would continue, on occasion, to be used to "make progress":[11]

> Beyond the situations when bills require urgent consideration for legal reasons, urgency could ultimately be justified to make progress if the Government's legislative programme has been unreasonably delayed in the House despite constructive attempts to negotiate arrangements in the Business Committee. There might also be an expectation that, immediately after an election, a Government might seek to implement its key campaign pledges quickly.

Our views as to urgency to implement campaign pledges were expressed in the previous chapter and do not need to be repeated here.[12] More generally, the danger is that, if urgency continues to fulfil a hybrid role and to be used to "make progress", the addition of the new "extended sitting" provision may turn out to have no appreciable impact at all on the political accountability mechanisms surrounding the urgency power.

III *Reserving Urgency for Urgent Situations*

This danger would be significantly alleviated if the Standing Orders Committee had adopted in full our next two recommendations. These were designed to improve the political accountability mechanisms surrounding urgency itself. Our argument was that, once an "extra time" provision was added to the Standing Orders, it would be possible to reserve "urgency" (enabling a stand-down period to be removed and/or the select committee stage to be omitted) for situations where there is a genuine reason to expedite the passage of the

---

10 See Geiringer, Higbee and McLeay, above n 1, at 12.
11 "Standing Orders Review 2011", above n 2, at 17.
12 Chapter Six, Part II.

particular piece of legislation.[13] We made two recommendations designed to improve the incentives for governments to do so. Unfortunately, the Committee only adopted one of these, and in a somewhat diluted form.

Our first recommendation in this regard was that the Standing Orders ought to stipulate that a motion to take urgency is limited to legislative business only in relation to one bill.[14] At present, one urgency motion may comprehend numerous items of legislative business relating to numerous bills. This means that it is not necessary for the Leader of the House, when moving the motion, to particularise his or her reasons in relation to each piece of legislation. Indeed, it is not uncommon for urgency motions, having listed particular items of legislative business to be considered under urgency, to end with a catch-all formula such as: "... and the introduction of government bills". In other words, governments do not always give notice in the urgency motion of all the items that will be considered under urgency, let alone the reasons justifying the urgency of each item.

A requirement of one legislative item per motion would enhance the opportunities for media scrutiny of parliamentary behaviour by highlighting what is at stake in each case and, thereby, increasing the incentives for governments to offer meaningful justifications for why they believe urgency is needed in the particular case. It is interesting to note in this respect that, in Australia, if more than one bill is to be included in a declaration of urgency, the Standing Orders must be suspended (although, as we noted in Chapter Two, we understand that there have been many cases over the years when that has, in fact, occurred).[15]

Our second recommendation in this respect related even more directly to the quality of reasons given in the urgency motion. Standing Order 54 requires the minister moving the urgency motion to "inform the House with some particularity why the motion is being moved." As noted in Chapter Three, although a Speaker's ruling in 1985 held that this required something more than a "bald statement that progress needed to be made", in fact, urgency motions often give little more than that. There is certainly no requirement in practice that the reasons given relate to the urgency of the particular items included in the motion.[16]

---

13   Geiringer, Higbee and McLeay, above n 1, at 13.
14   Geiringer, Higbee and McLeay, above n 1, at 13. If this proposal were to be adopted at some time in the future, we accept that consequential amendments to the Standing Orders would probably be required to make it workable. For example, under the Standing Orders, if the business that is being conducted under urgency is completed at a time the House would not otherwise be sitting, the House rises. This would need to be amended to enable the government to move successive urgency motions in a situation where a number of pieces of legislation were genuinely urgent.
15   Chapter Two, Part VII.
16   Chapter Three, Part I.

In our submission to the Standing Orders Committee we suggested that, once the Standing Orders had provided separately for an "extra time" provision, generalised reasons ought no longer to be considered sufficient to justify genuine "urgency"; nor should reasons that focus on the need to make progress rather than on why the particular legislation needs to be expedited. We recommended that the Standing Orders be reworded to require the minister when moving urgency to: "inform the House with some particularity why the particular item of business is urgent."[17]

We also suggested that a related innovation that might be worth considering would be to require urgency motions to be moved by the minister in charge of the particular legislation rather than, as is generally now the case, the Leader of the House. That would, again, highlight the fact that the reasons given need to relate to the urgency of the particular legislation. It would also locate ministerial responsibility where it should lie.[18]

In sympathy with the tenor of our submission, the Standing Orders Committee accepted that, in general, urgency should now be "confined to situations that genuinely require an urgent approach" and that the way to achieve this is to "strengthen the Government's political accountability for its proposals to accord urgency to business."[19] However, the Committee's proposal for how to achieve this enhanced political accountability was somewhat thin.

The Committee did not adopt our recommendation of limiting one urgency motion to one bill. This is disappointing but perhaps not surprising, given the inflexible nature of the "extended sitting" provision that the Committee has adopted and the Committee's view that it might still be appropriate, on occasion, to use urgency to "make progress". Politicians will be unlikely to take the additional step of limiting urgency motions to one bill at a time unless they can be confident that the extended sitting power makes adequate provision for the need to "make progress" without resort to urgency.

Turning to our suggestion that Standing Order 54 (relating to the reasons contained in an urgency motion) should be reworded, the Committee adopted the general thrust of this recommendation but not the precise wording proposed. Rather, it recommended that, on moving an urgency motion, a minister be required "to explain to the House with some particularity the circumstances that warrant the claim for urgency."[20] The intention behind this recommendation was expressed by the Committee as follows:[21]

17   Geiringer, Higbee and McLeay, above n 1, at 13–14.
18   Geiringer, Higbee and McLeay, above n 1, at 14.
19   "Standing Orders Review 2011", above n 2, at 17.
20   "Standing Orders Review 2011", above n 2, at 17.
21   "Standing Orders Review 2011", above n 2, at 17.

This would not require a Minister to provide information where it was not in the public interest to do so. But such cases are exceptional. We expect that specific information about the business to be accorded urgency, and the reasons why it is urgent, will be given if it can be given consistently with the public interest. The public interest would be for the Minister to judge.

Whether or not this new provision has its intended effect will depend on the norms of application that develop around it. As we noted above, in practice, the current requirement ("to inform the House with some particularity why the motion is being moved") has not been interpreted to require reasons specific to the particular items of business to be accorded urgency, and has often generated reasons that amount to little more than a bald statement that progress needs to be made. On its face, the language now to be adopted is equally capable of being interpreted and applied in this way. In contrast, the language that we had proposed focused more specifically on the reasons why "the particular item of business is urgent".

However, this is an area where norms and expectations are as important as text. The Standing Orders Committee has clearly signalled its view that the amended wording will, in the ordinary run of cases, require specific information about the business to be accorded urgency and it is to be hoped that the provision will be interpreted and applied in that light.

Ideally, we would hope that the Speaker would play a role in upholding these revised expectations and enforcing some minimum standards of specificity in the reasons given. However, recent practice suggests that this is unlikely. For example, at the beginning of the 2008–2011 Parliament, the Speaker refused in one case to assess whether a particular urgency motion contained any reason in it at all. He noted that, if the opposition felt that inadequate reason had been given, its remedy was to refuse to support the motion.[22]

In sum, the Standing Orders Committee accepted that the addition of a new "extended sitting" provision ought to mean that urgency is generally reserved for situations when there is a genuine need for haste in relation to the particular items of business. It also accepted that amendments to the Standing Orders would be helpful to underline this point and to sharpen the mechanisms of political accountability that surround the taking of urgency. The Committee's attempt to reword Standing Order 54 in order to tighten the requirement to give reasons is to be lauded. At the same time, the accountability mechanism that the Committee has adopted is fragile. The revised wording of Standing Order 54 is not, on its face, much more specific than the current wording and so much

---

22   (16 December 2008) 651 NZPD 728. Though we note that this appears to be inconsistent with speakers' rulings from the 1970s and 1980s: see (25 August 1976) 405 NZPD 2016 and 2019; (29 September 1978) 421 NZPD 4042 and 4047; (19 November 1985) 467 NZPD 8181.

will depend on the norms and expectations that solidify around it. It is also disappointing that the Committee did not take the extra step of adopting a one motion/one bill rule and it is to be hoped that the Committee might be prepared to revisit that issue once the House has had experience with the operation of the new "extended sitting" power.

IV *Additional Controls for Elimination of Select Committee Stage*

Up to this point, our submission to the Standing Orders Committee accepted, as its underlying premise, that the justifiability of urgency in any particular case is a political question and that the ultimate arbiters of political behaviour are the public. The proposed changes sought to enhance political sanctions for the use of urgency. To that extent, we were in sympathy with the Standing Orders Committee as to its general approach.

Our view, however, was that controls on the use of urgency to eliminate the select committee stage ought to go further than this. In our submission to the Standing Orders Committee, we suggested that the time had come to accord a role to the Speaker in approving this form of urgency, similar to the role that he or she plays in relation to extraordinary urgency. Standing Order 56 requires the minister moving extraordinary urgency to "inform the House of the nature of the business and the circumstances that warrant the claim for extraordinary urgency." Importantly, it then provides that extraordinary urgency may be claimed "only if the Speaker agrees that the business to be taken justifies it." Standing Orders do not specify a substantive criterion or standard for when extraordinary urgency would be "justified" or "warranted". Rather, it has been left to the Speaker, advised by the Office of the Clerk, to develop appropriate guidance.

We proposed that similar wording ought to be adopted in relation to any urgency motion that encompasses both the first and second stages of legislation (and therefore results in the select committee stage being bypassed). That would leave it to the Speaker and the Clerk of the House to develop guidance as to when the urgency of the situation is such that it is appropriate to eliminate select committee consideration.[23]

Unfortunately, the Standing Orders Committee rejected this submission. Its concern was that this would draw the Speaker into determinations about matters that could be highly controversial or politically sensitive, and that this carries the undesirable risk of politicising the office of the Speaker.[24]

The Standing Orders Committee nevertheless accepted that the use of urgency to eliminate the select committee stage was a matter of "significant public

---

23 Geiringer, Higbee and McLeay, above n 1, at 14.
24 "Standing Orders Review 2011", above n 2, at 17.

concern" on which it had received a number of submissions. It expressed the view that "the select committee process should be bypassed only in exceptional circumstances," and that "the Government is accountable for its decision to follow this course."[25]

Although its "first preference" was "for the select committee process not to be circumvented through the use of urgency", the Committee endorsed the use of truncated select committee processes in preference to the complete elimination of the select committee stage. However, it rejected a proposal from the Green Party to establish a procedure whereby all bills accorded urgency for the first and second stages would go to select committee for three to five sitting days. The Committee felt that there were already adequate powers in the Standing Orders to enable the Business Committee to facilitate truncated select committee processes of this kind. It was also concerned that the Greens' proposal might have the perverse effect of leading to greater reliance on extraordinary urgency.[26]

In short, despite high-sounding rhetoric about the undesirability of using urgency to eliminate the select committee stage, the Committee made no recommendations for amendments to the Standing Orders to control better this kind of urgency. It is disappointing that no political consensus has yet emerged for greater controls around this practice. The most troubling data produced by our study relate to the failure of MMP – at least during the forty-fifth and forty-ninth parliaments – to act as an effective constraint on this type of urgency. It will be remembered that these two parliaments (1996–1999 and 2008–2010) each used urgency on 20 occasions to bypass select committee scrutiny, and that the data on the forty-ninth Parliament related to an incomplete parliamentary term. Further, as we saw in Chapter Four, on around half the occasions when urgency was used in this way, there was no legitimate reason for haste in relation to the particular measure, let alone a reason sufficient to justify the complete elimination of the select committee stage.[27]

It is regrettable that the Committee was not prepared to consider a role for the Speaker, similar to the Speaker's role in relation to extraordinary urgency. The culture that has developed around Standing Order 56 and its predecessors has been strikingly effective in constraining the excessive use of extraordinary urgency. As noted above, there were only eight uses of extraordinary urgency in the entire 24-year period of our study. In our view, the use of urgency to eliminate select committee scrutiny ought to be almost as rare – an aspiration that is not unrealistic given that, during 10 years or partial years of post-MMP Labour-led Government, this kind of urgency was used on average 1.4 times per year.

25 "Standing Orders Review 2011", above n 2, at 18.
26 "Standing Orders Review 2011", above n 2, at 18–19.
27 Chapter Four, Part II.E.

The concern about politicisation of the Speaker's role is, in our view, overstated. The extraordinary urgency power has operated satisfactorily for 25 years without leading to politicisation of the Speaker's role. Certainly, expectations would need to be clarified around the circumstances that might justify urgency to eliminate the select committee stage. However, the expectations that have developed around extraordinary urgency (focusing on the reasons for immediacy as well as the need for an actual intention to bring the legislation into immediate effect) would provide a helpful starting point.

The Committee's stated preference was for measures that "strengthen the Government's political accountability" rather than "formally limiting the use of urgency".[28] That being so, it is a pity that the Committee did not consider additional political accountability measures specifically for urgency that removes select committee scrutiny. For example, we suggested in our submission that, if the Committee was not willing to take up our recommendation of one motion/one bill for all urgency motions, a halfway house would be to impose such a requirement in cases where the urgency motion would result in the select committee process being bypassed.[29] In the absence of such a requirement, it will still be possible to take urgency for the first and second reading of a particular bill by burying a reference to that bill in a long list of items to which urgency is to be accorded.

One final point of concern in this regard relates to the Standing Orders Committee's recommendation (discussed in Chapter Six) to make instructions to select committees debatable. On the face of things, this is a welcome reform. However, it may have an unfortunate and unanticipated consequence. If the government wishes to send a bill to select committee for a truncated period (of less than four months), there will now be a debate in the House. On the other hand, if the government were to eliminate select committee scrutiny altogether in relation to the same bill through the use of an urgency motion, that would not be debatable. This may create a perverse incentive to use urgency to remove the select committee stage rather than to send a bill to select committee for a truncated period. It is a pity, in that light, that the Committee did not also consider making urgency motions that eliminate select committee scrutiny debatable.

In short, while registering significant public concern about the overuse of this type of urgency, the Standing Orders Committee preferred not to single it out for special protection. Rather, the Committee preferred to subject this type of urgency to the same set of heightened accountability mechanisms as other forms of urgency. It is certainly to be hoped and expected that these heightened accountability mechanisms will make it more difficult for governments to use urgency to eliminate select committee scrutiny. And, indeed, the strong rhetoric

---

28 "Standing Orders Review 2011", above n 2, at 17.
29 Geiringer, Higbee and McLeay, above n 1, at 13.

in the Committee's report decrying this form of urgency may perhaps make this more likely. On the other hand, as we noted above, the overall package of enhanced accountability mechanisms that has been agreed to (consisting of the extended hours provision and the reworded requirement to give reasons) is not a strong one. Further, the importance of the select committee stage in New Zealand's unicameral legislative process, together with worrying data from our study on the overuse of this type of urgency during some recent parliamentary terms, makes this a matter of pressing concern.

In our view, a major cultural shift is required in relation to this type of urgency. That was able to be engineered in the mid-1980s in relation to all-night sittings by giving the Speaker a role in determining whether extraordinary urgency was justified. It is a pity that the House is not yet ready to contemplate a similar package of reforms in relation to urgency to eliminate select committee scrutiny.

V *Possibilities for Future Reform of the Standing Orders*

In stating these concerns, we would not wish to detract from the importance of the 2011 Standing Orders review process. As we explained in the previous chapter, the 2011 review became the occasion for a broad re-examination of the problem of parliamentary time and resulted in a package of recommendations designed to streamline the House's legislative business – primarily by providing incentives for constructive cross-party engagement through the vehicle of the Business Committee. The extended sitting provision is a valuable addition to the parliamentary armoury that, at least, has the potential to diminish reliance on urgency. The rewording of Standing Order 54 is also to be welcomed.

As significant as the recommendations themselves is the fact that a cross-party parliamentary committee has recorded its concern, in a public document, that excessive reliance on urgency does not enhance the reputation of Parliament as an effective institution. The Committee has also emphasised the importance of select committee scrutiny to New Zealand's parliamentary system.

Ultimately, only time will tell whether this package of reforms succeeds in imposing a more effective constraint on the use of urgency (or on particular uses of urgency). If, however, the revised rules do not prove adequate, further reform options are available. A number have already been touched on in the preceding analysis. They are:

- providing a more flexible "extended sitting" provision that allows for more than one extended sitting per week, or longer extended sittings;
- limiting urgency motions (or urgency motions that remove select committee scrutiny) to one bill per motion;
- making urgency motions that remove select committee scrutiny debatable (so as to bring them into line with the new position in relation to instructions to select committees);

- requiring urgency motions to be moved by the minister in charge of the particular legislation;
- rewording Standing Order 54 to make it clearer that the reasons given must relate to the need for haste in relation to the particular item or items of business included in the motion (and/or clarifying that the Speaker can determine whether or not the urgency motion contains reasons that are sufficiently specific);
- requiring, in the case of urgency that eliminates select committee scrutiny, that the urgency may be claimed "only if the Speaker agrees that the business to be taken justifies it."

We continue to endorse these reform options. Further, if even these measures were not successful, more dramatic measures might need to be considered. These might include:

- requiring a certain number of MPs to be present when voting on urgency motions (or voting on urgency motions that result in elimination of select committee scrutiny);
- requiring a personal vote rather than a party vote to be taken on urgency motions (or on urgency motions that result in elimination of select committee scrutiny);
- requiring a higher approval threshold (say, a two-thirds majority in the House) for urgency motions (or for urgency motions that result in elimination of select committee scrutiny);
- requiring all urgency motions to be debatable.

We do not put this final list of possibilities forward as recommendations but simply record them as possibilities worthy of future discussion. The broader point is that effective constraints on urgency (and, most especially, urgency to remove select committee scrutiny) are needed in order to uphold the democratic and constitutional legitimacy of New Zealand's legislative process. If the current package of reforms does not prove adequate, these and other reform options will need to be considered.

VI *The Term of Parliament*

Finally, we note with approval that the ministerial review of New Zealand's constitutional arrangements that was put in train in 2010 includes, as one of the issues to be considered: "The length of the term of Parliament and whether or not the term should be fixed".[30]

---

30 Office of the Deputy Prime Minister and Office of the Minister of Māori Affairs, "Consideration of Constitutional Issues" (2010) <www.beehive.govt.nz>; Bill English, Deputy Prime Minister, and Pita Sharples, Minister of Māori Affairs, "Govt Begins Cross-Party Constitutional Review" (press release, 8 December 2010) <www.beehive.govt.nz>.

As noted in Chapter Three, a number of interviewees suggested to us that the time pressure created by the three-year term is a factor that both motivates and, in their mind, justifies the use of urgency.[31] Some of that pressure could be alleviated significantly by a four-year term.

Reform of the term of Parliament is difficult to achieve. The three-year term is entrenched, meaning that, as a matter of convention if not law, it can only be altered by either a 75 per cent majority in the House or a majority of voters at a referendum.[32] Given that any such amendment would enhance the powers of the MPs who vote for it and diminish the rights of the electorate, there is a serious question as to whether the former method of amendment is constitutionally appropriate.[33] Ultimately, in order to acquire constitutional legitimacy, reform would probably need to be achieved by referendum.

The question whether the term should be extended to four years was put to the electorate in 1967 and again in 1990 and, on both occasions, a resounding majority voted to keep the three-year term. There is, therefore, reason to be sceptical as to the likelihood of change. Nevertheless, the fact that the term of Parliament will feature as one of the issues to be subject to public education and debate through the constitutional review process is a positive development.

VII Conclusion

Urgency is one of a range of mechanisms available to New Zealand governments to seek to expedite legislation through the parliamentary process. In broad terms, there are two methods available to legislatures to ease the passage of legislation. One is to put aside extra time in the House to debate the proposal. The other is to reduce the level of scrutiny that the proposal receives. Urgency always does the former (by extending the House's sitting hours and prioritising certain items of business) but can also do the latter (by removing stand-down periods and select committee scrutiny).

This dual role is confusing. It has led to a situation in which routine recourse to urgency to extend the House's sitting hours is undermining the reputation of Parliament and politicians. It has also made it difficult for public watchdogs such as the media to provide effective scrutiny when urgency is used in more democratically problematic ways.

Our research demonstrated the regularity with which governments had recourse to urgency during the period 1987–2010 and the staggering number

---

31 For example, Prebble email exchange; Palmer and Wilson interviews.
32 Election Act 1993, s 268. For discussion of the status and effect of this provision see, for example, Report of the Royal Commission on the Electoral System, *Towards a Better Democracy* (Government Press, Wellington, 1986) at [9.174]–[9.188].
33 Report of the Royal Commission on the Electoral System, above n 32, at [9.186]–[9.187].

of bills that were accorded urgency at some stage during this period. Some governments used urgency more than others did, and the advent of MMP undoubtedly provided a significant constraint on its use. However, MMP is an informal constraint that depends on a number of variables for its efficacy. Its impact on urgency has been somewhat erratic. Most troublingly, there have been periods since MMP was introduced when governments used urgency to avoid select committee scrutiny far too often, and without evidence of adequate justification.

Our research also disclosed that, for many decades, urgency has been viewed by politicians as a legitimate tool for extending the House's sitting hours. The prevailing view amongst the politicians whom we interviewed was that criticisms of urgency were misinformed and misplaced.

Against this background, the 2011 review of the Standing Orders is a welcome development, if for no other reason than it demonstrates an apparent sea change in attitudes to urgency in the House. Under pressure from a range of sources (including this study), politicians are coming to realise that, if nothing else, regular recourse to urgency does not enhance their reputations. There is also growing recognition of the undesirability (from the perspective of democratic and constitutional legitimacy) of using urgency to bypass the select committee stage.

If urgency is to be used less frequently, however, there must be some other mechanism available to the House to achieve an ad hoc extension of its sitting hours. The new "extended sitting" provision provides an alternative and better tailored mechanism for governments to seek such an extension to the House's sitting hours and, for that reason, it is to be welcomed.

However, the "extended sitting" provision will not contribute to significant culture change in relation to the use of urgency unless two factors are present. First, the "extended sitting" provision must itself prove sufficient to meet the level of need for extra sitting hours (so that governments are not still tempted to have recourse to urgency as an additional means to "make progress"). Secondly, there must be strong disincentives against the use of urgency itself – at least in the absence of appropriate justification.

Our concern is that it is not clear that either of these factors are present under the new regime. The "extended sitting" provision is restrictive in scope, and the new measures designed to strengthen public accountability in relation to urgency itself are weak. For that reason, a further round of reforms may well be required.

Finally, we remain particularly concerned about the absence of more formal constraints on the use of urgency to bypass select committee scrutiny. This form of urgency should only be tolerated in exceptional circumstances. Recent experience is that politicians have resorted to it far too readily. We doubt that the new public accountability mechanisms to be introduced as a result of the

2011 review will prove sufficient to engineer the dramatic cultural change that, it seems, is required in this respect.

In short, bills passed in a hurry too often offend against the principles of good democratic and constitutional practice. The changes to be introduced as a result of the 2011 review of the Standing Orders are to be welcomed. We doubt, however, that they go far enough.

The Research Team

Claudia Geiringer is Senior Lecturer in Law at Victoria University of Wellington, an Associate Director of the New Zealand Centre for Public Law and a barrister specialising in constitutional law and human rights. In addition to other research interests, she has previously published on the laws and processes of Parliament, including on the Māori seats, the processes around creation of electoral vacancies, and Parliament's responsibilities under the New Zealand Bill of Rights Act 1990. Prior to taking up her academic role, she was a Crown Counsel at the Crown Law Office. In that capacity, she advised and represented the government on a range of matters, including electoral issues and the laws of Parliament.

Polly Higbee graduated from Victoria University of Wellington with a LLB/BA(Hons) in Political Science and History in 2010. She was employed full time as a Research Fellow for the New Zealand Centre of Public Law from July to December 2010. Polly currently works as a solicitor at a commercial law firm in Wellington.

Until 2009, **Dr Elizabeth McLeay** was Professor of Political Science at Victoria University of Wellington, having specialised in comparative politics and government. Professor McLeay has published widely on Cabinet government, the transition to MMP, parliamentary and ministerial careers, political representation (especially of Māori and of women) and the policy process. She was a member of the International Board of Advisers, Parliamentary Studies Centre, Australian National University, between 2006 and 2011; and she was the Convenor of the New Zealand Chapter, Australasian Study of Parliament Group, between 2001 and 2006. During 2010 and 2011, Professor McLeay was affiliated to the New Zealand Centre for Public Law as a Visiting Senior Research Fellow.

Appendix A

List of Interviewees and Interview Topics

I List of Interviewees

A MPs and Former MPs

Name	Date of Interview
Hon Gerry Brownlee (National)	01/11/2010
Rt Hon Wyatt Creech (National)	01/10/2010
Hon Dr Michael Cullen (Labour)	24/09/2010
Hon Peter Dunne (United Future)	06/10/2010
Rt Hon Paul East QC (National)	23/09/2010
Hon Rodney Hide (ACT)	08/11/2010
Hon Darren Hughes (Labour)	08/09/2010 and 09/09/2010
Rt Hon Jonathan Hunt (Labour)	06/10/2010
Rahui Katene (Māori Party)	10/11/2010
Hon Sir Douglas Kidd (National)	20/09/2010
Rt Hon Sir Geoffrey Palmer SC (Labour)	09/11/2010
Hon Richard Prebble (Labour, ACT)	23/10/2010 (written response)
Hon Ken Shirley (Labour, ACT)	14/09/2010
Dr The Rt Hon Lockwood Smith (National)	13/10/2010
Hon Roger Sowry (National)	12/10/2010
Metiria Turei (Green Party)	14/10/2010
Hon Margaret Wilson (Labour)	12/10/2010

B Clerks of the House of Representatives

Name	Date of Interview
Mary Harris	30/09/2010
David McGee QC	13/09/2010

II Topics Covered in the Interviews

1. What role (or roles) do you play (or have you played in the past) in relation to the use of urgency motions in the New Zealand House of Representatives?
2. Urgency can be taken at various stages of the legislative process. How do governments decide on which stages to seek urgency?
3. Are there any particular principles that have guided governments in determining when they should seek urgency?
4. What distinguishes urgency from extraordinary urgency (apart from the fact that, under the Standing Orders, the Speaker must first approve a motion for extraordinary urgency)?
5. What roles are played by the Cabinet Legislation Committee and full Cabinet respectively in deciding to seek approval from the House to apply urgency to a bill?
6. What part is played by the Business Committee of the House of Representatives in guiding, enabling or preventing the use of urgency? Do opposition parties have any impact on whether or not urgency is employed?
7. Leaving aside the Business Committee processes, do governing parties consult other parties when they want to take urgency, and how do they do this?
8. What role is played by parliamentary officials in the process? Are they/you asked for advice?
9. Have some parties been more sympathetic towards the use of urgency than others?
10. How have the type, availability and use of urgency motions changed over time? What are the overall trends?
11. How has the advent of minority and coalition governments after the implementation of MMP affected the use of urgency motions?
12. Do you have suggestions of particular examples of the use of urgency that we might consider studying? Why are those examples of particular interest?
13. The use of urgency is one way of expediting legislation. What other processes and strategies are available to New Zealand governments for speeding up the legislative process?
14. How can opposition parties delay the progress of legislation through the House?
15. Do you have any knowledge of how governments expedite legislation in other jurisdictions? If so, how do they do this? Are these ways preferable to how New Zealand handles these matters, and why?

16. When can the use of urgency be justified? Can you provide examples of when urgency is, and is not, justified?
17. What sorts of uses of urgency are troubling from a constitutional or democratic legitimacy perspective?
18. Can you suggest any reforms to the legislative process – the Standing Orders – that would change the circumstances under which urgency should be requested and granted?

Appendix B

Bills Not Sent to Select Committee 1996–2010

Category "A"

Bills where an identifiable rationale for expediting the legislation was evident:

- (A1), there was an identifiable justification for urgency in relation to the particular measure, such as to reduce the potential for speculative behaviour, to respond to an unexpected event or court decision, to remedy an anomaly, oversight or uncertainty in existing legislation, or to respond to certain factors creating a deadline for the proposed legislative change.
- (A2), the bill was accorded extraordinary urgency (and therefore its fast-tracking was approved by the Speaker).
- (A3), the bill both received unanimous support in the House, as indicated by voting at the third reading, and the omission of the select committee stage was not criticised by MPs.
- (A4), the bill repealed an act that itself went through select committee scrutiny and the repealing legislation received widespread (if not complete) parliamentary support.

Category "B"

Bills that proposed substantial policy (including constitutional) change where we could identify no obvious rationale for expediting the legislation.

Category "C"

Tax measures.

Bill	Category
1996–1999 (20 Bills) *National–NZ First Coalition; and National-led Minority Governments*	
*Accident Insurance Amendment Bill 1999	B
*Broadcasting Amendment Bill (No. 3) 1999	B
*Copyright (Removal of Prohibition on Parallel Importing) Amendment Bill 1998	B
*Customs and Excise Amendment Bill 1998	A2
Education Amendment Bill 1998	B
*Estate Duty Repeal Bill 1999	A3
Farm and Fishing Vessel Ownership Savings Schemes (Closure) Bill 1998	A1
Fire Service Amendment Bill 1998	B
Immigration (Migrant Levy) Bill 1998	B
Immigration Amendment Bill (No. 2) 1999	A1
Māori Reserved Land Amendment Bill (No. 2) 1998	A1
Oaths and Declarations (Validation) Amendment Bill 1998	A1
*Social Security Amendment Bill (No. 5) 1998	B
Social Welfare (Transitional Provisions) Amendment Bill 1998	B
Stamp Duty Abolition Bill 1999	A2
State Sector Amendment Bill 1997	B
State-Owned Enterprises (Contact Energy Limited) Amendment Bill 1998	B
*State-Owned Enterprises (Meteorological Service of NZ Limited and Vehicle Testing NZ Limited) Amendment Bill 1999	B
Tariff (Zero Duty) Amendment Bill 1998	B
*Taxation (Parental Tax Credit) Bill 1999	C
1999–2002 (7 Bills) *Labour–Alliance Minority Government*	
Customs and Excise Amendment Bill 2000	A2
Customs and Excise Amendment Bill (No. 5) 2002	A2
Local Government (Prohibition of Liquor in Public Places) Amendment Bill 2001	B
Local Government (Rodney District Council) Amendment Bill 2000	A1
Road User Charges Amendment Bill 2002	A1
Tariff (Zero Duty Removal) Amendment Bill 2000	B
Taxation (Tax Rate Increase) Bill 1999	C
2002–2005 (4 Bills) *Labour–Progressive Minority Government*	
Customs and Excise (Alcoholic Beverages) Amendment Bill 2003	A2
Electoral (Vacancies) Amendment Bill 2003	B
*Future Directions (Working for Families) Bill 2004	C
Immigration Amendment Bill (No. 2) 2003	B

Bill	Category
2005–2008 *(4 Bills)* *Labour–Progressive Minority Government*	
Appropriation (Parliamentary Expenditure Validation) Bill 2006	B
Biosecurity (Status of Specified Ports) Amendment Bill 2005	A1
*Taxation (KiwiSaver and Company Tax Rate Amendments) Bill 2007	C
*Taxation (Personal Tax Cuts, Annual Rates, and Remedial Matters) Bill 2008	C
2008–2010 *(20 Bills)* *National Minority Government* (Note incomplete parliamentary term)	
Bail Amendment Bill 2008	B
Civil Aviation (Cape Town Convention and Other Matters) Amendment Bill 2010	A1 (and A3)
Corrections (Use of Court Cells) Amendment Bill 2009	B
Crown Retail Deposit Guarantee Scheme Bill 2009	A1
Education (National Standards) Amendment Bill 2008	B
Electoral Amendment Bill 2009	A4
Electricity (Renewable Preference) Repeal Bill 2008	B
Employment Relations (Film Production Work) Amendment Bill 2010	B
Employment Relations Amendment Bill 2008	B
Energy (Fuels, Levies and References) Biofuel Obligation Repeal Bill 2008	B
Environment Canterbury (Temporary Commissioners and Improved Water Management) Bill 2010	B
Excise and Excise-Equivalent Duties Table (Tobacco Products) Amendment Bill 2010	A2
Immigration Act 2009 Amendment Bill 2010	A1
Policing (Constable's Oaths Validation) Amendment Bill 2009	A1
Policing (Involvement in Local Authority Elections) Amendment Bill 2010	B
Sentencing (Offences Against Children) Amendment Bill 2008	B
Summary Proceedings Amendment Bill (No. 2) 2010	A1
*Taxation (Budget Measures) Bill 2010	C
*Taxation (Budget Tax Measures) Bill 2009	C
Taxation (Urgent Measures and Annual Rates) Bill 2008	C

*Asterisked legislation was included in a Budget day urgency motion.

Appendix C

Portfolio Groupings

This appendix explains the portfolio groups that the study adopted to produce the data displayed in Figure 4.12, which grouped the bills accorded urgency during the period of the study according to the portfolio area of the minister responsible for introducing the bill and shepherding it through the legislative process.

Energy
Minister of Energy and Resources

Transport
Minister of Civil Aviation and Meteorological Services
Minister of Transport

Health
Minister for Accident Insurance
Minister for Food Safety
Minister of Health
Minister for Disability Issues

Education
Minister for Tertiary Education
Minister of Education

Labour
Minister of Labour
Minister of Trade and Industry
Minister of Works and Development

Social Services and Employment
Minister of Housing
Minister for Senior Citizens
Minister Responsible for the Government Superannuation Fund
Minister of Veterans' Affairs
Minister of Social Services and Employment

Culture and Sport
Minister Responsible for Archives New Zealand
Minister of Broadcasting
Minister Responsible for the National Library
Minister for Racing
Minister for Arts, Culture and Heritage
Minister for Sport and Recreation

Māori Affairs
Minister in Charge of Treaty of Waitangi Negotiations
Minister of Māori Affairs

Finance
Minister of Revenue
Minister of Finance
Treasurer

Primary Production
Minister for Food, Fibre, Biosecurity and Border Control
Minister for Biosecurity
Minister of Forestry
Minister of Fisheries
Minister for Rural Affairs
Minister of Agriculture

Local Government
Minister of Civil Defence
Minister of Local Government

Justice
Minister for Courts
Minister of Justice
Minister of Corrections
Minister of Police

International
Minister for Disarmament and Arms Control
Minister of Foreign Affairs and Trade
Minister for Trade Negotiations
Minister of Defence

Commerce
Minister of Consumer Affairs
Minister for Building and Construction
Minister of Regional Development
Minister of Tourism
Minister of Commerce

Environment
Minister for Climate Change Issues
Minister for the Environment
Minister of Conservation

Domestic Affairs
Minister in Charge of the Public Trust Office
Minister of Customs
Minister in Charge of the New Zealand Security Intelligence Service
Minister for Land Information
Minister of Immigration
Minister of State Services
Minister of Internal Affairs

Technology
Minister for Information Technology
Minister of Communications
Minister for Research, Science and Technology

State-Owned Enterprises
Minister in Charge of the Rural Banking and Finance Corporation
Minister in Charge of the Valuation Department
Minister for State-Owned Enterprises

Individual Areas
Leader of the House
Prime Minister/Deputy Prime Minister
Attorney-General

Non-Government Bills
Local Bills
Private Bills
Members' Bills